Shuwayya 'An Nafsi

شوية عن نفسي

Listening, Reading, and Expressing Yourself in Egyptian Arabic

Matthew Aldrich

lingualism

© 2016 by Matthew Aldrich

revised 2021

The author's moral rights have been asserted.
All rights reserved. No part of this document may be reproduced or transmitted in any form or by any means, electronic, mechanical, photocopying, recording, or otherwise, without prior written permission of the publisher.

Cover art: Mona Mohamed

ISBN: 978-0692704950

website: www.lingualism.com

email: contact@lingualism.com

Table of Contents

Visit our website:

www.lingualism.com

Introduction

Shuwayya 'An Nafsi (شُوَيَّة عن نفْسي *šuwáyya 3an náfsi* **A Little About Myself**) will be of tremendous help to independent language learners who want to develop their conversational skills and increase their Arabic vocabulary.

Very simply, *Shuwayya 'An Nafsi* presents the results of a survey given to 10 Egyptians. Each of the 30 sections in the book begins with a question from the survey followed by the 10 responses and a breakdown of the vocabulary and concludes with a page where you are encouraged to give your own answer to the question using newly learned words and phrases.

This book was designed in such a way that it can be an effective learning tool for **learners at all levels**:

For **beginners**, even the most basic words are found in the glossaries with their English translations. Even if you find the sentences challenging and cannot understand some of the underlying grammar at work, you will be able to pick up useful phrases while building your vocabulary. All of the materials appear in three forms: Arabic script, phonemic transcription (that is, pronunciation in the Latin alphabet), and English translation.

For more **advanced learners**, the texts appear again in the back of the book without voweling (tashkeel) or translations to provide a more challenging reading experience without distractions. Modern Standard Arabic (MSA) translations of the texts are also given for learners who are more proficient in MSA and can benefit from comparing the similarities and differences between it and Egyptian Colloquial Arabic (ECA).

The accompanying MP3s, free to download from www.lingualism.com/san, make up an invaluable part of the learning process, allowing you to hear and mimic native speakers' pronunciation, pitch, intonation, and rhythm.

The author would like to thank all of the contributors for their participation in the *Shuwayya 'An Nafsi* project.

- Visit www.lingualism.com/san, where you can find:
- free accompanying audio to download or stream (at variable playback rates)
- a guide to the Lingualism orthographic (spelling and tashkeel) system
- links to accompanying materials (Anki flashcards, Premium Audio)

How to Use This Book

The sections are numbered, but that does not mean you have to do them in order. Sections do not build on previous sections, and words and phrases found in each section are given even if they appear in other sections. That said, if you are a **beginner**, you will want to do sections 1-10 first, as these lay out even the most basic words (pronouns, prepositions, conjunctions), which are largely excluded from the other sections.

Each section begins with a question presented in the masculine singular form, as is the norm on surveys.

Vocabulary from the question.

The feminine form of the question.

Key expressions may be given.

Nouns *Irregular plurals are normally given.*

Verbs *The corresponding conjugation table from the book* Egyptian Colloquial Arabic Verbs *is given in small square brackets.*

Adjectives

Adverbs

Function Words *Other parts of speech, such as conjunctions, prepositions, and pronouns.*

Vocabulary unique to each response appears in order of appearance.

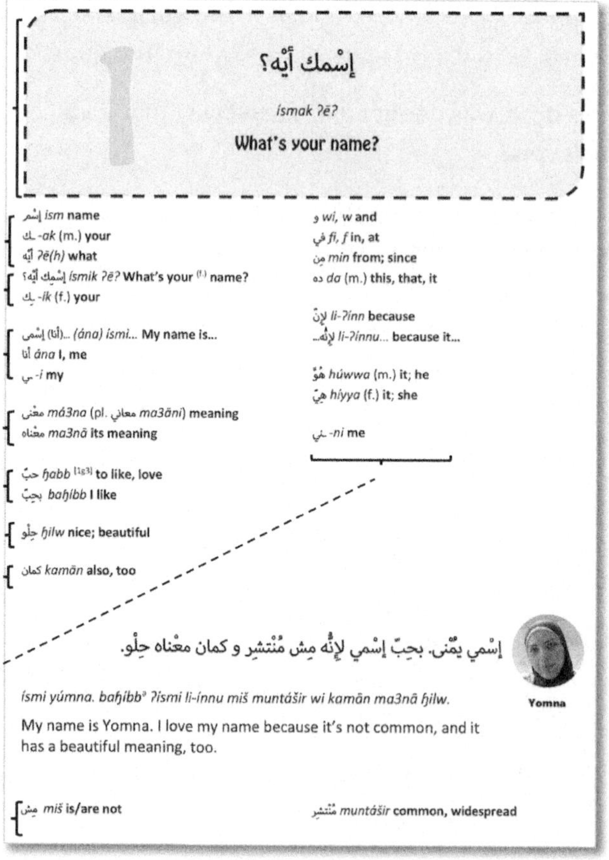
1

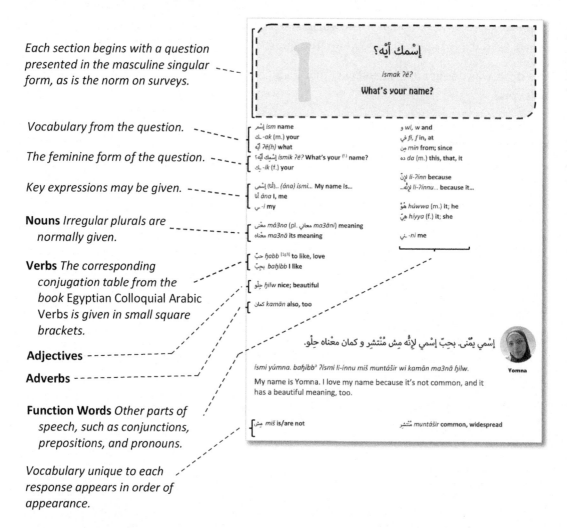

إسْمك أيْه؟

ísmak ʔē?

What's your name?

إسْم *ism* name
ـك *-ak* (m.) your
أيْه *ʔē(h)* what
إسْمِك أيْه؟ *ísmik ʔē?* What's your (f.) name?
ـِك *-ik* (f.) your

(أنا) إسْمي... *(ána) ísmi...* My name is...
أنا *ána* I, me
ـي *-i* my

معْنى *má3na* (pl. معاني *ma3āni*) meaning
معْناه *ma3nā* its meaning

حبّ *ḥabb* [1g3] to like, love
بحِبّ *baḥíbb* I like

حِلْو *ḥilw* nice; beautiful

كمان *kamān* also, too

و *wi, w* and
في *fi, f* in, at
مِن *min* from; since
ده *da* (m.) this, that, it

لإِنّ *li-ʔinn* because
لإِنُّه... *li-ʔínnu...* because it...

هُوّ *húwwa* (m.) it; he
هِيّ *híyya* (f.) it; she

ـني *-ni* me

إسْمي يُمْنى. بحِبّ إسْمي لإِنُّه مِش مُنْتشِر و كمان معْناه حِلْو.

ísmi yúmna. baḥíbbᵃ ʔísmi li-ínnu miš muntášir wi kamān ma3nā ḥilw.

My name is Yomna. I love my name because it's not common, and it has a beautiful meaning, too.

Yomna

مِش *miš* is/are not

مُنْتشِر *muntášir* common, widespread

Study the responses. Listen to the MP3s and read the responses. Notice how words are used together. Making notes of (or highlighting) groups of words used together in meaningful chunks and memorizing them will help you to produce more natural, idiomatic language. *(Note on MP3s: There is a three-second pause between each response—not enough time for you to repeat it, but this should give you time to pause the audio.)*

Give your own response. At the end of each section, there is a page where you can practice using words and phrases you have learned. First, write out the question in the "arrow" box.

Then write your own personal response to the question. As you can see, there are places for two more responses. Whose? Be creative:

- Interview an Egyptian friend.
- Interview your teacher or a classmate.
- Use the questions to talk to Egyptians online on a language exchange website or chat room.
- Interview a friend or family member (in English!), and translate (or paraphrase) their answers in Egyptian Arabic.
- Imagine you are interviewing a celebrity or public figure. What might their answers be? Use what you know about them, find out more online (Wikipedia, etc.), or just be imaginative.
- Create your own fictional character from Egypt to answer the questions!

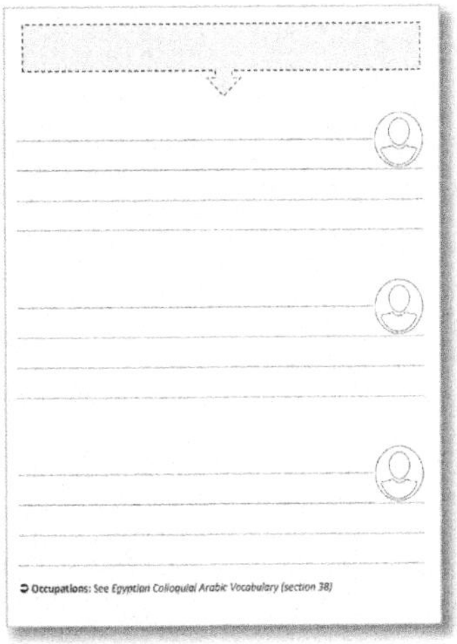
➲ Occupations: See *Egyptian Colloquial Arabic Vocabulary (section 38)*

Try your best when answering, but don't worry about making mistakes. These are part of the learning process. The book *Egyptian Colloquial Arabic Vocabulary* (available from Lingualism) contains additional words and phrases you may want in order to write your responses. References to suggested sections of this book are given at the bottom of the page. You can also use other references, of course, such as a dictionary or native speakers. If you still cannot find the word you are looking for, go ahead and substitute it in your sentence with the Modern Standard Arabic word or even the English translation. Perhaps later, you will have an opportunity to improve your responses.

Practice reading. The questions and responses appear again in Appendix C, written without voweling or the distraction of the phonemic transcriptions, translations, and glossaries. Practice reading them (with or without the audio).

Appendix C: The Egyptian Arabic Texts

1 إسمك أيه؟
إسمك أيه؟

يمنى: إسمي يمنى. بحب إسمي لإنه مش منتشر و كمان معناه حلو.
محمد: أنا إسمي محمد. أكيد إنتو عارفين إن ده أشهر إسم في العالم.
داليا: أنا إسمي داليا. و بحب إسمي جدا لإن داليا هي إسم زهرة شكلها و لونها حلو.
أندرو: أنا إسمي أندرو و الإسم ده نادر في مصر و من صغري بيقولولي دورا علشان رجلي صغيرة.
آيه: أنا إسمي آية. و معناه معجزة أو دليل زي الآيات في القرآن.
محمود: محمود أسامة، و معنى إسم محمود هو الشخص اللي بيمدح في الناس كتير.
رباب: إسمي رباب محمود. رباب يعني السحاب الأبيض و ممكن كمان يكون معناه ربابة (آلة موسيقية).
تامر: إسمي تامر. الإسم تركي الأصل و غالبا معظم الناس على النت بيفتكروني تركي.
شروق: إسمي شروق و معنى إسمي جاي من شروق الشمس و صحابي بينادوني شيرو.
فؤاد: إسمي فؤاد و ده إسم قديم شوية و معناه القلب. و اتسميت بيه تيمنا بجدي الله يرحمه.

Abbreviations

coll.	collective noun
f.	feminine
lit.	literally
m.	masculine
pl.	plural

Pronunciation

Egyptian Colloquial Arabic is a spoken dialect with no official status or rules of orthography. Egyptians tend to borrow spelling conventions from Modern Standard Arabic with some accommodations to account for ECA pronunciation. Arabic script, however, is ill suited to show the actual pronunciation of ECA and the sound changes that occur when words are inflected. (For a treatment of these sound changes, see the book *Egyptian Colloquial Arabic Verbs.*) Even if you are comfortable with Arabic script, it is advised that you pay close attention to the phonemic transcriptions to determine the exact pronunciation of words and phrases.

Consonants

The following sounds are also found in English and should pose no difficulties for learners:

			examples
b	ب	[b] as in **b**ed	*bána* بنى *(build)*
d	د	[d̪] as in **d**og, but with the tongue touching the back of the upper teeth	*dáras* درس *(study)*
f	ف	[f] as in **f**our	*fāz* فاز *(win)*
g	ج	[g] as in **g**as	*gíri* جري *(run)*
h	ه	[h] as in **h**ouse	*hágam* هجم *(attack)*
k	ك	[k] as in **k**id	*kal* كل *(eat)*
l	ل	[l] a light ***l*** as in **l**ove; but in the word الله [ɫ] a dark, velarized ***l*** as in ye**ll**.	*líbis* لِبس *(get dressed)*
m	م	[m] as in **m**oon	*māt* مات *(die)*
n	ن	[n] as in **n**ice	*nísi* نِسي *(forget)*
s	س ث	[s] as in **s**un	*sāb* ساب *(leave)*
š	ش	[ʃ] as in **sh**ow	*šakk* شكّ *(doubt)*
t	ت	[t̪] as in **t**ie, but with the tongue touching the back of the upper teeth	*taff* تفّ *(spit)*
w	و	[w] as in **w**ord	*wárra* ورّى *(show)*
y	ي	[j] as in **y**es	*yíktib* يِكْتِب *(he writes)*
z	ز ذ	[z] as in **z**oo	*zār* زار *(visit)*
ž	ج	[ʒ] as in plea**s**ure and bei**g**e; used in foreign borrowings and sometimes written چ to distinguish it from ج [g].	*žim* جيم *(gym)*
v	ف	[v] (sometimes spelled ڤ) and [p] (پ)	*seven ap* سفن أپ *(7 Up)*
p	ب	appear in some foreign borrowings, but may also be pronounced [f] and [b], respectively, by many speakers	

The following sounds have no equivalent in English and require special attention. However, some exist in other languages you may be familiar with.

r	ر	[ɾ] tapped (flapped) as in the Spanish cara, or the Scottish pronunciation of tree	*ráma* رمى *(throw)*
ɣ	غ	[ɣ] very similar to a guttural ***r*** as in the French Paris, or the German rot	*ɣāb* غاب *(be absent)*
x	خ	[x] as in the German do**ch**, Spanish rojo, or Scottish lo**ch**	*xad* خد *(take)*
q	ق	[q] like ***k*** but further back, almost in the throat, with the tongue touching the uvula	*qād* قاد *(lead)*
ɧ	ح	[ħ] like a strong, breathy ***h***, as if you were trying to fog up a window	*ɧáfar* حفر *(dig)*
3	ع	[ʕ] a voiced glottal stop, as if you had opened your mouth under water and constricted your throat to prevent choking and then released the constriction with a sigh	*3írif* عِرِف *(know)*
ʔ	ء ق	[ʔ] an unvoiced glottal stop, as [ʕ] above, but with a wispy, unvoiced sigh; or more simply put, like the constriction separating the vowels in uh-oh	*ʔíbil* قِبِل *(accept)* *ʔá3lan* أعْلن *(announce)*

The following sounds also have no equivalent in English but are emphatic versions of otherwise familiar sounds. An emphatic consonant is produced by pulling the tongue back toward the pharynx (throat), spreading the sides of the tongue wide as if you wanted to bite down on both sides of your tongue, and producing a good puff of air from the lungs.

ḍ	ض	[dˤ] emphatic ***d***	*ḍárab* ضرب *(hit)*
ṣ	ص	[sˤ] emphatic ***s***	*ṣamm* صمّ *(memorize)*
ṭ	ط	[tˤ] emphatic ***t***	*ṭáwa* طَوى *(fold)*
ẓ	ظ	[zˤ] emphatic ***z***	*ẓann* ظنّ *(believe)*

Vowels

			examples
a	ـَ	[æ] normally as in c**a**t (but with the jaw not quite as lowered as in English); [a] as in st**o**ck when in the same syllable with ***ɧ*** or ***3*** (with the tongue lower than [æ]); usually [ɑ] as in f**a**ther (but shorter) when in the same word as ***q, ḍ, ṣ, ṭ, ẓ,*** or, in most cases, ***r***	*kátab* كتب *(write)* *ɧámla* همْلى *(I will fill)* *mabá3š* مباعْش *(he didn't sell)* *ḍárab* ضرب *(hit)* *ɣáṣab* غصب *(force)*
ā	ـا	[æ:] / [a:] / [ɑ:] as with ***a*** above but longer	*nām* نام *(sleep)* *gā3* جاع *(get hungry)* *qād* قاد *(lead)*
ē	ـيْ	[e:] as in pl**ay** (but without the glide to [j])	*malēt* مليْت *(I filled)*
ə		[ə] as in tick**e**t. In ECA, ᵊ is inserted to avoid three adjacent consonants.	*kúntᵊ hína* كُنْت هِنا *(I was here)*
i	ـِ	[ɪ] as in k**i**d; [ɛ] as in b**e**d when in the same syllable with ***ɧ*** or ***3***; when in the same word as ***q, ḍ, ṣ, ṭ,*** or ***ẓ,*** [ɨ] with the tongue pulled back a bit	*3ílim* عِلِم *(know)* *biyíɧsib* بِيحْسِب *(he calculates)* *itẓāhir* اِتْظاهِر *(protest)*
ī	ـي	[i:] as in sk**i**; [ɛ:] and [ɨ:] as with **i** above (but longer)	*biygīb* بِيْجيب *(he brings)* *biybī3* بِيْبيع *(he sells)* *3āqib* عاقِب *(punish)*
ō	ـوْ	[o:] as with **o** above but longer	*nōm* نوْم *(sleep)*
u	ـُ	[ʊ] as in b**oo**k; [o] as in kn**ow** (but shorter and without the glide to [w]) when in the same syllable with ***ɧ*** or ***3***	*yúṭlub* يُطْلُب *(he orders)* *inbā3u* اِنْباعوا *(they sold)*
ū	ـو	[u:] as in m**oo**n; [o:] as in kn**ow** (but without the glide to [w]) when in the same syllable with ***ɧ*** or ***3***	*bitšūf* بِتْشوف *(you see)* *maba3ūš* مباعوش *(they didn't sell)*

إسْمك أيْه؟

ísmak ʔē?

What's your name?

إسْم *ism* **name**
ـك *-ak* (m.) **your**
أيْه *ʔē(h)* **what**
إسْمِك أيْه؟ *ísmik ʔē?* **What's your** (f.) **name?**
ـِك *-ik* (f.) **your**

(أنا) إسْمي... *(ána) ísmi...* **My name is...**
أنا *ána* **I, me**
ـي *-i* **my**

معْنى *má3na* (pl. معاني *ma3āni*) **meaning**
معْناه *ma3nā* **its meaning**

حبّ *ɦabb* [1g3] **to like, love**
بحِبّ *baɦíbb* **I like**

حِلْو *ɦilw* **nice; beautiful**

كمان *kamān* **also, too**

و *wi, w* **and**
في *fi, f* **in, at**
مِن *min* **from; since**
ده *da* (m.) **this, that, it**

لإِنّ *li-ʔínn* **because**
لإِنُّه... *li-ʔínnu...* **because it...**

هُوَّ *húwwa* (m.) **it; he**
هِيَّ *híyya* (f.) **it; she**

ـني *-ni* **me**

Yomna

إسْمي يمْنى. بحِبّ إسْمي لإِنُّه مِش مُنْتشِر و كمان معْناه حِلْو.

ísmi yúmna. baɦíbbᵊ ʔísmi li-ínnu miš muntášir wi kamān ma3nā ɦilw.

My name is Yomna. I love my name because it's not common, and it has a beautiful meaning, too.

مِش *miš* **is/are not**
مُنْتشِر *muntášir* **common, widespread**

Mohamed

أنا إسْمي مُحمّد. أكيد إنْتو عارْفين إنّ ده أشْهر إسْم في العالم.

ána ísmi muḫámmad. akīd íntu 3arfīn innᵊ da ášhar ismᵊ fi -l3ālam.

My name is Mohamed. I'm sure you know that it's the most popular name in the world.

أكيد *akīd* **for sure, undoubtedly**
إنْتو *íntu* (pl.) **you (guys)**
عارْفين *3arfīn* (pl.) **know(ing)**
إنّ... *inn...* **that...**
مشْهور *mašhūr* **famous, well known**
أشْهر *ášhar* (+ noun) **the most famous __**
عالم *3ālam* **world**
في العالم *fi -l3ālam* **in the world**

Dalia

أنا إسْمي دالْيا. و بحِبّ إسْمي جِدّاً لإنّ دالْيا هِيَّ إسْم زهرة شكْلها و لونْها حِلْو.

ána ísmi dálya. wi baḫíbbᵊ ʔísmi gíddan li-ʔínnᵊ dálya híyya ismᵊ záhara šakláha w lúnha ḫilw.

My name is Dalia. I really love my name because it is the name of a flower with a beautiful shape and color.

جِدّاً *gíddan* **really, a lot; very**
زهرة *záhara* **flower**
شكْل *šakl* **shape**
لوْن *lōn* (pl. ألْوان *alwān*) **color**
ـها *-ha, -áha* (f.) **its; her**
شكْلها *šakláha* **its shape**
لونْها *lúnha* **its color**

Andrew

أنا إسْمي أنْدْرو و الإسْم ده نادِر في مصْر و مِن صُغْري بِيْقولولي دورا علشان رِجْلي صْغيرّة.

ána ʔísmi ʔándru wi -lʔismᵊ da nādir fi maṣr, wi min ṣúɣri biyʔulūli dōra 3alašān rígli ṣɣayyára.

My name is Andrew. This name is rare in Egypt. And ever since I was a kid, people have called me Dora because my feet are small.*

الـ__ ده *il-__ da* (+ m. noun) **this __**
نادِر *nādir* **rare, uncommon**
مصْر *maṣr* (f.) **Egypt**
صُغر *ṣuɣr* **childhood, youth; smallness**
قال *ʔāl* [1h1] **to say, call**
بِيْقولوا *biyʔūlu* **they say, they call**
ـلي *-li* **to me**
علشان *3alašān* **because**
رِجْل *rigl* (f.) **foot; leg**
صُغيرّ *ṣuɣáyyar* **small**

Aya

أنا إسْمي آيَة. و معْناه مُعْجِزة أَوْ دليل زيّ الآيات في القُرآن.

ána ʔísmi ʔāya. wi ma3nā mu3gíza ʔaw dalīl zayy ilʔayāt fi -lqurʔān.

My name is Aya, and it means *miracle* or *attestation* like the verses of the Quran.

مُعْجِزة *mu3gíza* **miracle**
أَوْ *aw* **or**
دليل *dalīl* **sign, proof, evidence**
زيّ *zayy* **like, as, such as**
آيَة *āya* **Quranic verse;** (lit.) **miracle, sign**
القُرآن *ilqurʔān* **the Quran**

Mahmoud

محْمود أُسامة، و معْنى إسْم محْمود هُوَّ الشّخْص اللي بْيِمْدح في النّاس كِتير.

maɦmūd usāma, wi má3na ismᵊ maɦmūd húwwa -ššáxṣ ílli byímdaɦ fi -nnās kitīr.

Mahmoud Osama. Mahmoud means the person who praises people a lot.

شخْص *šaxṣ* (pl. أشْخاص *ašxāṣ*) **person**
اللي *ílli* **that, who; which**
مدح في [1s1] *mádaɦ fi* **to praise**
بيِمْدح في *biyímdaɦ fi* **he praises**
ناس *nās* **people**
كِتير *kitīr* **often, a lot; many**

Rabab

إسْمي رباب محْمود. رباب يَعْني السّحاب الأبْيَض و مُمْكِن كمان يِكون معْناه ربابة (آلة موسيقية).

ísmi rabāb maɦmūd. rabāb yá3ni -ssaɦāb ilʔábyaḍ wi múmkin kamān yikūn ma3nā rabāba (āla musiqíyya).

My name is Rabab Mahmoud. Rabab means *white clouds,* and it can also mean *rebec* (a musical instrument).

يَعْني *yá3ni* **means; that is...**
سحاب *saɦāb* (coll.) **clouds**
أبْيَض *ábyaḍ* **white**
مُمْكِن *múmkin* (+ imperfect) **may, might, could; possibly**
كان *kān* [1h1] **to be;** يِكون *yikūn* **is, be**
ربابة *rabāba* **rebec** (bowed string instrument)
آلَة *āla* **instrument**
موسيقي *musīqi* **musical** (f. موسيقية *musiqíyya*)

Tamer

إسْمي تامِر. الإسْم تُرْكي الأصْل و غالِباً مُعْظم النّاس على النّت بِيِفْتِكْروني تُرْكي.

ísmi tāmir. ilʔísmᵊ túrki -lʔaṣlᵊ w ɣāliban múʒẓam innās ʒála -nnet biyiftikrūni túrki.

My name is Tamer. The name is of Turkish origin, so most people on the Internet probably think that I'm Turkish.

الأصْل __ *ilʔáṣl* **of __ origin**
تُرْكي *túrki* **Turkish**
غالِباً *ɣāliban* **probably; usually**
مُعْظم __ *múʒẓam__* **most of __**
على النّت *ʒála -nnet* **on the Internet**
اِفْتكر *iftákar* [8s1] **to think**
بِيِفْتِكْروا *biyiftíkru* **they think**

Shorouk

إسْمي شُروق و معْنى إسْمي جايّ مِن شُروق الشّمْس و صُحابي بِيْنادوني شيرو.

ísmi šurūʔ wi máʒna ísmi gayyᵊ min šurūʔ iššáms, wi ṣuḥābi biynadūni šīru.

My name is Shorouk. The meaning of my name comes from *sunrise*, and my friends call me Shiro.

جايّ *gayy* **coming**
شُروق *šurūʔ* **(sun)rise**
شمْس *šams* **sun**
صاحِب *ṣāḥib* (pl. صُحاب *ṣuḥāb*) **friend**
نادى *nāda* [3h] **to call**
بِيْنادوا *biynādu* **they call**

Fouad

إسْمي فُؤاد و ده إسْم قديم شُوَيّة و معْناه القلْب. و اِتْسمّيْت بيه تَيَمُّناً بِجِدّي الله يِرْحمُه.

ísmi fuʔād wi da ismᵊ ʔadīm šuwáyya wi maʒnā ilʔálb. w itsammēt bī tayammúnan bi-gíddi, allāh yirḥámu.

My name is Fouad. This is a somewhat old name, and it means *heart*. I was named after my grandfather, God rest his soul.

قديم *ʔadīm* **old**
شُوَيّة *šuwáyya* **somewhat, a little**
قلْب *ʔalb* (pl. قلوب *ʔulūb*) **heart**
اِتْسمّى بِـ *itsámma bi-* [5d] **to be named/called**
بِـ *bi-* **with, by; in, at**
بيه *bī* **with it** (m.)**, by it**
اِتْسمّى تَيَمُّناً بِـ *itsámma tayammúnan bi-* **to be named after**
جِدّ *gidd* (pl. جُدود *gudūd*) **grandfather**
الله يِرْحمُه *allāh yirḥámu* **God rest his soul, R.I.P.**

Andrew's name: In recent years, it has become a minor trend in Egypt to give your child an English name. However, in the 1980s, when Andrew was born, it was quite rare. Andrew's father named him after a character in an American movie he had seen. Andrew's brother also has an English name, while his sister has a Greek name. Andrew's grandparents had trouble pronouncing his name at first and nicknamed him Dora. They told him it was because his feet were so small when he was little, although Andrew himself doesn't quite understand the connection between the nickname and small feet.

2

إنْتَ مْنينْ؟

ínta mnēn?

Where are you from?

إنْتَ *ínta* (m.) **you**
مِنيْن *minēn* **from where**
إنْتي مْنينْ؟ *ínti mnēn?* **Where are you** (f.) **from?**

أنا مِن... *ána min...* **I'm from...; I come from...**
أنا *ána* **I (am)**
مِن *min* **from**

مصْر *maṣr* (f.) **Egypt**
القاهِرة *ilqāhíra* **Cairo**
إسْكِنْدِرية *iskindiríyya* **Alexandria**
الجيزة *ilgīza* **Giza**

عاصِمة *3āṣíma* **capital (city)**
مُحافْظة *muɦáfẓa* **governorate, province**
بلد *bálad* (pl. بِلاد *bilād*) **land, country**
حيّ *ɦayy* (pl. أحْياء *aɦyā?*) **district, neighborhood**

عايِش *3āyiš* **living** (f. عايْشة *3áyša*)

تحْديداً *taɦdīdan* **specifically, to be precise**

و *wi, w* **and**

في *fi, f* **in, at**
مِن *min* **from; since; than**

هُوَّ *húwwa* (m.) **it; he**
هِيَّ *híyya* (f.) **it; she**

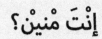

Yomna

أنا مِن مصْر، و تحْديداً مِن القاهِرة العاصِمة. و عِشْت أغْلب حَياتي في مُحافْظِةْ الجيزة المُلاصْقة لِلْقاهِرة.

ána min maṣr, wi taɦdīdan min ilqāhíra, il3āṣíma. wi 3išt áɣlab ɦayāti fi muɦáfẓit ilgīza, ilmuláṣqa li-lqāhíra.

I'm from Egypt—from the capital, Cairo, to be precise. I've lived most of my life in Giza, which is adjacent to Cairo.

عاش *3āš* [1h2] **to live**
عِشْت *3išt* **I lived**
أغْلب حَياتي *áɣlab ɦayāti* **most of my life**
أغْلب __ *áɣlab* __ (+ noun) **most of __**

حَياة *ɦáya* **life**
مُلاصِق لِـ *mulāṣiq li-* **adjacent to, bordering, attached to**

Mohamed

أنا أصْلاً مِن إسْكِنْدِرية، بلد البحْر المتُوَسِّط الرّايِق و البنات.

ána ʔáṣlan min iskindiríyya, bálad ilbáɦr ilmutawássiṭ irrāyiʔ wi -lbanāt.

I'm from Alexandria, the land of the tranquil Mediterranean Sea and girls.

أصْلاً *áṣlan* **originally**
البحْر المتُوَسِّط *ilbáɦr ilmutawássiṭ* **the Mediterranean Sea**
بحْر *baɦr* (pl. بِحار *biɦār*) **sea**
مُتَوَسِّط *mutawássiṭ* **mid-**
رايِق *rāyiʔ* **calm, tranquil**
بِنْت *bint* (pl. بنات *banāt*) **girl**

Dalia

أنا مِن مصْر و تحْديداً القاهِرة العاصِمة و كمان أنا طول عُمْري عايْشة في الجيزة و هِيَّ جمْبها.

ána min maṣr, wi taɦdīdan ilqāhíra il3āṣima wi kamān ána ṭūl 3úmri 3áyša fi -lgīza wi híyya gambáha.

I'm from Egypt, specifically from the capital, Cairo. I've lived all my life in Giza, which is next to Cairo.

كمان *kamān* **also, too**
طول عُمْري *ṭūl 3úmri* **all my life**
طول *ṭūl* **throughout**
عُمْر *3umr* **lifetime; age**
جمْبها *gambáha* **next to it**
جمْب *gamb* **next to**
ـها *-ha, -áha* (f.) **it; her**

Andrew

أنا مِن شُبْرا و هُوَّ حيّ شعْبي مَوْجود مِن أكْتر مِن ميتيْن سنة في القاهِرة.

ána min šúbra w húwwa ɦayyᵊ šá3bi mawgūd min áktar min mitēn sána fi -ilqāhíra.

I'm from Shoubra, a working-class district that's been around for more than two hundred years in Cairo.

شعْبي *šá3bi* **working-class-; popular**
مَوْجود *mawgūd* **present, existing, found**
أكْتر مِن *áktar min* **more than, over**
ميتيْن *mitēn* **two-hundred**
سنة *sána* (pl. سِنين *sinīn*) **year**

أنا مِن مصْر الجِديدة في القاهِرة، حيّ راقي جِدّاً و هادي.

ána min maṣr ilgidīda fi -lqāhíra, ɦayy^{ə} rāqi gíddan wi hādi.

Aya

I'm from Heliopolis in Cairo, an upscale, quiet neighborhood.

مصْر الجِديدة *maṣr ilgidīda* (f.) **Heliopolis**
جِديد *gidīd* **new**
راقي *rāqi* **middle-class-, upper-class-, upscale**
جِدّاً *gíddan* **very; really, a lot**
هادي *hādi* **quiet, calm**

مِن مصْر. دي أحْسن بلد في العالم و فيها تُلْتينْ أثار العالم.

min maṣr. di ʔáɦsan bálad fi -l3ālam wi fīha tultēn asār il3ālam.

Mahmoud

From Egypt, the best country in the world, which has two-thirds of the world's ancient monuments.

دي *di* (f.) **this, that, it**
أحْسن __ *áɦsan* __ (+ noun) **the best __**
عالم *3ālam* **world**
فيها *fīha* **in it** (f.)
تُلْتينْ *tultēn* **two-thirds**
أثر *ásar* (pl. أثار asār) **ancient monument, ruin**

أنا مِن مصْر، تحْديداً مِن مُحافْظِةْ الإسْكِنْدِرية، أجْمل مُحافْظات مصْر.

ána min maṣr, taɦdīdan min muɦáfẓit ilʔiskindiríyya, ágmal muɦafẓāt maṣr.

Rabab

I'm from Egypt, specifically from Alexandria, the most beautiful governorate in Egypt.

أجْمل *ágmal* **the most beautiful**

Tamer

أنا مِن إسْكِنْدِرِية مِن حيّ العجمي، منْطِقة في غرْب إسْكِنْدِرِية كانِت زمان مِن أفْضل المصايِف.

ána min iskindiríyya, min ḩayy il3ágami, manţíʔa f ɣarb iskindiríyya kānit zamān min áfḑal ilmaşāyif.

I'm from Alexandria, from the district Agami, an area in the west of Alexandria, which was once considered one of the best summer spots.

منْطِقة *manţíʔa* (pl. مناطِق *manāţiʔ*) **area, region**
غرْب *ɣarb* **west**
كانِت *kānit* **it** (f.) **was**
زمان *zamān* **long ago, in the past, used to (be)**
مِن أفْضل __ *min áfḑal__* (+ plural noun) **one of the best __**
أفْضل *áfḑal* **the best**
مصْيَف *máşyaf* (pl. مصايِف *maşāyif*) **summer spot, summer resort**

Shorouk

أنا مِن القاهِرة في مصْر بسّ كُنْت عايْشة فترْةْ طُفولْتي في الإمارات.

ána min ilqāhíra fi maşr, bass kuntᵊ 3áyša fátrit ţufúlti fi -lʔimarāt.

I'm from Cairo, Egypt, but I spent my childhood in the Emirates.

بسّ *bass* **but**
كُنْت عايْشة *kuntᵊ 3áyša* (f.) **I was living**
كُنْت *kunt* **I was**
فترْةْ طُفولْتي *fátrit ţufúlti* **during my childhood**
فترْة *fátra* **period (of time)**
طُفولة *ţufūla* **childhood**
الإمارات *ilʔimarāt* (f.) **the Emirates, the U.A.E.**

Fouad

مِن القاهِرة، مدينِةْ نصْر في الأساس، و لكِن أصْل العيْلة نفْسُه غيْر معْروف بِالنِّسْبة لي.

min ilqāhíra, madīnit naşrᵊ fi -lʔasās, wi lākin aşl il3ēla náfsu ɣēr ma3rūf bi-nnisbā-li.

From Cairo, basically Nasr City, but the origin of my family itself is unknown to me.

مدينة *madīna* (pl. مُدُن *múdun*) **city**
في الأساس *fi -lʔasās* **basically**
و لكِن *wi lākin* **but**
أصْل *aşl* **origin**
عيْلة *3ēla* **family**
نفْسُه *náfsu* **itself**
غيْر معْروف *ɣēr ma3rūf* **unknown**
غيْر *ɣēr* **un-, non-, not**
معْروف *ma3rūf* **known**
بِالنِّسْبة لي *bi-nnisbā-li* **as for me, personally**

Cairo is officially the city on the east bank of the Nile, while everything to the west of the Nile is **Giza**. However, both municipalities, along with other surrounding suburbs, are commonly referred to as *Greater Cairo* (القاهِرة الكُبْرى *ilqāhíra -lkúbra*).

➲ **Countries:** See *Egyptian Colloquial Arabic Vocabulary (section 39)*

3

سِنّك كام؟

sínnak kām?

How old are you?

سِنّ *sinn* **age**
ـك *-ak* (m.) **your**
كام *kām* **how much**
سِنّك كام؟ *sínnik kām?* **How old are you** [(f.)]**?**

سنة *sána* (pl. سِنين *sinīn*) **year**
سنِةْ __ *sánit* __ **in the year __**

شهْر *šahr* (pl. شُهور *šuhūr*) **month**
يوْم *yōm* (pl. أيّام *ayyām*) **day**
عيد ميلاد *3īd milād* (pl. أعْياد الميلاد *a3yād ilmilād*) **birthday**

اِتْوَلد *itwálad* [7s1] **to be born**
اِتْوَلدْت *itwaládt* **I was born**

تمّ *tamm* [1g3] **to turn __ (years old); to complete**
تمّيْت *tammēt* **I turned __ (years old)**
هتِمّ *hatímm* **I will turn __ (years old)**

أنا عنْدي __ سنة *ána 3ándi __ sána* **I am __ years old**
عنْدي *3ándi* **I have**

الجايّ *ilgáyy, iggáyy* **the next, coming**

كمان *kamān* **in __ more...; also, too**

و *wi* **and**

أنا *ána* **I, me; I am**
ـي *-i* **my**
ده *da* (m.) **this, that, it**
هُوَّ *húwwa* (m.) **it; he**

في *fi, f* **in, on, at**

Yomna

أنا سِنّي خمْسة و تلاتين سنة. و في شهْر نوفِمْبِر الجايّ هتِمّ سِتّة و تلاتين.
إنّما بِالتّقْويم الهِجْري هكون تمّيْت سِتّة و تلاتين خلاص.

ána sínni xámsa w talatīn sána. wi fi šahr[ə] nuvímbir ilgáyy hatímm sítta w talatīn. innáma bi-ttaqwīm ilhígri hakūn tammēt sítta w talatīn xalāṣ.

I'm thirty-five years old. Next November, I'll turn thirty-six. But I will have already completed my thirty-sixth year according to the Islamic calendar.*

أنا سِنّي __ سنة *ána sínni __ sána* **I am __ years old**
نوفِمْبِر *nuvímbir* **November**
إنّما *innáma* **however, but**
بِـ *bi-* **with, by; in, at**
تقْويم *taqwīm* **calendar**
هِجْري *hígri* **Hijri**
هكون تمّيْت *hakūn tammēt* **I will have completed**
خلاص *xalāṣ* **now, already**

Mohamed

أنا مِكمِّل سبْعة و عِشْرين سنة، كمان أُسْبوع بِالظَّبْط، يوْم اِتْنين إبْريل هُوَّ عيد ميلادي.

ána mikámmil sáb3a wi 3išrīn sána kamān usbū3 bi-ẓẓábṭ. yōm itnēn ibrīl húwwa 3īd milādi.

I'll be twenty-seven in exactly one week. My birthday is on April 2.

مِكمِّل *mikámmil* **completing**
أُسْبوع *usbū3* (pl. أسابيع *asabī3*) **week**
بِالظَّبْط *bi-ẓẓábṭ* **exactly, precisely**
إبْريل *ibrīl* **April**

Dalia

أنا عنْدي اِتْنيْن و عِشْرين سنة. اِتْوَلدْت يوْم واحِد أُكْتوبر ألْف تُسْعُمية تلاتة و تِسْعين و كمان اِتْوَلدْت في القاهِرة.

ána 3ándi -tnēn wi 3išrīn sána. itwaládt^ə yōm wāḫid uktōbar alf^ə tus3umíyya talāta w tis3īn wi kamān itwaládt^ə fi -lqāhíra.

I'm twenty-two years old. I was born on October 1, 1993, and I was born in Cairo.

أُكْتوبر *uktōbar* **October**
القاهِرة *ilqāhíra* **Cairo**

Andrew

أنا عنْدي تِسْعة و عِشْرين سنة لِإنِّي اتْوَلدْت في أُكْتوبر سنِةْ ألْف تُسْعُمية سِتّة و تمانين و بِالأخصّ في اليوْم تُلْتُمية في السّنة.

ána 3ándi tís3a w 3išrīn sána li-ínni itwaládt^ə fi uktōbar sánit alf^ə tus3umíyya sítta w tamanīn wi bi-lʔaxáṣṣ fi -lyōm tultumíyya fi -ssána.

I'm twenty-nine years old because I was born in October 1986 and specifically on the 300th day of the year.

لِإنِّي... *li-ínni...* **because I...**
أُكْتوبر *uktōbar* **October**
بِالأخصّ *bi-lʔaxáṣṣ* **specifically**

Aya

أنا عنْدي تلاتة و عِشْرين سنة. بسّ العُمْر مُجرّد رقم. الشّباب في الرّوح.

ána 3ándi talāta wi 3išrīn sána. bass il3úmr[ə] mugárrad ráqam. iššabāb fi -rrūḫ.

I'm twenty-three years old, but age is just a number. Youth is in the soul.

بسّ *bass* **but**
عُمْر *3umr* **age**
مُجرّد *mugárrad* **just**
رقم *ráqam* **number**
شباب *šabāb* **youth, being young**
روح *rūḫ* **soul**

Mahmoud

واحِد و عِشْرين سنة، عشان أنا مَوْلود سنِةْ ألْف تُسْعُمية أرْبعة و تِسْعين، يَعْني كمان شهْريْن هكمِّل اِتْنيْن و عِشْرين سنة.

wāḫid wi 3išrīn sána, 3ašān ána mawlūd sánit alf[ə] tus3umíyya arbá3a wi tis3īn, yá3ni kamān šahrēn hakámmil itnēn wi 3išrīn sána.

Twenty-one years old, as I was born in 1994. And this means that in two months I'll turn twenty-two.

مَوْلود *mawlūd* **born**
يَعْني *yá3ni* **this means; that is**
شهْريْن *šahrēn* **two months**
كمِّل *kámmil* [2s1] **to complete**
هـ *ha-* **(I) will**

Rabab

أنا عنْدي سبْعة و عِشْرين سنة و عيد ميلادي هَيْكون في شهْر مايو.

ána 3ándi sáb3a wi 3išrīn sána wi 3īd milādi haykūn fi šahr[ə] māyu.

I'm twenty-seven years old, and my birthday will be in May.

كان *kān* [1h1] **to be**
هَيْكون *haykūn* **it will be**
مايو *māyu* **May**

Tamer

عنْدي أرْبعة و تلاتين سنة و سِتّ شُهور و حِداشر يوْم تقْريباً.

3ándi arbá3a wi talatīn sána wi sitt^ə šuhūr wi ḫidāšar yōm taʔrīban.

I'm thirty-four years, six months, and almost eleven days old.

تقْريباً *taʔrīban* **approximately; almost**

Shorouk

دِلْوَقْتي اِتْنينْ و عِشْرين سنة و هتِمّ التّلاتة و عِشْرين شهْر عشرة الجايّ ده إن شاء الله.

dilwáʔti itnēn wi 3išrīn sána wi hatímm ittalāta wi 3išrīn šahr^ə 3ášara ilgáyy^ə da, in šāʔ allāh.

Now, twenty-two years old, and I'll be twenty-three next October, God willing.

دِلْوَقْتي *dilwáʔti* **now**

شهْر عشرة *šahr^ə 3ášara* **October** (lit. tenth month)

إن شاء الله *in šāʔ allāh* **God willing**

Fouad

سِتّة و عِشْرين سنة. و لكِن ناس كِتير بِيْقولولي إنْتَ شكْلك صُغيرّ أوي. ده بِسبب شكْل وِشّي طفولي أوي.

sítta wi 3išrīn sána. wi lākin nās kitīr biyʔulūli -nta šáklak ṣuɣáyyar áwi. da bi-sábab šakl^ə wíšši ṭfūli áwi.

Twenty-six years old. But a lot of people tell me that I look young, and that's because I have a babyface.

و لكِن *wi lākin* **but**

ناس كِتير *nās kitīr* **a lot of people**

بِيْقولولي *biyʔulūli* **they tell me**

إنْتَ *ínta* (m.) **you**

شكْل *šakl* **shape**

صُغيرّ *ṣuɣáyyar* **small, little**

أوي *áwi* **very**

بِسبب *bi-sábab* **because of**

وِشّ *wišš* (pl. وُشوش *wušūš*) **face**

طُفولي *ṭufūli* **childlike**

➲ **Numbers:** See **Appendix A**

➲ **Months:** See **Appendix B**

The Islamic Calendar: Yomna expressed that she was a year older according to the Islamic calendar. This is because a year in the Islamic calendar is some eleven days shorter than the 365 days of the solar Gregorian year.

4

تاريخ ميلادك إمْتى؟

tarīx milādak ímta?

What is your birthdate?

تاريخ *tarīx* **date**
ميلاد *milād* **birth**
ـك *-ak* (m.) **your**
إمْتى *ímta* **when**
تاريخ ميلادِك إمْتى؟ *tarīx milādik ímta?* **What is your**(f.) **birthdate?**

سنِةْ __ *sánit* __ **in the year __**
شهْر *šahr* (pl. شُهور *šuhūr*) **month**
يوْم *yōm* (pl. أيّام *ayyām*) **day**

اِتْوَلد *itwálad* [7s1] **to be born**
اِتْوَلدْت *itwaládt* **I was born**

أنا مِن مَواليد __ *ána min mawalīd* __ **I was born in/on __**

حبّ *ħabb* [1g3] **to like**
بحِبّ *baħíbb* **I like**

و *wi* **and**
و لكِن *wi lākin* **but**

أنا *ána* **I, me; I am**
ـي *-i* **my**
ـني *-ni* **me**
هُوَّ *húwwa* (m.) **it; he**
دي *di* (f.) **this, that, it**

مِن *min* **from; since; than**
في *fi, f* **in, on, at**

مِش *miš* **not; don't**

Yomna

أنا مِن مَواليد ١٤ نوفِمْبِر ١٩٨٠. و بِالتّقْويم الهِجْري ٧ مُحرّم ١٤٠١. مِش بحْتِفِل عادةً بِيوْم ميلادي بسّ بحِبّ الهدايا.

ána min mawalīd arba3tāšar nuvímbir álfᵊ tus3umíyya w tamanīn. wi bi-ttaqwīm ilhígri sáb3a muħárram álfᵊ rub3umíyya w wāħid. miš baħtífil 3ādatan bi-yōm milādi bássᵊ baħíbb ilhadāya.

I was born on November 14, 1980—or on 7 Muharram 1401, according to the Islamic calendar. I don't usually celebrate my birthday, but I love gifts.

نوفِمْبِر *nuvímbir* **November**
بِـ *bi-* **with, by; in, at**
التقْويم الهِجْري *ittaqwīm ilhígri* **the Islamic calendar**
مُحرّم *muħárram* **Muharram** (first month of the Islamic calendar)

اِحْتفل بِـ *iħtáfal bi-* [8s1] **to celebrate**
مِش بحْتِفِل بِـ *miš baħtífil bi-* **I don't celebrate**
عادةً *3ādatan* **usually**
بسّ *bass* **but**
هدية *hadíyya* (pl. هدايا *hadāya*) **present, gift**

Mohamed

تاريخ ميلادي يوْم ٢ إبْريل. اِتْوَلدْت يوْم حدّ في رمضان.

tarīx milādi yōm itnēn ibrīl. itwaládtᵊ yōm ɦaddᵊ f ramaḏān.

My birthday is on April 2. I was born on a Sunday in Ramadan.

إبْريل *ibrīl* **April**
يوْم حدّ *yōm ɦadd* **a Sunday**
يوْم الحدّ *yōm ilɦadd* **(on) Sunday**
رمضان *ramaḏān* **Ramadan** (ninth month of the Islamic calendar)

Dalia

أنا تاريخ ميلادي ١ أُكْتوبر ١٩٩٣ و اِتْوَلدْت يوْم جُمْعة و بحِبّ تاريخ ميلادي لإِنُّه مُميِّز و أوِّل الشّهْر.

ána tarīx milādi wāɦid uktōbar alfᵊ tus3umíyya talāta w tis3īn w itwaládtᵊ yōm gúm3a wi baɦíbbᵊ tarīx milādi li-ínnu mumáyyiz w áwwil iššáhr.

My birthdate is October 1, 1993. I was born on a Friday. I like my birthday because it's a special day and it's on the first of the month.

أُكْتوبر *uktōbar* **October**
يوْم جُمْعة *yōm gúm3a* **a Friday**
يوْم الجُمْعة *yōm iggúm3a* **(on) Friday**
لإِنُّه... *li-ʔínnu...* **because it...**
مُميِّز *mumáyyiz* **special, distinctive**
أوِّل *áwwil* **first, beginning**

Andrew

يوْم ٢٧ مِن شهْر أُكْتوبر سنِةْ ١٩٨٦.

yōm sáb3a w 3išrīn min šahr uktōbar sánit alfᵊ tus3umíyya sítta w tamanīn.

On October 27, 1986.

أُكْتوبر *uktōbar* **October**

Aya

تاريخ ميلادي واحِد واحِد ١٩٩٣. كان دايْماً عيد ميلادي بِيْكون في وَقْت الاِمْتِحانات.

tarīx milādi wāḫid wāḫid alfᵊ tus3umíyya talāta wi tis3īn. kān dáyman 3īd milādi biykūn fi waʔt ilʔimtiḫanāt.

I was born on January 1, 1993. My birthday would always fall during the exam period.

كان *kān* [1h1] **to be; it was**
كان بِيْكون *kān biykūn* **it would be; it used to be**
دايْماً *dáyman* **always**
عيد ميلاد *3īd milād* (pl. أعْياد ميلاد *a3yād milād*) **birthday**
وَقْت *waʔt* (pl. أوْقات *awʔāt*) **time**
اِمْتِحان *imtiḫān* **exam, test**

Mahmoud

سبْعة خمْسة ١٩٩٤، يوْم سبْعة و شهْر خمْسة و اِتْوَلدْت في السُّعودية مدينْة الرِّياض.

sáb3a xámsa alfᵊ tus3umíyya arbá3a wi tis3īn, yōm sáb3a wi šahrᵊ xámsa w itwaládtᵊ fi -ssu3udíyya madínt irriyāḍ.

7-5-1994 (the seventh day and fifth month), and I was born in the city of Riyadh, Saudi Arabia.

السُّعودية *issu3udíyya* **Saudi Arabia**
مدينْة الرِّياض *madínt irriyāḍ* **the city of Riyadh**
مدينة *madīna* (pl. مُدُن *múdun*) **city**
الرِّياض *irriyāḍ* **Riyadh**

Rabab

اِتْوَلدْت يوْم ٢٥ مايو سنِةْ ١٩٨٨.

itwaládtᵊ yōm xámsa w 3išrīn māyu sánit alfᵊ wi tus3umíyya tamánya w tamanīn.

I was born on May 25, 1988.

مايو *māyu* **May**

Tamer

أنا مِن مَواليد شهْر سبْتمْبِر سنِةْ ٨٢ و بُرْجي هُوَّ العذْراء.

ána min mawalīd šáhr^{ə} sabtámbir sánit itnēn wi tamanīn wi búrgi húwwa il3azrāʔ.

I was born in September ’82, and I’m a Virgo.

سبْتمبِر *sabtámbir* **September**

بُرْج *burg* **sign of the zodiac**

العذْراء *il3azrāʔ* **Virgo**

Shorouk

أنا اتْوَلدْت يوْم ٣ مِن شهْر أُكْتوبر اللي هُوَّ عشرة مِن سنِةْ ١٩٩٣.

ána -twaládt^{ə} yōm talāta min šahr uktōbar, ílli húwwa 3ášara min sánit alf^{ə} tus3umíyya talāta wi tis3īn.

I was born on October 3 (the tenth month) in 1993.

أُكْتوبر *uktōbar* **October**

اللي *ílli* **that, which**

اللي هُوَّ... *ílli húwwa...* **which is...**

Fouad

اِتْناشر اِتْناشر ١٩٨٩، و لكِن دي حاجة خلِّتْني أخُشّ الدِّراسة بدْري أوي و كُنْت ببْقى معَ ناس أكْبر مِنّي.

itnāšar itnāšar alf^{ə} tus3umíyya tís3a w tamanīn, wi lākin di ḫāga xallítni ʔaxúšš iddirāsa bádri ʔáwi wi kunt^{ə} bábʔa má3a nās ákbar mínni.

I was born on 12-12-1989. But this made me start school quite early, so I was with students who were older than me.

حاجة *ḫāga* **thing, something**

خلّى *xálla* [2d] **to make, cause**

خلِّتْني *xallítni* **it** (f.) **made me**

خشّ *xašš* [1g2] **to enter;** اخُشّ *axúšš* **I enter**

دِراسة *dirāsa* **studies**

بدْري *bádri* **early**

أوي *áwi* **very, quite**

كُنْت ببْقَى معَ *kunt^{ə} bábʔa má3a* **I would be with**

ناس *nās* **people**

أكْبر مِنّي *ákbar mínni* **older than me**

➲ **Numbers:** See **Appendix A**
➲ **Dates:** See **Appendix B**

بِتِشْتغل أيْه؟

bitištáɣal ʔē?

What do you do?

اِشْتغل *ištáɣal* [8s2] **to work (as)**
بِتِشْتغل *bitištáɣal* **you** (m.) **work**
أيْه *ʔē(h)* **what**
بِتِشْتغلى أيْه؟ *bitištáɣali ʔē?* **What do you** (f.) **do?**

بشْتغل *baštáɣal* **I work (as)**

بقالي *baʔāli* **I've been... for** (+ length of time)

شِرْكة *šírka* (pl. شرِكات *šarikāt*) **company**
عمْل *3ámal* **work, job**
شبكة *šábaka* (pl. شبكات *šabakāt*) **network**
مُهنْدِس *muhándis* **engineer**

حاليّاً *ḫalíyyan* **now, presently**
مثلاً *másalan* **for example, for instance**

أنا *ána* **I, me; I am**

فيها *fīha* **in it** (f.)
في *fi, f* **in, at**
ـها *-ha, -áha* (f.) **it; her**

و *wi, w* **and**

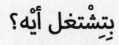

Yomna

أنا مُهنْدِسة مِعْمارية. بشْتغل في مشْروع إنْشاء المتْحف المصْري الكِبير.

ána muhandísa mi3maríyya. baštáɣal fi mašrū3 inšāʔ ilmátḫaf ilmáṣri -lkibīr.

I'm an architect, and I'm working on the construction project for the Grand Egyptian Museum.

مِعْمارى *mi3māri* **architectural**
مشْروع *mašrū3* (pl. مشاريع *mašarī3*) **project**
إنْشاء *inšāʔ* **construction**

متْحف *mátḫaf* (pl. متاحِف *matāḫif*) **museum**
مصْرى *máṣri* **Egyptian**
كِبير *kibīr* **grand, great; big, large**

Mohamed

أنا بشْتغل مُهنْدِس اِتّصالات. أنا شغّال في شِرْكِةْ اِتّصالات مصْر.

ána baštáɣal muhándis ittaṣalāt. ána šaɣɣāl fi šírkit ittaṣalāt maṣr.

I work as a telecommunications engineer. I'm employed at the company *Etisalat Egypt*.

اِتّصالات *ittaṣalāt* **telecommunications**
شغّال *šaɣɣāl* **employed**
مصْر *maṣr* (f.) **Egypt**

Dalia

أنا بشْتغل مُترْجِمة في شِرْكِةْ ترْجمة في المُهندِسين و بشْتغل فيها بقالي سِتّ شُهور و باخُد خِبْرة كْويِّسة.

ána baštáɣal mutargíma fi šírkit targáma fi -lmuhanadisīn wi baštáɣal fīha baʔāli sittᵊ šuhūr wi bāxud xíbra kwayyísa.

I'm a translator at a translation agency in Mohandeseen, and I've been working there for six months, and I'm gaining a lot of experience.

مُترْجِم *mutárgim* **translator** (f. مُترْجِمة *mutargíma*)
ترْجمة *targáma* **translation**
المُهندِسين *ilmuhanadisīn* **Mohandeseen** (district in Giza; lit. the engineers)
سِتّ *sitt* (+ pl. noun) **six**
شهْر *šahr* (pl. شُهور *šuhūr*) **month**
أخد *áxad* [i3] **to take;** باخُد *bāxud* **I take**
خِبْرة *xíbra* **experience**
كُوَيِّس *kuwáyyis* **good**

Andrew

أنا بشْتغل في شِرْكِةْ مشْروبات غازية في قِسْم التّسْويق التُّجاري.

ána baštáɣal fi šírkit mašrubāt ɣazíyya fi qism ittaswīʔ ittugāri.

I work at a soft drink company in the commercial marketing department.

مشْروبات غازْية *mašrubāt ɣazíyya* **soft drinks**
مشْروب *mašrūb* **drink, beverage**
غازي *ɣāzi* **gaseous**
قِسْم *qism* (pl. أقْسام *aqsām*) **department, section**
تسْويق *taswīʔ* **marketing**
تُجاري *tugāri, tigāri* **commercial**

Aya

بشْتغل مُحلِّلة في مجال أبْحاث السّوق. بِنْحلِّل بَيانات عن طبيعةْ اِسْتِهْلاك المنْتجات مثلاً.

baštáɣal muɦallíla fi magāl abɦās issūʔ. binɦállil bayanāt 3an ţabī3it istihlāk ilmuntagāt másalan.

I'm an analyst in the field of market research. We analyze data on product consumption habits, for instance.

مُحلِّل *muɦállil* **analyst** (f. مُحلِّلة *muɦallíla*)
مجال *magāl* **field, sector**
بحْس *baɦs* (pl. أبْحاس *abɦās*) **research, study**
سوق *sūʔ* (pl. أسْواق *aswāʔ*) **market**
حلِّل *ɦállil* [2s1] **to analyze;** بِنْحلِّل *binɦállil* **we ~**
بَيانات *bayanāt* (pl.) **data**
عن *3an* **about; on**
طبيعة *ţabī3a* **nature, trait, character**
اِسْتِهْلاك *istihlāk* **consumption**
مُنْتجات *muntagāt* (pl.) **products**

Mahmoud

بشْتغل جْرافيك ديزايْنر مُسْتقِلّ مُتخصِّص في عمل اللّوجوهات لِلشّرِكات الجِديدة.

baštáɣal grāfik dizáynar mustaqíll, mutaxáşşiş fi 3ámal illōgōhāt li-ššarikāt iggidīda.

I work as a freelance graphic designer, specializing in designing logos for new companies.

جْرافيك ديزايْنر *grāfik dizáynar* **graphic designer**
مُسْتقِلّ *mustaqíll* **independent, freelance-**
مُتخصِّص *mutaxáşşiş* **specializing; specialist**
لوجو *lōgō* (pl. لوجوهات *lōgōhāt*) **logo**
لِـ *li-* **to**
جِديد *gidīd* **new**

Rabab

بشْتغل مُهنْدِسةْ شبكات في شِرْكِةْ أورنْج، مِن أقْوى و أنْجح الشّرِكات العالمية.

baštáɣal muhandísit šabakāt fi šírkit Orange. *min áqwa w ángaɦ iššarikāt il3alamíyya.*

I'm a network engineer at the company *Orange*. It is one of the most powerful and successful companies in the world.

مِن *min* (+ elative + pl. noun) **one of the most __**
أقْوى *áqwa* **the strongest**
أنْجح *ángaɦ* **the most successful**
عالمي *3ālami* **global, world-, international**

Tamer

أنا بشْتغل مُدير شبكات و نُظُم في شِرْكِةْ مِلاحة بقالي تلات سِنين.

ána baštáɣal mudīr šabakāt wi núẓum fi šírkit milāḫa baʔāli tálat sinīn.

I've been working as a network and systems director at a shipping company for three years.

مُدير *mudīr* **director**
نِظام *niẓām* (pl. نظم *núẓum*) **system**
مِلاحة *milāḫa* **shipping, navigation**
تلات *tálat* (+ pl. noun) **three**
سنة *sána* (pl. سِنين *sinīn*) **year**

Shorouk

كُنْت بشْتغل في عِيادة و سِبْتها عشان تِعِبْت فترْة و حالِيّاً بشْتغل فْري لانْسِر.

kuntᵊ baštáɣal fi 3iyāda wi sibtáha 3ašān ti3íbtᵊ fátra wi ḫalíyyan baštáɣal frīlansir.

I used to work at a clinic, but I left because I was sick for a while, and now I work as a freelancer.

كُنْت *kunt* **I was**
عِيادة *3iyāda* **clinic, doctor's office**
ساب *sāb* [1h2] **to leave**
سِبْت *sibt* **I left**
عشان *3ašān* **because**
تِعِب *tí3ib* [1s4] **to be sick/ill, get tired**
تِعِبْت *ti3íbt* **I got sick**
فترْة *fátra* **for a while**
فْري لانْسِر *frīlansir* **freelancer**

Fouad

بشْتغل حالِيّاً في العمل الحُرّ و خُصوصاً رسْم الكوميكْس الياباني و ألْعاب الأنْدْرويْد.

baštáɣal ḫalíyyan fi -l3ámal ilḫúrr, wi xuṣūṣan rasm ilkōmiks ilyabāni w al3āb ilʔandrōyd.

Now, I'm a freelancer, specifically in drawing Japanese comics and Android games.

حُرّ *ḫurr* **free, unrestricted**
خُصوصاً *xuṣūṣan* **specifically**
رسْم *rasm* **drawing**
كوميكْس *kōmiks* **comics**
ياباني *yabāni* **Japanese**
لِعْبة *lí3ba* (pl. ألْعاب *al3āb*) **game**
أنْدْرويْد *andrōyd* **Android**

➲ **Occupations:** See *Egyptian Colloquial Arabic Vocabulary (section 9)*

6

عايِش فينْ؟

3āyiš fēn?

Where do you live?

عايِش *3āyiš* **living** (f. عايْشه *3áyša*)
فينْ *fēn* **where**
عايْشة فينْ؟ *3áyša fēn?* **Where do you** (f.) **live?**

مصْر *maṣr* (f.) **Egypt**
القاهِرة *ilqāhíra* **Cairo**
إسْكِنْدِرية *iskindiríyya* **Alexandria**
الجيزة *ilgīza* **Giza**
المعادي *ilma3ādi* **Maadi** (district in Cairo)

منْطِقة *manṭíʔa* (pl. مناطِق *manāṭiʔ*) **area, region**
مدينة *madīna* (pl. مُدُن *múdun*) **city**

قُريِّب مِن *ʔuráyyib min* **close to, near**

أوي *áwi* **very; a lot, really**
كِتير *kitīr* **a lot, much, many**
هِنا *hína* **here**

و *wi* **and**
بسّ *bass* **but**

أنا *ána* **I, me; I am**
هِيَّ *híyya* (f.) **it (is); she (is)**
ـها *-ha, -áha* (f.) (object) **it, her;** (possessive) **its, her**

ده *da* (m.) **this, that, it**
دي *di* (f.) **this, that, it**

في *fi, f* **in, at, on**
مِن *min* **from**

Yomna

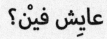

عايْشة في مصْر، تحْديداً في مُحافْظِةْ الجيزة قُريِّب أوي مِن الأهْرامات.

3áyša f maṣr, taḫdīdan fi muḫáfẓit ilgīza ʔuráyyib áwi min ilʔahramāt.

I live in Egypt, or more precisely in the governorate of Giza, very close to the Pyramids.

تحْديداً *taḫdīdan* **specifically, to be precise**
مُحافْظة *muḫáfẓa* **governorate, province**

هرم *háram* (pl. أهْرام *ahrām*) **pyramid**
الأهْرامات *ilʔahramāt* **the Great Pyramids**

Mohamed

أنا أصْلاً مِن إسْكِنْدِرية بسّ أنا عايِش في القاهِرة عشان شُغْلي.

ána áṣlan min iskindiríyya, bass ána 3āyiš fi -lqāhíra 3ašān šúɣli.

I'm originally from Alexandria, but I live in Cairo because of my work.

أصْلاً *áṣlan* **originally**
عشان *3ašān* **because of, for**
شُغْل *šuɣl* **job, work**
ـي *-i* **my**

Dalia

أنا عايْشة في الجيزة في منْطِقة إسْمها المُهنْدِسين و دي منْطِقة تُعْتبر راقْيَة عن مناطِق تانْيَة.

ána 3áyša fi -lgīza fi manṭíʔa ismáha -lmuhandisīn wi di manṭíʔa tu3tábar ráqya 3an manāṭiʔ tánya.

I live in Giza in an area called Mohandeseen. It's an area considered more upscale than other areas.

إسْم *ism* **name**
المُهندِسين *ilmuhanadisīn* **Mohandeseen** (district in Giza; lit. the engineers)
اِعْتبر *i3tábar* [8s1] **to consider**
تُعْتبر *tu3tábar* (passive) **it** (f.) **is considered**
راقي *rāqi* **middle-class-, upper-class-, upscale**
عن *3an* (adjective +) **more __ than**
تاني *tāni* **another, other** (f. تانْيه *tánya*)

Andrew

أنا عايِش في القاهِرة و هِيَّ عاصِمِةْ مصْر و القاهِرة مِن المُدُن اللي مِش بِتْنام.

ána 3āyiš fi -lqāhíra wi híyya 3āṣimit maṣr, wi -lqāhíra min ilmúdun ílli miš bitnām.

I live in Cairo, the capital of Egypt. Cairo is a city that never sleeps.

عاصمة *3āṣíma* **capital (city)**
عاصِمِةْ __ *3āṣímit* __ **the capital of __**
مِن __ *min* __ (+ plural noun) **one of the __**
اللي *ílli* **that, which**
مش *miš* **not; don't**
نام *nām* [1h3] **to sleep**
بِتْنام *bitnām* **it** (f.) **sleeps; she sleeps**

Aya

عايْشة في مدينِةْ نصْر في القاهِرة. ده حيّ كْبير و قُريِّب مِن كُلّ حاجة.

3áyša f madīnit naṣr^{ə} *fi -lqāhíra. da ɦayy*^{ə} *kbīr wi ʔuráyyib min kull*^{ə} *ɦāga.*

I live in Nasr City, Egypt. It is a large district and is close to everything.

مدينِةْ نصْر *madīnit naṣr* **Nasr City**
حيّ *ɦayy* (pl. أحْياء *aɦyāʔ*) **district, neighborhood**
كِبير *kibīr* **big, large**
كُلّ حاجة *kull*^{ə} *ɦāga* **everything**
كُلّ *kull* **every, all**
حاجة *ɦāga* **thing**

Mahmoud

في الجيزة، و معْنى كِلْمِةْ الجيزة في اللُّغة العربية هِيَّ الوادي.

fi -lgīza, wi má3na kílmit ilgīza fi -llúɣa -l3arabíyya híyya -lwādi.

I'm from Giza. And in Arabic, Giza means valley.

معْنى *má3na* **meaning**
كِلْمة *kílma* **word**
كِلْمِةْ __ *kílmit* __ **the word "__"**
اللُّغة العربية *illúɣa -l3arabíyya* **the Arabic language**
لُغة *lúɣa* **language**
عربي *3árabi* **Arabic; Arab**
وادي *wādi* (pl. وِدْيان *widyān*) **valley**

Rabab

عايْشة في القاهِرة في المعادي، أهْدى مكان في القاهِرة. أنا محْظوظة إنّي ساكْنة في المعادي.

3áyša fi -lqāhíra fi -lma3ādi, áhda makān fi -lqāhíra. ána maɦẓūẓa ínni sákna fi -lma3ādi.

I live in Maadi, Cairo. It's the quietest area in Cairo. I'm lucky that I live in Maadi.

أهْدى *áhda* **the quietest** (elative of هادي *hādi*)
مكان *makān* (pl. أماكِن *amākin*) **place**
محْظوظ *maɦẓūẓ* **lucky, fortunate** (f. محْظوظة *maɦẓūẓa*)
إنّي... *ínni...* **that I...**
ساكِن *sākin* **living** (f. ساكْنة *sákna*)

Tamer

أنا عايِش في بيْت عيْلة في إسْكِنْدِرية، أبويا و أُمّي في الدّوْر الأوّل و أنا في التّاني.

ána 3āyiš fi bēt 3ēla f iskindiríyya. abūya w úmmi fi -ddōr ilʔáwwal wi ána fi -ttāni.

I live in a family house in Alexandria. My parents live on the first floor, and I live on the second one.*

بيْت *bēt* (pl. بيوت *biyūt*) **house**
عيْلة *3ēla* **family**
أبويا و أُمّي *abūya w úmmi* **my parents**
أبّ *abb* **father, dad**
أُمّ *umm* **mother, mom**
دوْر *dōr* (pl. أدْوار *adwār*) **floor, story**
أوّل *áwwal* **first**
تاني *tāni* **second; other**

Shorouk

دِلْوَقْتي أنا عايْشة في القاهِرة في مصْر بسّ و أنا صُغيرّة كُنْت عايْشة في الإمارات.

dilwáʔti ána 3áyša fi -lqāhíra fi maṣr, bassᵊ w ána ṣuɣayyára kuntᵊ 3áyša fi -lʔimarāt.

Now, I live in Cairo, Egypt, but when I was little, I lived in the Emirates.

دِلْوَقْتي *dilwáʔti* **now**
و أنا... *w ána...* **when I was...**
صُغيرّ *ṣuɣáyyar* **small** (f. صُغيرّة *ṣuɣayyára*)
كُنْت عايْشة *kuntᵊ 3áyša* **I used to live**
كُنْت *kunt* **I was**
الإمارات *ilʔimarāt* **the Emirates, the U.A.E.**

Fouad

عايِش في الرِّحاب. الحدائِق هِنا كْتير و بِتْساعِد أوي في راحْةْ البال لمّا بْتِمْشي فيها الصُّبْح.

3āyiš fi -rriħāb. ilħadāʔiʔ hína ktīr wi bitsā3id áwi f raħt ilbāl lámma btímši fīha -ṣṣubħ.

I live in Al Rehab City. There are a lot of gardens here, which really helps you relax when you go for a walk in the morning.

حديقة *ħadīʔa* (pl. حدائِق *ħadāʔiʔ*) **garden**
ساعِد في *sā3id fi* [3s] **to help with**
بِتْساعِد في *bitsā3id fi* **it** (f.) **helps with**
راحة *rāħa* **relaxation, calmness**
بال *bāl* **mind**
لمّا *lámma* **when**
مِشي *míši* [1d5] **to walk**
بِتِمْشي *bitímši* **you walk**
الصُّبْح *iṣṣúbħ* **in the morning**

A family house is, for example, an apartment building built and owned by one family. Married family members each have their own apartments in the building.

7 إنْتَ مِتْجوِّز؟

ínta mitgáwwiz?

Are you married?

إنْتَ *ínta* (m.) **you**
مِتْجَوِّز *mitgáwwiz* **married**
إنْتي مِتْجَوِّزة؟ *ínti mitgawwíza?* **Are you** (f.) **married?**

سنة *sána* (pl. سِنين *sinīn*) **year**
سنتينْ *sanatēn* **two years**
__ـينْ *__-ēn* (dual suffix) **two __**
سِنّ *sinn* **age**
أرْبعة *arbá3a* **four**
سِتّة *sítta* **six**
عِشْرين *3išrīn* **twenty**
خُطوبة *xuṭūba* **engagement**
النّاس *innās* **people**

اِتْجَوِّز *itgáwwiz* [5s1] **to get married**
اِتْخطب *itxáṭab* [7s1] **to get engaged**
عنْدي *3ándi* **I have**

مخْطوب *maxṭūb* **engaged**
كِبير *kibīr* **big, large; old**

أه *ā, āh* **yes**
أَيْوَه *áywa* **yes**
لا *láʔ, láʔa* **no**
مِش *miš* **not**
لِسّه *líssa* **still**

و *wi* **and**
بسّ *bass* **but**

أنا *ána* **I, me; I am**
هُوَّ *húwwa* (m.) **it; he**

في *fi, f* **in, at, on**
مِن *min* **for, since; than; from**

Yomna

أنا مِتْجوِّزة مِن حَوالي سِتّ سْنين و عنْدي طِفْلينْ. الطّريق لِأُسْرة سعيدة هُوَّ إظْهار الحُبّ، التّفاهُم و الاِحْتِرام.

ána mitgawwíza min ḥawāli sittᵊ snīn wi 3ándi ṭiflēn. iṭṭarīʔ li-úsra sa3īda húwwa iẓhār ilḥúbb, ittafāhum wi -lʔiḥtirām.

I've been married for about six years, and I have two children. The secret to a happy family is showing love, understanding, and respect.

حَوالي *ḥawāli* **about, approximately**
طِفْل *ṭifl* (pl. اطْفال *aṭfāl*) **child, kid**
طريق *ṭarīʔ* (pl. طُرُق *ṭúruʔ*) **way, method**
لِـ *li-* **to**
أُسْرة *úsra* **family**

سعيد *sa3īd* **happy**
إظْهار *iẓhār* **showing, demonstration**
حُبّ *ḥubb* **love**
تفاهُم *tafāhum* **understanding**
اِحْتِرام *iḥtirām* **respect**

أه، مِتْجوِّز. اِتْجوِّزْت و أنا سِنّي صُغيرّ و أنا عنْدي أرْبعة و عِشْرين سنة.

Mohamed

āh, mitgáwwiz. itgawwízt[ə] w ána sínni ṣuɣáyyar w ána 3ándi arbá3a w 3išrīn sána.

Yes, I'm married. I got married when I was young, when I was twenty-four years old.

اِتْجَوِّزْت *itgawwízt* **I got married**
و أنا... *w ána...* **when I was...**
صُغيرّ *ṣuɣáyyar* **young; small, little**

لا، مِش مِتْجوِّزة ولا كمان مخْطوبة و كُنْت هتْخِطِب بسّ الظُّروف و النّصيب منعوا الخُطوبة.

Dalia

laʔ, miš mitgawwíza wála kamān maxṭūba, wi kúnt[ə] hatxíṭib bass iẓẓurūf wi -nnaṣīb mána3u -lxuṭūba.

No, I'm neither married nor engaged. I was going to get engaged, but circumstances and destiny prevented the engagement.

مِش... وَلا كمان... *miš... wála kamān...* **neither... nor...**
كُنْت *kunt* (+ future tense) **I was going to**
هتْخِطِب *hatxíṭib* **I will get engaged**
ظرْف *ẓarf* (pl. ظُروف *ẓurūf*) **circumstance, condition**
نصيب *naṣīb* **destiny, fortune, lot**
منع *mána3* [1s1] **to prohibit, forbid**
منعوا *mána3u* **they prohibited**

لا و كُلّ النّاس مِسْتنِّية اليوْم ده لإِنّ سِنّي بقى كْبير شُوَيّة.

Andrew

láʔa, wi kull innās mistanníyya -lyōm da li-ínn[ə] sínni báʔa kbīr šuwáyya.

I'm not married, but everyone is waiting for that day as I'm getting older.

كُلّ النّاس *kull innās* **everybody**
كُلّ *kull* **every, all**
مِسْتنّي *mistánni* **waiting**
اليوْم ده *ilyōm da* **that day**
لإِنّ *li-ʔínn* **because**
بقَى *báʔa* **it became;** [1d1] **to become; to be**
شُوَيّة *šuwáyya* **somewhat, a little**

Aya

لا، أنا مِش مِتْجوِّزة لكِن مُرْتبِطة و مُمْكِن أتْجوِّز خِلال سنتيْن.

la?, ána miš mitgawwíza, lākin murtábiṭa w múmkin atgáwwiz xilāl sanatēn.

No, I'm not married, but I'm in a relationship, and I may get married in a couple of years.

مُرْتبِط *murtábiṭ* **in a relationship;** (lit.) **bound, connected**

مُمْكِن *múmkin* (+ imperfect) **may, might, could**

خِلال *xilāl* **within, in; during**

Mahmoud

لا، مُعْظم النّاس في مصْر بْيِتْجوِّز عنْد سِنّ خمْسة و عِشْرين عُقْبال ما يِتْخرّج و يِقْدر يِكوِّن نفْسُه.

la?, mú3ẓam innās fi maṣrᵊ byitgáwwiz 3andᵊ sinnᵊ xámsa w 3išrīn 3u?bāl ma yitxárrag wi yí?dar yikáwwin náfsu.

No. Most people in Egypt marry at the age of twenty-five, by the time that they graduate and are establishing themselves.

مُعْظم __ *mú3ẓam__* **most (of) __**

مصْر *máṣr* (f.) **Egypt**

عنْد *3and* **at**

عُقْبال ما *3u?bāl ma* **by the time**

اِتْخرّج *itxárrag* [5s2] **to graduate**

قِدِر *?ídir* [1s4] **to be able to**

يِقْدر *yí?dar* **he can**

كوِّن *káwwin* [2s1] **to establish; develop**

يِكوِّن *yikáwwin* **he establishes**

نفْسُه *náfsu* **himself**

Rabab

أَيْوَه. أنا مِتْجوِّزة بقالي سنتيْن و مبْسوطة جِدّاً معاه. هُوَّ إنْسان أكْتر مِن رائع.

áywa, ána mitgawwíza ba?āli sanatēn wi mabsūṭa gíddan ma3ā. húwwa insān áktar min rā?i3.

Yes, I've been married for two years, and I'm very happy with him. He is an absolutely amazing man.

بقالي *ba?āli* **I've been... for** (+ length of time)

مبْسوط *mabsūṭ* **happy**

جِدّاً *gíddan* **very**

معَ *má3a* **with**

معاه *ma3ā* **with him**

إنْسان *insān* **person**

أكْتر مِن رائع *áktar min rā?i3* **absolutely amazing** (lit. more than great)

أكْتر مِن *áktar min* **more than**

رائع *rā?i3* **great, terrific, fantastic**

Tamer

أنا الحمْدُ لله مِتْجوِّز و عنْدي وَلديْن، آسِر و عُدّيّ، و عُمْرُهُم أرْبع سِنين و سنتيْن.

ána -lɧámdu l-illāh mitgáwwiz wi 3ándi waladēn, āsir wi 3uddáyy, wi 3umrúhum árba3 sinīn wi sanatēn.

I'm married, praise God. I have two boys, Asser and Uday. They are four years old and two years old.

الحمْدُ لله *ilɧámdu li-llāh* **praise (be to) God**
وَلد *wálad* (pl. وِلاد *wilād*) **son; boy**
عُمْر *3umr* **age**
ـهُم *-hum* **their**

Shorouk

لا، أنا لِسّه سينْجِل و اِتْخطبْت مرّة بسّ فرْكِشْت الخُطوبة عشان مكانْش مُناسِب لِيّا.

la?, ána líssa síngil w itxaṭábt[ə] márra, bass[ə] farkíšt ilxuṭūba 3ašān ma-kánš[ə] munāsib líyya.

No, I'm single. I was engaged once, but we broke up because he wasn't right for me.

سينْجِل *síngil* **single**
مرّة *márra* **once, one time**
فرْكِش *fárkiš* [11s1] **to break off, end**
عشان *3ašān* **because**
مكانْش *ma-kánš* **he wasn't**
كان *kān* **he was**
مـ ـش *ma-__-š* **not; didn't**
مُناسِب *munāsib* **proper, appropriate, suitable**
لِيّا *líyya* **for me, to me**

Fouad

لا، لِسّه بدْري عليّا في مَوْضوع الزَّواج علشان دي مسْؤولية كْبيرة و بِتِحْتاج مادِّيّات و اِتِّزان نفْسي.

la?, líssa bádri 3aláyya fi mawḍū3 izzawāg 3alašān di mas?ulíyya kbīra wi bitiɧtāg maddiyyāt wi -ttizān náfsi.

No, it's too soon for me to get married because it's a big responsibility and you need a lot of money and maturity.

بدْري *bádri* **early, soon**
عليّا *3aláyya* **for me**
مَوْضوع *mawḍū3* (pl. مَواضيع *mawaḍī3*) **subject**
زَواج *zawāg* **marriage**
علشان *3alašān* **because**
مسْؤولية *mas?ulíyya* **responsibility**
اِحْتاج *iɧtāg* [8h] **to need;** بِتِحْتاج *bitiɧtāg* **you need**
مادِّيّات *maddiyyāt* (pl.) **assets**
اِتِّزان *ittizān* **balance, composure, rationality**
نفْسي *náfsi* **mental, psychological**

➲ **Marriage and relationships:** See *Egyptian Colloquial Arabic Vocabulary (section 3)*

8 عنْدك إخْوات؟

3ándak ixwāt?

Do you have any brothers or sisters?

عنْد *3and* (preposition) **have; at**
ـك *-ak* (m.) (object) **you;** (possessive) **your**
إخْوات *ixwāt* (pl.) **siblings**
عنْدِك إخْوات؟ *3ándik ixwāt?* **Do you** (f.) **have any brothers or sisters?**

اخّ *axx* (pl. إخْوات وِلاد *ixwāt wilād*) **brother**
أُخْت *uxt* (pl. إخْوات بنات *ixwāt banāt*) **sister**
بِنْت *bint* (pl. بنات *banāt*) **girl**
كُلّيّة *kullíyya* **college, university**
سنة *sána* (pl. سِنين *sinīn*) **year**

واحِد *wāħid* **one**
اِتْنين *itnēn* **two**
___ـيْن ___-*ēn* (dual suffix) **two __**

أكْبر *akbar* **older;** (+ noun) **the oldest**
أصْغر *áşyar* **younger;** (+ noun) **the youngest**
مِنّي *mínni* **than me**

كِتير *kitīr* **often, a lot; many**

و *wi* **and**
بسّ *bass* **but; only, just**

أنا *ána* **I, me; I am**
هُمّا *húmma* **they (are)**
ـي *-i* (possessive) **my;** (preposition +) **me**
ـنا *-na* (object) **us;** (possessive) **our**
ـُه *-u* (m.) (object) **him, it;** (possessive) **his, its**
ـها *-ha, -áha* (f.) (object) **her, it;** (possessive) **her, its**
ـهُم *-hum* (object) **them;** (possessive) **their**

في *fi, f* **in, at, on**
معَ *má3a* **with**
بِـ *bi-* **by** (how many months, years, etc.)

Yomna

عنْدي أُخْت و أخّ أصْغر مِنّي. مِش بشوفْهُم كِتير نتيجِةْ اِنْشِغالْنا بسّ بنحاوِل نِلاقي طُرُق لِلِّقاء.

*3ándi úxt wi axx, áşyar mínni. miš bašúfhum kitīr natīgit inšiyálna báss*ᵊ *binħāwil nilāʔi ţúruʔ li-lliqāʔ.*

I have a younger sister and brother. I don't see them much because we are so busy, but we try to find ways to meet.

مِش *miš* **not; don't**
شاف *šāf* [1h1] **to see**
بشوف *bašūf* **I see**
__ نتيجِةْ *natīgit* __ **because of __**
اِنْشِغال *inšiyāl* **being busy**

حاوِل *ħāwil* [3s] **to try;** بِنْحاوِل *binħāwil* **we try**
لاقى *lāʔa* [3d] **to find;** نِلاقي *nilāʔi* **(that) we find**
طريق *ţarīʔ* (pl. طُرُق *ţúruʔ*) **way, method**
لِـ *li-* **to**
لِقاء *liqāʔ* **meeting**

Mohamed

أنا عنْدي أخّ واحِد أصْغر مِنّي بِأرْبع سِنين، لِسّه في الكُلّية.

ána 3ándi ax(xᵊ) wāĥid áṣɣar mínni bi-árba3 sinīn, lissa fi -lkullíyya.

I have one brother who is four years younger than me and is still in college.

بِأرْبع سِنين *bi-árba3 sinīn* **by four years**

لِسّه *líssa* **still**

Dalia

عنْدي أخّ واحِد بسّ و معنْديش إخْوات بنات و كان نِفْسي يْكون عنْدي إخْوات كِتير ألْعب معاهُم.

3ándi ax(xᵊ) wāĥid báss, wi ma-3andīš ixwāt banāt wi kān nífsi ykūn 3ándi ixwāt kitīr ál3ab ma3āhum.

I just have one brother, but I don't have any sisters. I wanted to have a lot of siblings to play with.

معنْديش *ma-3andīš* **I don't have**
كان نِفْسي *kān nífsi* **I wanted**
نِفْسـ *nifs-* (+ pronoun suffix) **to want**
نِفْسي *nífsi* (+ imperfect) **I want**

يِكون *yikūn* (here: untranslated); **it is; that there be**
لِعِب *lí3ib* [1s4] **to play**
ألْعب *ál3ab* **(that) I play**
معاهُم *ma3āhum* **with them**

Andrew

عنْدي أخّ و أُخْت و هُمّا الاِتْنينْ أكْبر مِنّي و مِتْجوِّزين و كُلّ واحِد فيهُم عنْدُه بِنْت.

3ándi ax(xᵊ) w úxt, wi húmma litnēn ákbar mínni wi mitgawwizīn wi kullᵊ wāĥid fīhum 3ándu bint.

I have a brother and a sister. They are both older than me and are married. Each of them has a daughter.

الاِتْنينْ *litnēn* **both**
مِتْجوِّز *mitgáwwiz* **married**

بِنْت *bint* (pl. بنات *banāt*) **daughter**

Aya

أَيْوَه عنْدي خمس إخْوات كُلُّهُم بنات. دايْماً بِنِتْخانِق معَ بعْض بسّ منِقْدرْش نِسْتغْنى عن بعْض.

áywa, 3ándi xámas ixwāt kullúhum banāt. dáyman binitxāniʔ má3a bá3ḍᵊ báss ᵊ ma-niʔdáršᵊ nistáɣna 3an ba3ḍ.

Yes, I have five siblings, all girls. Although we always fight, we can't live without each other.

أَيْوَه *áywa* **yes**
خمس *xámas* (+ pl. noun) **five**
دايْماً *dáyman* **always**
اِتْخانِق *itxāniʔ* [6s] **to fight**
بِنِتْخانِق *binitxāniʔ* **we fight**
بعْض *ba3ḍ* **each other**
قدِر *ʔídir* [1s4] **to be able to**
منِقْدرْش *ma-niʔdárš* **we can't**
اِسْتغْنى عن *istáɣna 3an* [10d1] **to do without, live without**

Mahmoud

أه، عنْدي أخّيْن، واحِد أكْبر مِنّي و مْخلِّص كُلّية و تاني أصْغر مِنّي بِسنتيْن.

āh, 3ándi axxēn, wāħid ákbar mínni wi mxálliṣ kullíyya wi tāni áṣɣar mínni bi-sanatēn.

Yes, I have two brothers, one older than me and he has graduated from college, while the other is two years younger than me.

آه *ā, āh* **yes**
مِخلّص *mixálliṣ* **a graduate; having graduated**
تاني *tāni* **the other one**

Rabab

عنْدي أخّ أصْغر مِنّي بِسبع سِنين يَعْني عنْدُه واحِد و عِشْرين سنة.

3ándi axx áṣɣar mínni bi-sába3 sinīn, yá3ni 3ándu wāħid wi 3išrīn sána.

I have a brother who is seven years younger than me, so he's twenty-one years old.

بِسبع سِنين *bi-sába3 sinīn* **by seven years**
يَعْني *yá3ni* **this means; that is**
عِشْرين *3išrīn* **twenty**

Tamer

عنْدي أخّ و أُخْتينْ. أنا أكْبرْهُم و بعْدي أُخْت و بعْدها أخّ و أصْغرْنا أُخْت.

3ándi áxx^{ə} w uxtēn. ána akbárhum wi bá3di úxt, wi ba3dáha áxx, wi aṣɣárna uxt.

I have one brother and two sisters. I'm the oldest, followed by a sister, then a brother, and the youngest is a sister.

بعْد *ba3d* **after**

Shorouk

أه، عنْدي. هُمّا بِنْتينْ و وَلد. الفرْق بينْ كُلّ واحِد فينا سنتينْ و أنا أكْبرْهُم.

āh, 3ándi. húmma bintēn wi wálad. ilfárʔ^{ə} bēn kúll^{ə} wāɦid fīna sanatēn w ána akbárhum.

Yes, I do. Two sisters and one brother. The [age] difference between each of us is two years, and I'm the oldest.

وَلد *wálad* (pl. وِلاد *wilād*) **boy; son**
فرْق *farʔ* **difference**
كُلّ واحِد فينا *kúll^{ə} wāɦid fīna* **every one of us**

Fouad

عنْدي اتْنينْ و أنا الوُسْطاني. صعْب تِلاقي حدّ ملوش أخّ أَوْ أُخْت في مصْر.

3ándi -tnēn w ána -lwusṭāni. ṣa3b^{ə} tlāʔi ɦadd^{ə} ma-lūš axx aw uxt^{ə} fi maṣr.

I have two siblings. I'm the middle child. It's hard to find someone who doesn't have a brother or sister in Egypt.

وُسْطاني *wusṭāni* **mid-, middle**
صعْب *ṣa3b* **difficult, hard**
لاقى *lāʔa* [3d] **to find;** تِلاقي *tilāʔi* **(that) you** (m.) **find**
حدّ *ɦadd* **someone**
ملوش *ma-lūš* **he doesn't have**
أَوْ *aw* **or**
مصْر *maṣr* (f.) **Egypt**

➲ **Family:** See *Egyptian Colloquial Arabic Vocabulary (section 2)*

9

بِتِتْكلِّم لُغات؟

bititkállim luɣāt?

Do you speak any foreign languages?

اِتْكلِّم *itkállim* [5s1] **to speak**
لُغة *lúɣa* (pl. لُغات *luɣāt*) **language**
بِتِتْكلِّمي لُغات؟ *bititkallími luɣāt?* **Do you** (f.) **speak any foreign languages?**

لُغة أُمّ *lúɣa ʔumm* **native language, mother tongue**
إنْجِليزي *ingilīzi* **English**
فرنْساوي *faransāwi* **French**
عربي *3árabi* **Arabic**

اِتْكلِّم *itkállim* [5s1] **to speak**
بتْكلِّم *batkállim* **I speak**
اِتْعلِّم *it3állim* [5s1] **to learn**
بتْعلِّم *bat3állim* **I learn**
عِرِف *3írif* [1s4] **to know**
بعْرف *bá3raf* **I know**

شُوَيِّة__ *šuwáyyit*__ **a little __**

كُوَيِّس *kuwáyyis* **well**
جِدّاً *gíddan* **very; really, a lot**
بِطلاقة *bi-ṭalāqa* **fluently**

يَعْني *yá3ni* **well, you know**

و *wi* **and**

مِن *min* **from; than**

هِيَّ *híyya* (f.) **it; she**
دي *di* (f.) **this, that, it**

Yomna

اللُّغة العربية هِيَّ لُغتي الأُمّ و بعْرف أتْكلِّم إنْجِليزي. الفرنْساوي أعْرفُه شْوَيّة و نِفْسي أتْعلِّمُه كْويِّس.

illúɣa -l3arabíyya híyya lúɣiti -lʔúmm, wi bá3raf atkállim ingilīzi. ilfaransāwi, a3ráfu šwáyya wi nífsi at3allímu kwáyyis.

Arabic is my mother tongue, and I can speak English. French, I know a bit of, and I want to learn it well.

شُوَيّة *šuwáyya* **a little, a bit**

نِفْسي *nífsi* (+ imperfect) **I want**

Mohamed

بتْكلِّم عربي و إنْجِليزي بِطلاقة و شْويِّةْ فرنْساوي مِكسّر على قدّي.

batkállim 3árabi w ingilīzi bi-ţalāqa, wi šwáyyit faransāwi mikássar 3ála ʔáddi.

I speak Arabic and English fluently, and broken, limited French.

مِكسّر *mikássar* **broken**

على قدّ *3ála ʔádd-* (+ pronoun suffix) **limited, mediocre**

على قدّي *3ála ʔáddi* **limited (for me)**

Dalia

بتْكلِّم لُغات زيّ الإنْجْليش و العربي و الفرنْساوي و بتْعلِّم لُغات زيّ الأسْباني و الإيطالي و الألْماني.

batkállim luɣāt zayy ilʔíngliš wi -l3árabi wi -lfaransāwi wi bat3állim luɣāt zayy ilʔasbāni wi -lʔiţāli wi -lʔalmāni.

I speak languages like English, Arabic, and French. And I'm learning languages such as Spanish, Italian, and German.

زيّ *zayy* **like, as, such as**

إنْجْليش *íngliš* **English**

أسْباني *asbāni* **Spanish**

إيطالي *iţāli* **Italian**

ألْماني *almāni* **German**

Andrew

طبْعاً العربي و هِيَّ اللُّغة الأُمّ و بتْكلِّم إنْجِليزي و أعْرف شِويِّةْ فرنْساوي بِحُكْم الدِّراسة لِمُدِّةْ سبع سِنين.

ţáb3an il3árabi wi híyya -llúɣa -lʔumm, wi batkállim ingilīzi, wi á3raf šiwáyyit faransāwi bi-ħúkm iddirāsa li-múddit sába3 sinīn.

Arabic, of course. It's my native language. And I speak English, and I know a little French thanks to seven years of studies.

طبْعاً *ţáb3an* **of course, naturally**

بِحُكْم *bi-ħúkm* **thanks to, because of**

دِراسة *dirāsa* **studies**

__ لِمُدِّةْ *li-múddit* __ **for (a period of) __**

سبع سِنين *sába3 sinīn* **seven years**

Aya

أَيْوَه، بتْكلِّم عربي و إنْجِليزي. اِتْعلِّمْت الإنْجِليزي كُوَيِّس مِن الأفْلام و المُسلْسلات.

áywa, batkállim 3árabi w ingilīzi. it3allímt ilʔingilīzi kuwáyyis min ilʔaflām wi -lmusalsalāt.

Yes, I speak Arabic and English. I learned English well from movies and TV series.

أَيْوَه *áywa* **yes**
فيلْم *film* (pl. أفْلام *aflām*) **movie, film**
مُسلْسلة *musálsala* (pl. مُسلْسلات *musalsalāt*) **TV series**

Mahmoud

أه، بتْكلِّم لُغتينْ: اللُّغة الأُولى عربي و اللُّغة التّانْيَة إنْجِليزي.

āh, batkállim luɣatēn: illúɣa -lʔūla 3árabi wi -llúɣa -ttánya ingilīzi.

I speak two languages: the first language is Arabic, and the second language is English.

لُغتينْ *luɣatēn* (dual) **two languages**
أوّل *áwwal* (f. أولى *ūla*) **first**
تاني *tāni* (f. تانْية *tánya*) **second**

Rabab

بتْكلِّم إنْجِليزي كْويِّس جِدّاً. بسْتخْدِمُه طول الوَقْت في الشُّغْل عشان بتْعامِل معَ مُسْتخْدِمين برّه مصْر.

batkállim ingilīzi kuwáyyis gíddan. bastaxdímu ṭūl ilwáʔtᵊ fi -ššúɣl, 3ašān bat3āmil má3a mustaxdimīn bárra maṣr.

I speak English very well. I use it all the time at work because I deal with customers abroad.

اِسْتخْدِم *istáxdim* [10s1] **to use**
بسْتخْدِمُه *bastaxdímu* **I use it**
طول الوَقْت *ṭūl ilwáʔt* **all the time, constantly**
شُغْل *šuɣl* **work, job**
عشان *3ašān* **because**
اِتْعامِل معَ *it3āmil má3a* [6s] **to deal with**
مُسْتخْدِم *mustáxdim* (pl. مُسْتخْدِمين *mustaxdimīn*) **customer; user**
برّه *bárra* **outside (of); outside; abroad**
مصْر *maṣr* (f.) **Egypt**

بتْكلِّم إنْجِليزي كْوِيِّس، يِمْكِن أَكْتر مِن العربي و الفرنْساوي يَعْني شْوَيَّة.

batkállim ingilīzi kuwáyyis, yímkin áktar min il3árabi wi -lfaransāwi yá3ni šwáyya.

Tamer

I speak English well, maybe better than Arabic, and French, well, a little.

يِمْكِن *yímkin* (+ imperfect) **may, might, could; possibly**

أَكْتر مِن *áktar min* **more than**

هُوَّ مِش لُغات أَوي يَعْني بتْكلِّم إنْجِليزي و شْوَيَّةٌ كلِمات ياباني و لِسَّه بتْعلِّم.

húwwa miš luɣāt áwi yá3ni. batkállim ingilīzi wi šwáyyit kalimāt yabāni wi líssa bat3állim.

Shorouk

Well, not so many languages, but I can speak a little English and a few words in Japanese, but I'm still learning.

هُوَّ *húwwa* (softening particle) **well; it's just that...**

مِش *miš* **not**

أَوى *áwi* **very**

كِلْمة *kílma* (pl. كلِمات *kalimāt*) **word**

ياباني *yabāni* **Japanese**

لِسَّه *líssa* **still**

بتْكلِّم اللُّغة الإنْجِليزية بِطلاقة و دي حاجة مُهِمّة جِدّاً لِأَيّ مصْري نظراً لإنّنا بلد سِياحي.

batkállim illúɣa -lʔingilizíyya bi-ṭalāqa, wi di ḥāga muhímma li-áyyᵊ máṣri náẓaran li-innína bálad siyāḥi.

Fouad

I speak English fluently. That's something important for any Egyptian because we are a touristic country.

حاجة *ḥāga* **thing, something**

مُهِمّ *muhímm* **important**

لِ *li-* **for, to**

أَيّ *ayy* **any**

مصْري *máṣri* **Egyptian**

نظراً لإنّ *náẓaran li-ínn* **because**

بلد *bálad* (pl. بِلاد *bilād*) **country; land, place**

سِياحي *siyāḥi* **touristic**

➲ **Languages:** See *Egyptian Colloquial Arabic Vocabulary (section 38)*

10

أيْه هُوَّ أكْتر لوْن بِتْفضّلُه؟

ʔē húwwa ʔáktar lōn bitfaḍḍálu?

What's your favorite color?

أيْه *ʔē(h)* **what**
هُوَّ *húwwa* (m.) **it; he**
أكْتر *áktar* **most**
لوْن *lōn* (pl. ألْوان *alwān*) **color**
فضّل *fáḍḍal* [2s2] **to prefer**
أيْه هُوَّ أكْتر لوْن بِتْفضّليه؟ *ʔē húwwa áktar lōn bitfaḍḍalī?* **What's your** (f.) **favorite color?**

إِسْوِد *íswid* **black**
أحْمر *áḥmar* **red**
أخْضر *áxḍar* **green**
أزْرق *ázraʔ* **blue**
بنفْسِجي *banafsígi* **purple**

حبّ *ḥabb* [1g3] **to like; to love**
بحِبّ *baḥíbb* **I like**
حسّ *ḥass* [1g3] **to feel**
بحِسّ *baḥíss* **I feel**

مُفضّل *mufáḍḍal* **favorite, preferred**
غامِق *ɣāmiʔ* (pl. غَوامِق *ɣawāmiʔ*) **dark**

جِدّاً *giddan* **really, a lot; very**
كمان *kamān* **also, too**

و *wi* **and**
إنّ... *inn...* **that...**

أنا *ána* **I, me; I am**
هُوَّ *húwwa* (m.) **it; he**
ـُه *-u* (m.) **it; (object) him; (possessive) his, its**
ـي *-i* **my**

لِ *li-* **of; for; to**

Yomna

بفضّل تلات ألْوان: الأخْضر و البنفْسِجي و البمْبي. لكِن اِخْتِياري لِلالْوان مُرْتبِط عادةً بِحالْتي المِزاجية.

bafáḍḍal tálat alwān: ilʔáxḍar wi -lbanafsígi wi -lbámbi. lākin ixtiyāri li-lʔalwān murtábiṭ 3ādatan bi-ḥálti -lmizagíyya.

I prefer three colors: green, purple, and pink. But my choice of colors is usually linked to my mood.

تلات *tálat* (+ pl. noun) **three**
بمْبي *bámbi* **pink**
لكِن *lākin* **but**
اِخْتِيار *ixtiyār* **choice**
مُرْتبِط بِـ *murtábiṭ bi-* **connected to**

عادةً *3ādatan* **usually**
حالة *ḥāla* **condition, state**
حالْتي *ḥálti* **my state**
مِزاجي *mizāgi* **moody, temperamental**

Mohamed

أكْتر لوْن بحِبُّه هُوَّ الأحْمر. و كمان بحِبّ الأخْضر، لوْن الزّرْع.

áktar lōn baɧíbbu húwwa -lʔáɧmar. wi kamān baɧíbb ilʔáxdar, lōn izzár3.

My favorite color is red. I also like green, the color of plants.

زرْع *zar3* **plants, greenery**

Dalia

أنا بحِبّ اللّوْن الإسْوِد لإنّي بحِسّ إنُّه ملِك الألْوان و بحِبّ كمان البنفْسِجي و الأحْمر و الكُحْلي و الأبْيَض.

ána baɧíbb illōn ilʔíswid li-ínni baɧíss ínnu málik ilʔalwān wi baɧíbb^{ə} kamān ilbanafsígi wi -lʔáɧmar wi -lkúɧli wi -lʔábyad.

I like black because I feel that it's the king of colors. I also like purple, red, navy blue, and white.

لإنّي *li-ínni* **because I**
ملِك *málik* **king**
كُحْلي *kúɧli* **navy blue**
أبْيَض *ábyad* **white**

Andrew

أكْتر لوْن بفضّلُه هُوَّ الأحْمر علشان بيْحسِّسْني بِالفرْحة و حتّى النّادي اللي بشجّعُه بيِلْبِس أحْمر.

áktar lōn bafaddálu húwwa -lʔáɧmar, 3alašān biyɧassísni bi-lfárɧa wi ɧátta -nnādi illi bašaggá3u byílbis áɧmar.

Red is my favorite color because it makes me feel happy. Even the [soccer] team I support wears red.

علشان *3alašān* **because**
حسِّس بِ *ɧássis bi-* [2s1] (+ noun) **to make feel**
بيْحسِّسْني *biyɧassísni* **it makes me feel**
فرْحة *fárɧa* **joy, happiness**
حتّى *ɧátta* **even**
نادي *nādi* **club**
اللي *ílli* **that, which**
شجّع *shágga3* [2s2] **to support, encourage**
لِبس *líbis* [1s5] **to wear; to get dressed**

Aya

أكْتر لوْن بحِبُّه هُوَّ الأزْرق الغامِق، لوْن البحْر، و بحِسُّه لوْن نقي جِدّاً.

áktar lōn baɧíbbu húwwa -lʔázraʔ ilɣāmiʔ, lōn ilbáɧr, wi baɧíssu lōn náqi gíddan.

My favorite color is dark blue, the color of the sea. I feel it's a really pure color.

بحْر *baɧr* (pl. بِحار *biɧār*) **sea**

نقي *náqi* **pure**

Mahmoud

الأزْرق، ده أكْتر لوْن بِيوحي بِالفخامة و العظمة و الهِدِوّ و سُكون اللّيْل.

ilʔázraʔ, da ʔáktar lōn biyūɧi bi-lfaxāma wi -l3áẓama wi -lhidíwwᵊ w sukūn illēl.

Blue. It signifies luxury, greatness, calm, and the still of the night.

ده *da* (m.) **this, that, it**

أَوْحى *áwɧa* [(4d)] **to indicate, suggest**

فخامة *faxāma* **luxury**

عظمة *3áẓama* **greatness, splendor**

هِدِوّ *hidíww* (=هُدوء *hudūʔ*) **calm, tranquility**

سُكون *sukūn* **stillness, tranquility**

ليْل *lēl* **night**

Rabab

الإسْوِد. أنا أعْشق الإسْوِد لإِنُّه بِيْمثِّل الأناقة و الشِّياكة بِالنِّسْبة لي.

ilʔíswid. ána á3šaq ilʔíswid li-ínnu biymássil ilʔanāqa wi -ššiyāka bi-nnisbā-li.

Black. I love black because it represents fashion and elegance for me.

عِشِق *3íšiq, 3íšiʔ* [1s4] **to love (passionately)**

أعْشق *á3šaq, á3šaʔ* **I love**

لإِنُّه *li-ínnu* **because it**

مثِّل *mássil* [2s1] **to represent**

أناقة *anāqa* **fashion, style**

شِياكة *šiyāka* **elegance, chicness**

بِالنِّسْبة لي *bi-nnisbā-li* **for me**

Tamer

الإسْوِد هُوَّ أكْتر لوْن بحِبُّه بِالرَّغْم مِن إنّ ناس كِتير بِتْقول إنُّه كئيب.

ilʔíswid húwwa áktar lōn baħíbbu bi-rráɣmᵊ min innᵊ nās kitīr bitʔūl ínnu kaʔīb.

Black is my favorite color, even though a lot of people say it's gloomy.

بِالرَّغْم مِن إنّ... *bi-rráɣmᵊ min ínn...* **in spite of the fact that...; even though...**
ناس كِتير *nās kitīr* **a lot of people**
قال *ʔāl* [1h1] **to say**
كئيب *kaʔīb* **gloomy, depressing**

Shorouk

بحِبّ الإسْوِد و الجْراي و البنفْسِجي جِدّاً بِدرجاتُه كُلّها و البينْك بسّ الغَوامِق أكْتر.

baħíbb ilʔíswid wi -lgrē wi -lbanafsígi gíddan bi-daragātu kulláha wi -lbínk, bass ilɣawāmiʔ áktar.

I really love black, gray, all shades of purple, and pink, but darker [shades] more.

جْراي *grē* **gray**
بِـ *bi-* **in; with**
درجة *dáraga* **degree, shade, grade**
كُلّها *kulláha* **all of them**
بينْك *bink, pink* **pink**

Fouad

لوْني المُفضّل هُوَّ الإسْوِد. اللّوْن الإسْوِد هُوَّ لوْن بِيْدِلّ على الغُموض.

lōni -lmufáḍḍal húwwa -lʔíswid. illōn ilʔíswid húwwa lōn biydíllᵊ 3ála -lɣumūḍ.

My favorite color is black. Black is a color that signifies mystery.

دلّ على *dall 3ála* [1g3] **to signify, indicate**
غُموض *ɣumūḍ* **mystery, uncertainty, obscurity**

➲ **Colors:** See *Egyptian Colloquial Arabic Vocabulary (section 46)*

11

بِتِلْعب رِياضة؟

bitíl3ab riyāḍa?

Do you play any sports?

لِعِب *lí3ib* [1s4] **to play**
رِياضة *riyāḍa* **sport(s); physical activity, exercise**
بِتِلْعبى رِياضة؟ *bitil3ábi riyāḍa?* **Do you** (f.) **play any sports?**

سِباحة *sibāħa* **swimming**
نادي *nādi* (pl. نَوادي *nawādi,* أنْدية *andíyya*) **club**
فريق *farīʔ* (pl. فِرق *fíraʔ*) **team**

كُنْت *kunt* (+ bi-imperfect) **I used to**

آه *ā, āh* **yes**
أَيْوَه *áywa* **yes**
لا *láʔ, láʔa* **no**

حاليّاً *ħalíyyan* **now, presently**

Yomna

حالِيّاً لا. لكِن كُنْت بمارِس المشْي و السِّباحة و بحاوِل أمارِسْهُم كُلّ ما تُتاحْلي الفُرْصة.

ħalíyyan laʔ. lākin kuntᵊ bamāris ilmášy, wi -ssibāħa. wi baħāwil amaríshum kullᵊ ma tutáħli -lfúrṣa.

Not presently, but I used to walk and swim. I try to exercise whenever I have the chance.

مارِس *māris* [3s] **to practice, exercise, engage in**
مشْي *mášy* **walking**
حاوِل *ħāwil* [3s] **to try**
كُلّ ما *kullᵊ ma* **whenever**
تُتاحْلى الفُرْصة *tutáħli -lfúrṣa* **I have the chance** (lit. I am allowed the opportunity)
أتاح لِـ *atāħ li-* **to allow;** تُتاح لِـ *tutāħ* (passive) **it** (f.) **is allowed for** (someone)
فُرْصة *fúrṣa* **opportunity, chance**

Mohamed

بلْعب سِباحة في النّادي، و بروح الجيم تلات أَوْ أرْبع أيّام.

bál3ab sibāɦa fi -nnādi, wi barūɦ ilžīm tálat aw árba3 ayyām.

I go swimming at the club, and I go to the gym three or four days [a week].

راح *rāɦ* [1h1] **to go (to)**
جيم *žīm* **gym**

تلات *tálat* (+ pl. noun) **three**
أرْبع *árba3* (+ pl. noun) **four**
يوْم *yōm* (pl. أيّام *ayyām*) **day**

Dalia

بلْعب رِياضة بسّ مِش دايْماً يَعْني مُمْكِن الصُّبْح ألْعب رِياضة شْوَيّة أَوْ مُمْكِن أنْزِل و أمْشي.

bál3ab riyāḍa bassᵊ miš dáyman. yá3ni múmkin iṣṣúbɦ ál3ab riyāḍa šwáyya aw múmkin ánzil w ámši.

I exercise, but not regularly. You know, I may exercise in the morning a little or go for a walk.

دايْماً *dáyman* **always**
يَعْني *yá3ni* **that is; you know**
مُمْكِن *múmkin* (+ imperfect) **may, might, could; possibly**

الصُّبْح *iṣṣúbɦ* **in the morning**
شْوَيّة *šuwáyya* **a little, a bit**
نِزِل *nízil* [1s5] **to go out** (of the house)
مِشي *míši* [1d5] **to walk**

Andrew

لا، بسّ زمان كُنْت بلْعب بينْج بونْج و اِشْتركْت مرّة في مُسابْقِةْ الجامْعة بسّ محقّقْتِش جَوايِز.

laʔ, bassᵊ zamān kuntᵊ bál3ab pīng pōng w ištaráktᵊ márra fi musábʔit ilgám3a bassᵊ ma-ɦaʔʔáʔtiš gawāyiz.

No, but I used to play ping pong. I once participated in a college competition but didn't get any awards.

زمان *zamān* **in the past, used to**
بينْج بونْج *pīng pōng* **ping pong, table tennis**
اِشْترك في *ištárak fi* [8s1] **to participate in**
مرّة *márra* **once, one time**

مُسابْقة *musábʔa* **competition**
جامْعة *gám3a* **university, college**
حقّق *ɦáʔʔaʔ* [2s2] **to get, obtain, win, achieve**
جائْزة *gáyza* (pl. جَوايِز *gawāyiz*) **award, prize**

Aya

أه، بلْعب إسْكْواش. رِياضة جميلة جِدّاً مِحْتاجة ترْكيز و ردّ فِعْل سريع.

āh, bál3ab iskwāš, riyāḍa gamīla gíddan miḫtāga tarkīz wi radd[ə] fi3l[ə] sarī3.

Yes, I play squash, a very nice sport that requires focus and quick reaction.

إسْكْواش *iskwāš* (sport) **squash**
جميل *gamīl* **nice; beautiful**
مِحْتاج *miḫtāg* **requiring; needing**
ترْكيز *tarkīz* **focus**
ردّ فِعْل *rádd[ə] fí3l* **reaction**
سريع *sarī3* **quick, fast**

Mahmoud

أه، بلْعب سِباحة و في فريق النّادي بقالي اتْناشر سنة و دخلْت بُطولات كِتير.

āh, bál3ab sibāḫa wi fi farīʔ innādi baʔāli itnāšar sána wi daxált[ə] buṭulāt kitīr.

Yes, I swim, and I've been on the club's team for 12 years and have competed in many championships.

بقالي *baʔāli* **I've been... for** (+ length of time)
اِتْناشر *itnāšar* **twelve**
سنة *sána* (pl. سِنين *sinīn*) **year**
دخل *dáxal* [1s3] **to enter**
بُطولة *buṭūla* **championship**

Rabab

أَيْوَه. بلْعب سِلاح و دي لِعْبة تِحْتاج سُرْعة و دِقّة عشان تِغْلِب خِصْمك.

áywa. bál3ab silāḫ, wi di lí3ba tiḫtāg súr3a wi díqqa 3ašān tíɣlib xíṣmak.

Yes, I fence, and this sport requires speed and accuracy for you to defeat your opponent.

سِلاح *silāḫ* **fencing; weapon**
لِعْبة *lí3ba* (pl. ألعاب *al3āb*) **sport; game**
اِحْتاج *iḫtāg* [8h] **to require; to need**
سُرْعة *súr3a* **speed**
دِقّة *díqqa* **accuracy, precision**
غلب *ɣálab* [1s2] **to defeat, overcome**
خِصْم *xiṣm* (pl. خُصوم *xuṣūm*) **opponent**

Tamer

كُنْت بلْعب كوْرِةْ قدم و كونْغ فو و أنا صُغيرّ بسّ جالي إصابة في رُكْبِتي مِن الكوْرة.

kuntᵊ bál3ab kōrit qádam wi kōng fū w ána ṣuɣáyyar, bassᵊ gā-li iṣāba fi rukbíti min ilkōra.

I used to play soccer and kung fu when I was young, but my knee got injured in soccer.

كوْرِةْ قدم *kōrit qádam* **soccer**
صُغيرّ *ṣuɣáyyar* **small**
جالي إصابة *gā-li iṣāba* **I got injured** (lit. an injury came to me)
جهْ *gih* [i1] **to come**
إصابة *iṣāba* **injury**
رُكْبة *rúkba* (pl. رُكب *rúkab*) **knee**
الكوْرة *ilkōra* **soccer**

Shorouk

أه، حالِيّاً بلْعب زومْبا و زمان أيّام المدْرسة كُنْت مِشْترِكْة في فريق كُرِةْ سلّة.

āh, ḫalíyyan bál3ab zúmba, wi zamān ayyām ilmadrása kuntᵊ mištírka f farīʔ kúrit sálla.

Yes, I do Zumba, and back in school, I used to be on a basketball team.

زومْبا *zúmba* **Zumba** (aerobic fitness program)
مدْرسة *madrása* (pl. مدارِس *madāris*) **school**
مِشْترِك *mištírik* **participating; participant**
كُرِةْ سلّة *kúrit sálla* **volleyball**

Fouad

بلْعب رفْع أثْقال و دي غالِباً أكْتر رِياضة مُفضّلة عنْد المصْرِيِّين و ليها شعْبية كْبيرة أوي في مصْر.

bál3ab raf3 asqāl wi di ɣāliban áktar riyāḍa mufaḍḍála 3and ilmaṣriyyīn wi līha ša3bíyya kbīra áwi f maṣr.

I do weight-lifting, and this is probably the favorite sport among Egyptians, and it's really popular in Egypt.

رفْع أثْقال *raf3 asqāl* **weight-lifting**
غالِباً *ɣāliban* **probably**
مُفضّل *mufáḍḍal* **favorite, preferred**
عنْد *3and* **among; at**
مصْري *máṣri* **Egyptian**
ليها *līha* **it** (f.) **has**
شعْبية *ša3bíyya* **popularity**
كِبير *kibīr* **big, large**
مصْر *maṣr* (f.) **Egypt**

➲ **Sports:** See *Egyptian Colloquial Arabic Vocabulary (section 23)*

12

أكلْت أيْه عَ الغدا إمْبارِح؟

akált^ə ʔē 3a -lɣáda ʔimbāriħ?

What did you eat for lunch yesterday?

أكل *ákal* [i3] (also: كل *kal*) **to eat**
أيْه *ʔē(h)* **what**
عَ *3a* **for; on, at**
غدا *ɣáda* **lunch**
إمْبارِح *imbāriħ* **yesterday**
أكلْتي أيْه عَ الغدا إمْبارِح؟ *akálti ʔē 3a -lɣáda ʔimbāriħ?*
What did you (f.) **eat for lunch yesterday?**

أكْلة *ákla* **food**
رُزّ *ruzz* (coll.) **rice**
سلطة *sálaṭa* **salad; side dish**
فِراخ *firāx* **chicken**
لحْمة *láħma* **meat; beef**
محْشي *máħši* (pl. محاشي *maħāši*) **stuffed vegetables**
مكروْنة *makarōna* **pasta**
صلْصة *ṣálṣa* **sauce**
بانيْه *banēh* **breaded chicken breast**

مشْوي *mášwi* **grilled, roasted**
مصْري *máṣri* **Egyptian**

على *3ála* **for; on, at**

Yomna

أكلْت إمْبارِح فِراخ بانَيْه و مكروْنة بِالصّلْصة و البصل و طبق سلطة ضخْم.

akált imbāriħ firāx banēh wi makarōna bi-ṣṣálṣa wi -lbáṣal wi ṭábaʔ sálaṭa ḍaxm.

Yesterday, I ate breaded chicken breast, pasta with sauce, onions, and a large salad.

بصل *báṣal* (coll.) **onions**
طبق *ṭábaʔ* (pl. أطْباق *aṭbāʔ*) **plate, dish**

ضخْم *ḍaxm* **huge, very large**

Mohamed

أكلْت مكرونة بشاميل و فِراخ مشْوية و شِويّةْ خُضار سوتَيْه.

akált^ə makarōna bašamīl wi firāx mašwíyya wi šiwáyyit xuḍār sutēh.

I ate pasta with white sauce, grilled chicken, and some sauteed vegetables.

بشاميل *bašamīl* **Béchamel sauce, white sauce, cream sauce**
__شُوَيّةْ *šuwáyyit__* **a little __**
خُضار *xuḍār* (coll.) **vegetables**
سوتَيْه *sutēh* **sauteed**

Dalia

إمْبارِح على الغدا كلْت محْشي و مُلوخية و شورْبة و فِراخ مشْوية و بطاطِس و سلطة و عَيْش و مِخلِّل و بِتِنْجان.

imbāriḥ 3ála -lɣáda kalt^ə máḥši w muluxíyya wi šúrba wi firāx mašwíyya w baṭāṭis wi sálaṭa w 3ēš wi mixállil wi bitingān.

Yesterday, I had for lunch stuffed vegetables, molokheyyah, soup, grilled chicken, potatoes, salad, bread, pickles, and eggplant.

مُلوخية *muluxíyya* **molokheyyah**
شورْبة *šúrba* **soup**
بطاطِس *baṭāṭis* (coll.) **potatoes**
عيْش *3ēš* **bread**
مِخلِّل *mixállil* (coll.) **pickles**
بِتِنْجان *bitingān* (coll.) **eggplant**

Andrew

إمْبارِح علشان كُنْت في الشُّغْل أكلْت على الغدا كُشري و دي أكْلة شعْبية مصْرية.

imbāriḥ 3alašān kunt^ə fi -ššuɣl akált^ə 3ála -lɣáda kúšari wi di ákla ša3bíyya maṣríyya.

Yesterday, because I was at work, I had koshari, a popular Egyptian dish, for lunch.

شُغْل *šuɣl* **work, job**
كُشري *kúšari* **koshari** (rice, pasta, and lentils)
شعْبي *šá3bi* **popular**

Aya

أكلْت إمْبارِح على الغدا رُزّ و فِراخ و كوسة. أُخْتي هِيَّ اللي عملِت الأكْل لإِنّها مِش بِتِشْتغل.

akált imbāriḫ 3ála -lɣáda rúzz^{ə} wi firāx wi kōsa. úxti híyya -lli 3ámalit ilʔákl^{ə} li-innáha miš bitištáɣal.

Yesterday, I had rice, chicken, and zucchini. My sister is the one who made the food because she doesn't work.

كوْسة *kōsa* **zucchini**
هُوَّ اللي *húwwa -lli* **is the one who** (f. هِيَّ اللي *híyya -lli*)
عمل *3ámal* [1s2] **to make; to do**
أكْل *akl* **food**
لإِنّها... *li-innáha...* **because it** (f.)...
اِشْتغل *ištáɣal* [8s2] **to work**

Mahmoud

كلْت مكروْنة و رُزّ و لحْمة في الصّلْصة و بانَيْه و ديك رومي.

kalt^{ə} makarōna wi ruzz^{ə} wi láḫma fi -ṣṣálṣa wi banēh wi dīk rūmi.

Yesterday I ate pasta, rice, meat with sauce, breaded chicken breast, and turkey.

ديك رومي *dīk rūmi* **turkey**

Rabab

أكلْنا أنا و جَوْزي لحْمة مشْوية و سبانِخ و رُزّ و سلطة.

akálna ʔána wi gōzi láḫma mašwíyya wi sabānix wi rúzz^{ə} wi sálaṭa.

Yesterday, my husband and I had grilled meat, spinach, rice, and salad.

جوْز *gōz* **husband**
سبانخ *sabānix* **spinach**

Tamer

إمْبارِح أكلْت محْشي و هُوَّ الأكْلة المُفضّلة لِلشّعْب المصْري و كان معاه فِراخ مِحمّرة.

imbāriḫ akált^{ə} *máḫši wi húwwa -lʔákla -lmufaḍḍála li-ššá3b ilmáṣri wi kān ma3ā firāx miḫammára.*

Yesterday, I ate stuffed vegetables, Egyptians' favorite dish, and also grilled chicken.

مُفضّل *mufáḍḍal* **favorite, preferred**
شعْب *ša3b* **people, populace**
معاه *ma3ā* **with it** (m.)
مِحمّر *miḫámmar* **baked**

Shorouk

إمْبارِح كُنْت في مهْرجان، فا أكلْت برّه معَ صُحابي رُزّ و كُفْتة داوود باشا.

imbāriḫ kúnt^{ə} *f mahragān, fa akált*^{ə} *bárra má3a ṣuḫābi rúzz, wi kúfta dāwud bāša.*

Yesterday, I was at a festival, so I ate out with my friends: rice and meatballs.

مهْرجان *mahragān* **festival**
فا *fa, fā* **(and) so, therefore**
برّه *bárra* **out, outside**
صاحِب *ṣāḫib* (pl. صُحاب *ṣuḫāb*) **friend**
كُفْتة *kúfta* **meat ball(s)**
كُفْتة داوود باشا *kúfta dāwud bāša* **meat balls with tomato sauce**

Fouad

أكلْت كنْتاكي و زوِّدْت ليه رُزّ مامْتي كانِت عامْلاه علشان أنا بحِبّ الرُّزّ الأبْيَض أوي.

akált^{ə} *kantāki wi zawwídt*^{ə} *lī ruzz, mámti kānit 3amlā 3alašān ána baḫíbb irrúzz ilʔábyaḍ áwi.*

I ate KFC, and I added rice to it that my mom made because I really like white rice.

كنْتاكي *kantāki* **KFC; Kentucky**
زوِّد *záwwid* [2s1] **to add**
ليه *lī* **to it** (m.)
ماما *māma* **mom**
مامْتي *mámti* **my mom**
عامْلة *3ámla* (f.) **making**
عامْلاه *3amlā* (f.) **making it** (m.)
حبّ *ḫabb* [1g3] **to like**
أبْيَض *ábyaḍ* **white**

➲ **Food:** See *Egyptian Colloquial Arabic Vocabulary (section 8)*

13

مِتْعوِّد تِصْحى السّاعة كام؟

mit3áwwid tíṣħa -ssā3a kām?

What time do you usually get up?

مِتْعوِّد *mit3áwwid* (+ imperfect) **usually; to be accustomed to**
صِحي *ṣíħi* [1d4] **to wake up, get up**
السّاعة كام *issā3a kām* **what time**
مِتْعوِّدة تِصْحي السّاعة كام؟ *mit3awwída tíṣħi -ssā3a kām?* **What time do you** (f.) **usually get up?**

شُغْل *šuɣl* **job, work**

راح *rāħ* [1h1] **to go (to)**
لِحِق *líħiʔ* [1s4] (+ imperfect) **to have time to**

بدْري *bádri* **early**
الصُّبْح *iṣṣúbħ* **in the morning**
عادةً *3ādatan* **usually**

السّاعة __ *issā3a* __ **at __ o'clock**
سبْعة *sáb3a* **seven**
تمانْية *tamánya* **eight**
تِسْعة *tís3a* **nine**

على *3ála* **at** (an hour)

Yomna

عادةً بصْحى سِتّة الصُّبْح. آخِر الأُسْبوع بِنْحاوِل نِصْحى مِتْأخّر لكِن كُلّ البيْت بِيْكون مِتْعوِّد يِصْحى بدْري.

3ādatan báṣħa sítta -ṣṣubħ. āxir ilʔusbū3 binħāwil níṣħa mitʔáxxar lākin kull ilbēt biykūn mit3áwwid yíṣħa bádri.

I usually wake up at 6 a.m. On the weekend, we try to get up late, but everyone in the house is used to getting up early.

آخِر أُسْبوع *āxir usbū3* **weekend**
حاوِل *ħāwil* [3s] (+ imperfect) **to try to**

مِتْأخّر *mitʔáxxar* **late**
بيْت *bēt* (pl. بِيوت *biyūt*) **house**

Mohamed

أنا بصْحى على تمانْيَة الصُّبْح. أفْطر و أسْتحمّى و أروح الشُّغْل.

ána báṣħa 3ála tamánya -ṣṣubħ. áfṭar w astaħámma w arūħ iššúɣl.

I get up at 8 in the morning, have breakfast, shower, and go to work.

فِطِر *fíṭir* [1s4] **to eat breakfast**

اِسْتحمّى *istaħámma* [10.2d] **to bathe**

Dalia

أنا مِتْعوِّدة أصْحى كُلّ يوْم السّاعة تِسْعة الصُّبْح و اِتْعوِّدْت أصْحى كِده لِإِنّ بِيْكون عنْدي شُغْل.

ána mit3awwída áṣħa kull^ə yōm issā3a tís3a -ṣṣubħ, w it3awwídt áṣħa kída li-ínn^ə biykūn 3ándi šuɣl.

I usually wake up every day at 9 a.m, and I've gotten used to getting up this early because I have a job.

كُلّ يوْم *kull^ə yōm* **every day**

اِتْعوِّد *it3áwwid* [5s1] (+ imperfect) **to become accustomed to**

كِده *kída* **in this way, like this, thus**

Andrew

عادةً بصْحى السّاعة تمانية الصُّبْح علشان الشُّغْل و في الأجازات مُمْكِن أصْحى على عشرة.

3ādatan báṣħa -ssā3a tamánya -ṣṣubħ, 3alašān iššúɣl, wi fi -lʔagazāt múmkin áṣħa 3ála 3ášara.

I usually wake up for work at 8 a.m. and on my days off at 10 a.m.

أجازة *agāza* **day off; holiday**

مُمْكِن *múmkin* (+ imperfect) **may, might, could; possibly**

Aya

مِتْعوِّدة أَصْحى السّاعة سبْعة الصُّبح، معاد مُناسِب إنيّ أَجْهز و أروح الشُّغْل.

mit3awwída áṣḫa -ssā3a sáb3a -ṣṣubḫ, ma3ād munāsib ínni ághaz w arūḫ iššúɣl.

I usually get up at 7 a.m. in time for me to get ready and go to work.

معاد *ma3ād, mi3ād* **set time; appointment**
مُناسِب *munāsib* **appropriate, right**
إنّ... *inn...* **that...**
جِهِز *gíhiz* [1s4] **to get ready**

Mahmoud

مِتْعوِّد أَصْحى السّاعة سبْعة الصُّبح عشان أَلْحق أرْكب المُواصْلات و أروح الكُلّية.

mit3áwwid áṣḫa -ssā3a sáb3a -ṣṣubḫ 3ašān álḫaʔ árkab ilmuwaṣlāt w arūḫ ilkullíyya.

I usually wake up at 7 a.m., so I have time to take public transportation to get to college.

رِكِب *ríkib* [1s4] **to ride, take** (transportation)
مُواصْلات *muwaṣlāt* (pl.) **public transportation**
كُلّية *kullíyya* **college, university**

Rabab

السّاعة سبْعة عشان أُتوبيس الشُّغْل بِيِيْجيلي السّاعة تمانْيَة و بكون في الشُّغْل السّاعة تِسْعة.

issā3a sáb3a 3ašān utubīs iššuɣlᵊ biygīli -ssā3a tamánya wi bakūn fi -ššúɣl issā3a tís3a.

I usually wake up at 7 a.m. because the company shuttle comes at eight, and I get to work at nine.

أُتوبيس *utubīs* **bus**
جِه *gih* [i1] **to come**
ـلي *-li* **to me**

Tamer

المفْروض أصْحى لِلشُّغْل السّاعة سبْعة الصُّبح بسّ ساعات وِلادي بيِصحّوني قبْل كِده كمان.

ilmafrūḍ áṣḫa li-ššúɣl issā3a sáb3a -ṣṣubḫ bassᵊ sa3āt wilādi biyṣaḫḫūni ʔablᵊ kída kamān.

I have to get up for work at seven, but sometimes my kids wake me up before this, too.

المفْروض *ilmafrūḍ* (+ imperfect) **must, have to**
ساعات *sa3āt* **sometimes**
وَلد *wálad* (pl. وِلاد *wilād*) **son; boy**
صحّى *ṣáḫḫa* [2d] **to wake** (someone) **up**
قبْل كِده *ʔáblᵊ kída* **before this, beforehand**

Shorouk

غالِباً بصْحى بعْد الضُّهْر عشان بسْهر كِتير بسّ الأيّام دي بصْحى بدْري بِسبب الجامْعة.

ɣāliban báṣḫa ba3d iḍḍúhr, 3ašān báshar kitīr bass ilʔayyām di báṣḫa bádri bi-sábab ilgám3a.

I usually get up in the afternoon because I stay up all night a lot, but these days I wake up early because of university.

غالِباً *ɣāliban* **usually; probably**
بعْد الضُّهْر *ba3d iḍḍúhr* **in the afternoon**
بعْد *ba3d* **after**
ضُهْر *ḍuhr* **noon**
سِهِر *síhir* [1s4] **to stay up all night**
الأيّام دي *ilʔayyām di* **these days**
بِسبب *bi-sábab* **because of**
جامْعة *gám3a* **university, college**

Fouad

مِتْعوِّد أصْحى السّاعة تِسْعة الصُّبْح. لازِم ألْحق أتْمشّى في الشّمْس عشان دي حاجة الجِسْم مِحْتاجْها.

mit3áwwid áṣḫa -ssā3a tís3a -ṣṣubḫ. lāzim álḫaʔ atmášša fi -ššáms, 3ašān di ḫāga ilgísmᵊ miḫtágha.

I usually get up at nine. I need to have time to go for a walk in the sun because it's something the body needs.

لازِم *lāzim* (+ imperfect) **must, have to**
اِتْمشّى *itmášša* [5d] **to go for a walk**
شمْس *šams* **sun**
حاجة *ḫāga* **thing, something**
جِسْم *gism* **body**
مِحْتاج *miḫtāg* **needing, in need of**

14

أيْه هِيَّ أكْلتك المُفضّلة؟

ē? híyya ?aklítak ilmufaḍḍála?

What is your favorite food?

أيْه *?ē(h)* **what**
هِيَّ *híyya* (f.) **it; she**
أكْلة *ákla* **food**
ـك *-ak* (m.) **your**
مُفضّل *mufáḍḍal* **favorite, preferred**
أيْه هِيَّ أكْلِتك المُفضّلة؟ *ē? híyya aklítik ilmufaḍḍála?*
What is your (f.) **favorite food?**

أكْل *akl* **food**
سُبّيْط *subbēṭ* **calamari**
سمك *sámak* **fish**
محْشي *máḫši* (pl. محاشي *maḫāši*) **stuffed vegetables**

أكل *ákal* [i3] (also: كل *kal*) **to eat**
حبّ *ḫabb* [1g3] **to like**

مصْري *máṣri* **Egyptian**

مُمْكِن *múmkin* (+ imperfect) **can; might, may; possibly**

خُصوصاً *xuṣūṣan* **especially**

على *3ála* **on**

Yomna

الأكْل كُلُّه بِالنِّسْبة لي مُفضّل. أنا باعْتِبِر الأكْل مِن أجْمل نِعم ربِّنا عليْنا.

*il?ákl*ᵊ *kúllu bi-nnisbā-li mufáḍḍal. ána ba3tíbir il?ákl*ᵊ *min ágmal ní3am rabbína 3alēna.*

All food is preferable to me. I consider food one of God's most beautiful blessings upon us.

كُلّه *küllu* **all of it** (m.)
بِالنِّسْبة لي *bi-nnisbā-li* **as for me, personally**
مِن *min* (+ elative + pl. noun) **one of the most __**
أجْمل *ágmal* **the most beautiful**

نِعْمة *ní3ma* (pl. نِعم *ní3am*) **blessing, favor, kindness**
ربِّنا *rabbína* **our Lord, God**
ربّ *rabb* **lord**
عليْنا *3alēna* **upon us, on us**

أنا بحِبّ السّمك. أكْتر أكْلة بحِبّها شْوَيِّةْ سمك على سُبِّيْط على جمْبري.

Mohamed

ána baħíbb issámak. áktar ákla baħibbáha šwáyyit sámak 3ála subbēṭ 3ála gambári.

I love fish. My favorite food is fish with calamari and shrimp.

__شُوَيِّةْ__ *šuwáyyit__* **a little __**

جمْبري *gambári* **shrimp**

أكْلتي المُفضّلة هِيَّ البيتْزا الأيطالي رغْم إنّ فيه أكْل مصْري برْضُه يِجنِّن زيّ الكُشري و الفلافِل.

Dalia

aklíti -lmufaḍḍála híyya -lbítsa -lʔiṭāli, raɣm innᵊ fī aklᵊ máṣri bárḍu yigánnin zayy ilkúšari wi -lfalāfil.

My favorite food is Italian pizza, although there is also some delicious Egyptian food, such as koshari and falafel.

بيتْزا *bítsa, pítsa* **pizza**

إيطالي *iṭāli* **Italian**

رغْم إنّ *raɣmᵊ ʔinn* **in spite of the fact that, although**

فيه *fī* **there is, there are**

برْضُه *bárḍu, bárdu* **also, too, as well**

جنِّن *gánnin* [2s1] **to delight; to make crazy**

زيّ *zayy* **like, as, such as**

فلافِل *falāfil* **falafel**

بحِبّ أوي الفول و الجِبْنة بِالسّلطة و دوْل أكْتر اِتْنين مُمْكِن أكْل مِنْهُم مِن غيْر ما أشْبع.

Andrew

baħíbbᵊ áwi -lfūl wi -lgíbna bi-ssálaṭa wi dōl áktar itnēn múmkin ākul mínhum min ɣēr m- ášba3.

I love beans, and cheese with salad—and these are the two things I can eat and eat.

فول *fūl* **beans**

جِبْنة *gíbna* **cheese**

دوْل *dōl* **these, those, they**

اِتْنين *itnēn* **two**

مِن غيْر ما *min ɣēr ma* (+ imperfect) **without**

شِبِع *šíbi3* [1s4] **to get full, feel satiated**

أكْلِتي المُفضّلة هِيَّ وَرق عِنب معاه لحْمة مشْوية. الأكْلة دي بِتِتْعِمِل كِتير في العُزومات.

Aya

aklíti -lmufaḍḍála híyya wára? 3ínab, ma3ā láɦma mašwíyya. il?ákla di bitit3ímil kitīr fi -l3uzumāt.

My favorite food is vine leaves with grilled meat. This food is made a lot for dinner parties.

وَرق عِنب *wára? 3ínab* **stuffed vine leaves**
معاه *ma3ā* **with it** (m.)
لحْمة *láɦma* **meat; beef**
مشْوي *mášwi* **grilled, roasted**
اِتْعمل *it3ámal* [7s1] **to be made**
عُزومة *3uzūma* **dinner party**

البِسِلّة. هِيَّ نوْع مِن النباتات تبع الفصيلة البُقولية مِن رُتْبِةْ الفولِيات.

Mahmoud

ilbisílla. híyya nō3 min ilnabatāt tába3 ilfaṣīla ilbuqulíyya min rútbit ilfuliyāt.

Peas. They're a kind of plant belonging to the legumes class, to the fabales order.

بِسِلّة *bisílla* **peas**
نوْع مِن *nō3 min* **a kind of**
نبات *nabāt* **plant**
تبع *tába3* **belonging to**
فصيلة *faṣīla* (biology) **class**
بُقول *buqūl* **legumes**
بُقولى *buqūli* **leguminous**
رُتْبة *rútba* (biology) **order**
فولِيات *fuliyāt* **fabales**

السُّبّيْط. أنا بموت فيه بِجدّ، مُمْكِن أقْعُد آكُل مِنُّه إلى ما لا نِهايَة.

Rabab

issubbēṭ. ána bamūt fī bi-gádd. múmkin á?3ud ākul mínnu íla ma la nihāya.

Calamari. I love it to death. I can keep eating it without end.

مات في *māt fi* [1h1] **to die for, really love**
بِجدّ *bi-gádd* **seriously**
قعد *?á3ad* [1s3] (+ imperfect) **to keep __ing, continue to**
إلى ما لا نِهايَة *íla ma la nihāya* **without end**

Tamer

أكْلِتي المُفضّلة المحْشي و الدّيك الرّومي، خُصوصاً لَوْ مطْبوخ كُوَيِّس بِيِبْقى حِلْو أوي.

aklíti -lmufaḑḑála, ilmáħši wi -ddīk irrūmi. xuşūşan law maţbūx kuwáyyis biyíbʔa ħilwᵊ áwi.

My favorite food is stuffed vegetables and turkey. Especially when it's cooked well, it's really nice.

ديك رومي *dīk rūmi* **turkey**
لَوْ *law* **if**
مطْبوخ *maţbūx* **cooked**
كُوَيِّس *kuwáyyis* **well**
بقى *báʔa* [1d1] **to be, become**
حِلْو *ħilw* **nice; beautiful**

Shorouk

أنا بعْشق حاجة إسْمها مِسقّعة بِالذّات اللي بِتْكون بِالبشاميل و بحِبّ المكروْنة جِدّاً كمان.

ána bá3šaʔ ħāga ismáha misaʔʔá3a bi-zzāt ílli bitkūn bi-lbašamīl wi baħíbb ilmakarōna gíddan kamān.

I love something called moussaka, especially the one made with cream sauce, and I love pasta a lot.

عشق *3íšiʔ, 3íšiq* [1s4] **to love**
حاجة *ħāga* **thing, something**
إسْمُه *ísmu* **called** (f. اِسْمها *ismáha*)
مِسقّعة *misaʔʔá3a* **moussaka** (dish with eggplant and ground meat)
بِالذّات *bi-zzāt* **especially, particularly**
...اللي *ílli...* **the one that...**
بشاميل *bašamīl* **Béchamel sauce, white sauce, cream sauce**
مكروْنة *makarōna* **pasta**

Fouad

بحِبّ آكُل المحاشي و خُصوصاً الكُرونْب. الكُرونْب مِن أرْخص الأكْلات المصْرية و لكِن صعْبة التّحْضير.

baħíbb ākul ilmaħāši wi xuşūşan ilkurúmb. ilkurúmbᵊ min árxaş ilʔaklāt ilmaşríyya wi lākin şá3ba -ttaħḑīr.

I love stuffed vegetables, especially cabbage. Stuffed cabbage is one of the cheapest foods in Egypt, but it's hard to prepare.

كُرونْب *kurúmb* **cabbage; stuffed cabbage**
أرْخص *árxaş* **the cheapest**
و لكِن *wi lākin* **but**
صعْب *şa3b* **difficult, hard**
تحْضير *taħḑīr* **preparation**

➲ **Food:** See *Egyptian Colloquial Arabic Vocabulary (section 8)*

15

مين المُمثِّل أَوْ المُمثِّلة المُفضّلة ليك؟

mīn ilmumássil aw ilmumassíla ilmufaddála līk?

Who is your favorite actor or actress?

مين *mīn* **who**
مُمثِّل *mumássil* **actor**
أَوْ *aw* **or**
مُمثِّلة *mumassíla* **actress**
مُفضّل *mufáddal* **favorite, preferred**
ليك *līk* **to you** (m.)**, for you**
مين المُمثِّل أَوْ المُمثِّلة المُفضّلة ليكي؟ *mīn ilmumássil aw ilmumassíla -lmufaddála līki?* **Who is your** (f.) **favorite actor or actress?**
ليكي *līki* **to you** (f.)**, for you**

فيلْم *film* (pl. أفْلام *aflām*) **movie, film**

حبّ *ḥabb* [1g3] **to like;** (+ imperfect) **to like to**

هادِف *hādif* **meaningful**

زيّ *zayy* **like, as, such as**

__ بِتاع *bitā3* __ **of** __ (f. __ بِتاعِةْ *bitā3it* __)

لِيّا *líyya* **for me, to me**

Yomna

بحِبّ المُمثِّلين الكُبار زيّ فاتِن حمامة و عُمر الشّريف و روبِرْت دينيرو و أل باتْشينو.

baḥíbb ilmumassilīn ilkubār záyyᵊ fātin ḥamāma, 3úmar iššarīf, Robert De Niro *wi* Al Pacino.

I love the great actors, such as Faten Hamama, Omar Sharif, Robert De Niro, and Al Pacino.

كِبير *kibīr* (pl. كُبار *kubār*) **great; big, large**

Mohamed

مُمثِّلي المُفضّل هُوَّ أل باتْشينو. أنا بعْشق أفْلام المافْيا بِتاعْتُه زيّ الأبّ الرّوحي.

mumassíli -lmufáḍḍal húwwa Al Pacino. *ána bá3šaʔ aflām ilmáfya bitá3tu zayy ilʔább irrūɦi.*

My favorite actor is Al Pacino. I love his mafia films, like the God Father.

عِشِق *3íšiʔ, 3íšiq* [1s4] **to love**
مافْيا *máfya* **mafia**
بِتاعْتُه *bitá3tu* (noun +) **his**

أبّ روحي *abb^{ə} rūɦi* **god father**
أبّ *abb* **father**
روحي *rūɦi* **spiritual**

Dalia

مِن المُمثِّلين المُفضّلين عنْدي، بحِبّ أحْمد السّقا. بحِبّ أفْلامُه الأكْشِن و بحِبّ مُنى ذكي تمِثِّل معاه.

min ilmumassilīn ilmufaḍḍalīn 3ándi, baɦíbb áɦmad issáʔa. baɦíbb aflāmu ilʔákšin wi baɦíbb^{ə} múna záki timássil ma3ā.

One of my favorite actors is Ahmed El Sakka. I love his action movies, and I like it when Mona Zaki is acting with him.

مِن *min* **one of**
عنْدي *3ándi* **I have**

أكْشِن *ákšin* **action**
مثِّل *mássil* [2s1] **to act**

Andrew

أنا مِش مِتابِع التّمْثيل بسّ بحِبّ أتْفرّج على أفْلام أحْمد حِلْمي لإِنُّه بِيْقدِّم أفْلام هادْفة.

ána miš mitābi3 ittamsīl, bass^{ə} baɦíbb atfárrag 3ála aflām áɦmad ɦílmi li-ínnu biyʔáddim aflām hádfa.

I don't follow actors, but I love watching Ahmed Helmy movies because he puts out meaningful films.

مِتابِع *mitābi3* **following; follower**
تمْثيل *tamsīl* **acting**

اِتْفرّج على *itfárrag 3ála* [5s2] **to watch**
قدِّم *2áddim* [2s1] **to present, put forward**

Aya

المُمثِّل المُفضّل لِيّا هُوَّ آسِر ياسْين. بحِبُّه علشان بِيِتْقمّص الدّوْر كُوَيِّس أوي و نظْراتُه مِعبرّة و وَسيم.

ilmumássil ilmufáḍḍal líyya húwwa āsir yasīn. baḫíbbu 3alašān biyitqámmaṣ iddōr kuwáyyis áwi wi naẓrātu mi3abbára wi wasīm.

My favorite actor is Asser Yassin. I like him because he incarnates his role really well and has expressive looks, and is handsome.

اِتْقمّص *itqámmaṣ* [5s2] **to imitate, take on the attributes of**
دوْر *dōr* (pl. أدْوار *adwār*) **role**
نظْرة *náẓra* **look, glance**
مِعبرّ *mi3ábbar* **expressive**
وَسيم *wasīm* **handsome, good-looking**

Mahmoud

أحْمد حِلْمي، ده أكْتر مُمثِّل كوْميدي في مصْر و الشّرْق الأَوْسط.

áḫmad ḫílmi. da áktar mumássil kōmidi fi maṣr^{ə} wi -ššárq ilʔáwsaṭ.

Ahmed Helmy. He's the biggest comedic actor in Egypt and the Middle East.

كوْميدي *kōmidi* **comedy**
مصْر *maṣr* (f.) **Egypt**
الشّرْق الأَوْسط *iššárʔ ilʔáwsaṭ* **the Middle East**
شرْق *šarq, šarʔ* **east**
أَوْسط *áwsaṭ* **mid-, middle**

Rabab

بحِبّ عُمر الشّريف الله يِرْحمُه. كان مُمثِّل أكْتر مِن رائِع و فنّان فِعْلاً مَوْهوب.

baḫíbb^{ə} 3úmar iššarīf allāh yirḫámu. kān mumássil áktar min rāʔi3 wi fannān fí3lan mawhūb.

I like Omar Sharif, God rest his soul. He was an amazing actor and a truly gifted artist.

الله يِرْحمُه *allāh yirḫámu* **God rest his soul, R.I.P.**
أكْتر مِن رائِع *áktar min rāʔi3* (lit. more than great) **absolutely amazing**
فنّان *fannān* **artist**
فِعْلاً *fí3lan* **truly, really; in fact**
مَوْهوب *mawhūb* **beloved**

Tamer

المُمثِّلة المُفضّلة ليّا هِيَّ ياسْمين عبْدُ العزيز، تقْريباً كُلّ جيلي بِيْحِبّ المُمثِّلة دي.

ilmumassíla -lmufaḍḍála líyya híyya yasmīn 3ábdu -l3azīz, taʔrīban kull^{ə} *gīli biyħíbb ilmumassíla di.*

My favorite actress is Yasmin Abdulaziz. Practically all my generation loves this actress.

تقْريباً *taʔrīban* **approximately; almost**
كُلّ *kull* **all, every**
جيل *gīl* **generation**

Shorouk

مفيش حدّ مُعينّ بِصراحة بسّ بحِبّ سْكارْلِت جوهانْسِن بِتاعِةْ فيلْم لوسي جِدّاً.

ma-fīš ħadd^{ə} *mu3áyyan bi-ṣarāħa, bass*^{ə} *baħíbb*^{ə} Scarlett Johansson *bitā3it fílm*^{ə} Lucy *gíddan.*

There's no specific one, but to be honest, I love Scarlett Johansson, who was in the film *Lucy*.

مفيش *ma-fīš* **there isn't, there aren't**
حدّ *ħadd* **someone**
مُعيّن *mu3áyyan* **specific**
بِصراحة *bi-ṣarāħa* **to be honest, frankly**

Fouad

ويلّ سْميث. بِتِعْجِبْني أفْلامُه أدّ أيْه. بِتْكون هادْفة و إنُّه بِيْحاوِل يِبْني حاجة معَ عيلْتُه.

Will Smith. *biti3gíbni ʔaflāmu ʔadd*^{ə} *ʔē. bitkūn hádfa w ínnu biyħāwil yíbni ħāga má3a 3íltu.*

Will Smith. I love his films so much. They're meaningful, and he tries to create something with his family.

عجب *3ágab* [1s2] **to please**
بيِعْجِبْني *biyi3gíbni* **I like him/it** (m.) (f. بِتِعْجِبْني *biti3gíbni*) (lit. it pleases me)
أدّ ايْه *ʔadd*^{ə} *ʔē* **so much**
حاوِل *ħāwil* [3s] **to try**
بنى *bána* [1d2] **to build**
حاجة *ħāga* **something; thing**
عيْلة *3ēla* **family**

16

لابِس أيْه النّهارْده؟

lābis ʔēh innahárda?

What are you wearing today?

لابِس *lābis* **wearing**
أيْه *ʔē(h)* **what**
النّهارْده *innahárda* **today**
لابْسة ايْه النّهارْده؟ *lábsa ʔēh innahárda?* **What are you** [(f.)] **wearing today?**

قميص *ʔamīṣ* (pl. قُمْصان *ʔumṣān*) **shirt**
طرْحة *ṭárḫa* (pl. طُرح *ṭúraḫ*) **headscarf**
لوْن *lōn* (pl. ألْوان *alwān*) **color**
لِبْس *libs* **clothes**
بنْطلوْن *banṭalōn* **(a pair of) pants**
بنْطلوْن جينْز *banṭalōn žinz* **jeans**
جوّ *gaww* **weather**
بُلوْفر *bulōvar* **sweater**
جاكيت *žākit* (pl. جَواكِت *žawākit*) **jacket**
بيْت *bēt* (pl. بِيوت *biyūt*) **house**

حبّ *ḫabb* [1g3] (+ imperfect) **to like**
لِبِس *líbis* [1s5] **to wear**

فاتِح *fātiḫ* (color) **light**
كُحْلي *kúḫli* **navy blue**
بمْبي *bámbi* **pink**
أبْيَض *ábyaḍ* **white** (f. بيْضا *bēḍa*)
رمادي *ramādi* **gray**
إسْوِد *íswid* **black**
واسِع *wāsi3* **loose, baggy; broad**
مُريح *murīḫ* **comfortable**

Yomna

لابْسة جيبة بُنّي فاتِح و قميص كُحْلي سادة و طرْحة بمْبي. بحِبّ أدخّل كذا لوْن في لِبْسي.

lábsa žība búnni fātiḫ wi ʔamīṣ kúḫli sāda wi ṭárḫa bámbi. baḫíbb adáxxal káza lōn fi líbsi.

I'm wearing a light brown skirt, a plain navy blue shirt, and a pink headscarf. I like to add several colors to what I'm wearing.

جيبة *žība* **skirt**
بُنّي *búnni* **brown**
سادة *sāda* **plain, solid**

دخّل *dáxxal* [2s2] **to put in, add**
كذا *káza* (+ singular noun) **several**

Mohamed

النّهارْده عشان رُحْت الشُّغْل فا أنا لازِم ألْبِس سيمي كاجْوال. يَعْني قميص و بنْطلوْن.

innahárda 3ašān ruĥt iššúɣl, fa ána lāzim álbis sīmi kāžwal. yá3ni ʔamīṣ wi banṭalōn.

Today, because I went to work, I had to dress semi-casually, that is, a shirt and pants.

راح *rāĥ* [1h1] **to go (to)**
شُغْل *šuɣl* **job, work**
فا *fa, fā* **(and) so, therefore**
لازِم *lāzim* (+ imperfect) **must, have to**
سيمي كاجْوال *sīmi kāžwal* **semi-casual**
يَعْني *yá3ni* **that is; you know**

Dalia

النّهارْده كُنْت لابْسة بنْطلوْن جينْز و عليْه بِلوزة لونْها كُحْلي مِنقّطة بِأبْيَض و الحقيقة برْتاح فيها و بحِبّها.

innahárda kunt^{ə} lábsa banṭalōn žinz, wi 3alē bilūza lúnha kúĥli minaʔʔáṭa bi-ábyaḍ wi -lĥaʔīʔa bartāĥ fīha wi baĥibbáha.

Today, I was wearing jeans with a navy blue blouse with white polka dots, and actually I feel comfortable in them and like them.

عليْه *3alē* **over it, on top of it**
بِلوزة *bilūza* **blouse**
مِنقّط *mináʔʔaṭ* **(polka-)dotted**
الحقيقة *ilĥaʔīʔa* **actually, really**
اِرْتاح *irtāĥ* [8h] **to relax, rest**

Andrew

النّهارْده الجوّ حِلْو. لابِس بُلوفر رمادي خفيف و بنْطلوْن جينْز و كوتْشي.

innahárda ilgáww^{ə} ĥílw. lābis bulōvar ramādi xafīf wi banṭalōn žinz, wi kútši.

Today the weather is nice. I'm wearing a thin, gray sweater, jeans, and sneakers.

حِلْو *ĥilw* **nice; beautiful**
خفيف *xafīf* **light, thin**
كوتْشي *kútši* **sneakers**

Aya

لابْسة بنْطلوْن إسْوِد و بِلوزة رمادي فاتِح و جزْمة رمادي. اِخْترْت اللِّبْس ده علشان مُريح.

lábsa banṭalōn íswid wi bilūza ramādi fātiḫ wi gázma ramādi. ixtárt illíbs[ə] *da 3alašān murīḫ.*

I have black pants, a light gray blouse, and gray shoes on. I chose them because they're comfortable.

جزْمة *gázma* **shoes**

اِخْتار *ixtār* [8h] **to choose**

Mahmoud

لابِس تي شِرْت و جاكيت عشان الجوّ مُتقلِّب شُوَيّة حرّ و شْوَيّة برْد.

lābis tī širt[ə] *wi žākit 3ašān ilgáww*[ə] *mutaqállib, šuwáyya ḫarr*[ə] *wi šwáyya bard.*

I'm wearing a t-shirt and jacket because the weather is fluctuating, a bit hot and a bit cold.

تي شِرْت *tī širt* **t-shirt**

مُتقلِّب *mutaqállib* **changeable, fluctuating**

شُوَيّة *šuwáyya* **somewhat, a little**

حرّ *ḫarr* **hot**

برْد *bard* **cold**

Rabab

لابْسة بنْطلوْن إسْوِد و بُلوفَر إسْوِد و طرْحة بَيْضا و جاكيت إسْوِد.

lábsa banṭalōn íswid wi bulōvar íswid wi ṭárḫa bēḍa wi žākit íswid.

I'm wearing black pants, a black sweater, a white headscarf, and a black jacket.

Tamer

و أنا خارِج بفضّل اللِّبْس الكّاجْوال أكْتر مِن الرّسْمي و في البيْت بلْبِس ترِنْج أَوْ بيجامة.

w ána xārig bafáḍḍal illíbs ikkāžwal áktar min irrásmi, wi fi -lbēt bálbis tiráng aw bižāma.

When I go out, I prefer dressing casual rather than formal, and when I'm at home, I wear a tracksuit or pajamas.

و أنا... *w ána...* **when I...**
خارِج *xārig* **going out**
فضّل *fáḍḍal* [2s2] **to prefer**
كاجْوال *kāžwal* **casual**
رسْمي *rásmi* **formal; official**
ترِنْج *tiráng* **tracksuit**
بيجامة *bižāma* **pajamas**

Shorouk

لابْسة لِبْس بيْت عِبارة عن بنْطلوْن لَيْجِن إسْوِد و سْويت شيرْت واسِع مِقلِّم ألْوان كتِير.

lábsa líbsᵊ bēt 3ibāra 3an banṭalōn lēgin íswid wi swīt šírtᵊ wāsi3 miʔállim alwān kitīr.

I'm wearing my house clothes, which consist of black leggings and a loose, multi-colored striped sweatshirt.

عِبارة عن *3ibāra 3an* **consisting of**
بنْطلوْن ليْجِن *banṭalōn lēgin* **leggings**
سْويت شيرْت *swīt širt* **sweatshirt**
مِقلِّم *miʔállim* **striped**

Fouad

لابِس لِبْس مُريح في الحركة. مِش بحِبّ يِكون لِبْسي ضيِّق أَوْ واسِع أَوْ فيه رُسومات.

lābis libsᵊ murīḥ fi -lḥáraka. miš baḥíbbᵊ yikūn líbsi ḍáyyiʔ aw wāsi3 aw fī rusumāt.

I'm wearing clothes that are easy to move in. I don't like my clothes to be tight or loose or have pictures on them.

حركة *ḥáraka* **movement**
ضيِّق *ḍáyyiʔ* **tight, fitting; narrow**
فيه *fī* **in it** (m.)**, on it; there is, there are**
رسْم *rasm* (pl. رُسومات *rusumāt*) **picture, drawing**

➲ **Clothing:** See *Egyptian Colloquial Arabic Vocabulary (section 6)*

17

بتِعْيا كام مرّة في السّنة؟

bití3ya kam márra fi -ssána?

How many times a year do you get sick?

عيي *3íyi* [1d4] **to get sick**
كام مرّة في السّنة *kam márra fi -ssána* **how many times a year**
كام *kam* (+ singular noun) **how many**
مرّة *márra* **time**
بتِعْيي كام مرّة في السّنة؟ *bití3yi kam márra fi -ssána?* **How often do you** [(f.)] **get sick?**

مرّة *márra* **time; once, one time**
عيا *3áya* **illness, sickness**
صِحّة *ṣiɧɧa* **health**
تغْيير *taɣyīr* **change**

تلات *tálat* (+ pl. noun) **three**
أرْبع *árba3* (+ pl. noun) **four**

عدّ *3add* [1g3] **to count**

كُوَيِّس *kuwáyyis* **good**

حَوالي *ɧawāli* **about, approximately**
عادةً *3ādatan* **usually**
الصّراحة *iṣṣarāɧa* **to be honest, frankly**
تقْريباً *taʔrīban* **approximately, or so**
يَعْني *yá3ni* **that is; you know**

Yomna

حَوالي تلات - أرْبع مرّات في السّنة. عادةً حدّ مِن الوِلاد بيِعْيا و بعْديْن باقي البيْت بيِتْعِدي مِنُّه.

ɧawāli tálat - árba3 marrāt fi -ssána. 3ādatan ɧáddᵊ min ilwilād biyí3ya wi ba3dēn bāʔi -lbēt biyit3ídi mínnu.

About three or four times a year. Usually, one of the kids gets sick, and then the rest of the house catches it from him.

حدّ مِن *ɧaddᵊ min* **one of**
وَلد *wálad* (pl. وِلاد *wilād*) **son; boy**
بعْديْن *ba3dēn* **then, after that**

باقي *bāʔi* (+ def. noun) **the rest of**
بيْت *bēt* (pl. بِيوت *biyūt*) **house**
اِتْعدى *it3áda* [7d1] **to be infected**

Mohamed

مِش عارِف. عُمْري ما حسبْتها الصّراحة. ربِّنا مَيْجيبْش عَيا لِحدّ.

miš 3ārif. 3úmri ma ɧasabtáha -ṣṣarāɧa. rabbína ma-ygíbš^{ə} 3áya li-ɧadd.

I don't know. I've never counted, to be honest. May God not bring sickness to anyone.

عارِف *3ārif* **knowing**
عُمْرُه ما *3úmru ma* (+ perfect verb) **has never**
حسب *ɧásab* [1s2] **to calculate**
ربِّنا *rabbína* **our Lord, God**
جاب *gāb* [1h2] **to bring**
حدّ *ɧadd* **someone, anyone**

Dalia

الحمْدُ لله أنا صِحِّتي كْويِّسة و بحافِظ على أكْلي و الرِّياضة فا مِش بعْيا أكْتر مِن مرّتيْن في السّنة.

ilɧámdu li-llāh ána ṣiɧɧíti kwayyísa wi baɧāfiẓ 3ála ákli wi -rriyāḍa, fa miš bá3ya áktar min marratēn fi -ssána.

Thank God, I'm in good health, and I watch what I eat and exercise, so I don't get sick more than twice a year.

الحمْدُ لله *ilɧámdu li-llāh* **praise (be to) God**
حافِظ على *ɧāfiẓ 3ála* [3s] **to pay attention to**
أكْل *akl* **food**
رِياضة *riyāḍa* **physical activity, exercise; sport(s)**
فا *fa, fā* **(and) so, therefore**

Andrew

حَوالي أرْبع مرّات و عادةً بِيْكون معَ تغْيير الفُصول و عادةً بِيْكون جِيوب أنْفية.

ɧawāli árba3 marrāt wi 3ādatan biykūn má3a taɣyīr ilfuṣūl wi 3ādatan biykūn giyūb anfíyya.

About four times, and it's usually with the change of seasons, and it's usually my sinuses.

فصْل *faṣl* (pl. فُصول *fuṣūl*) **season**
جِيوب أنْفية *giyūb anfíyya* **sinuses**

Aya

بعْيا مثلاً خمس مرّات في السّنة. أغْلبْهُم معَ تغْيير الجوّ عشان عنْدي حساسية.

bá3ya másalan xámas marrāt fi -ssána, aɣlábhum má3a taɣyir ilgáww, 3alašān 3ándi ɧasasíyya.

I get sick about five times a year, and it's usually with the change of weather because I have allergies.

مثلاً *másalan* **approximately; for example**
خمس *xámas* (+ pl. noun) **five**
أغْلبْهُم *aɣlábhum* **most of them**
جوّ *gaww* **weather**
حساسية *ɧasasíyya* **allergy**

Mahmoud

مرّة واحْدة تقْريباً عشان عامِل عمليةْ اللوْز و مناعْتي كْويِّسة.

márra wáɧda taʔrīban 3ašān 3āmil 3amalíyyit illōz wi maná3ti kwayyísa.

Only one time or so because I had my tonsils out, and my immune system is strong.

واحْدة *wáɧda* (f. noun +) **one**
عامِل *3āmil* **doing**
عملية *3amalíyya* **surgery, operation**
لوْز *lōz* **tonsils; almonds**
مناعة *manā3a* **immune system**

Rabab

قُليِّل يَعْني تقْريباً تلات مرّات بِالسّنة بسّ لمّا بعْيا العيا بِيْكون جامِد أوي.

ʔuláyyil yá3ni taʔrīban tálat marrāt bi-ssána, bassᵊ lámma bá3ya -l3áya biykūn gāmid áwi.

Rarely, about three times a year, but when I get sick, it is severe.

قُليِّل *ʔuláyyil* **rarely, seldom; little**
لمّا *lámma* **when**
جامِد *gāmid* **severe**

مجرّبْتِش أعِدّ الصّراحة قبْل كِده بسّ أنا عُموماً صِحّتي كْويِّسة، يَعْني مِش بعْيا بِسُهولة.

Tamer

ma-garrábtiš a3ídd iṣṣarāḫa ʔablᵊ kída, bass ána 3umūman ṣiḫḫíti kwayyísa, yá3ni miš bá3ya bi-suhūla.

I've honestly never tried to count, but my health is generally good; that is, I don't get sick easily.

جرّب *gárrab* [2s2] (+ imperfect) **to try to**
قبْل كِده *ʔablᵊ kída* **before this, beforehand**
عُموماً *3umūman* **generally, in general**
بِسُهولة *bi-suhūla* **easily** (lit. with ease)
سُهولة *suhūla* **ease**

لا، كام مرّة دي متْعدِّش. أنا بعْيا أكْتر مِن أيّ حاجة تانْيَة في حَياتي.

Shorouk

laʔ, kam márra di ma-t3áddiš. ána bá3ya áktar min áyyᵊ ḫāga tánya fi ḫayāti.

No, how many times can't be counted. I get sick more than anything else in my life.

أيّ حاجة تانْيَة *áyyᵊ ḫāga tánya* **anything else**
حاجة *ḫāga* **thing; something**
أيّ *ayy* **any**
تاني *tāni* **another, other** (f. تانْيَة *tánya*)
حَياة *ḫáya* **life**

مُمْكِن تمانْ أَوْ تِسع مرّات و بِيْكونوا برْد. و لكِن مُؤخّراً بدأْت أهْتِمّ بِصِحّتي أكْتر و أفْهم أكْتر ليْه بْنِمْرض.

Fouad

múmkin táman aw tísa3 marrāt wi biykūnu bard. wi lākin muʔaxxáran badáʔt ahtímmᵊ bi-ṣiḫḫíti áktar w áfham áktar lē bnímraḍ.

Maybe eight or nine times, and it's usually a cold. But recently, I've begun to take care of my health more and better understand why we get sick.

تمان *táman* (+ pl. noun) **eight**
تِسع *tísa3* (+ pl. noun) **nine**
برْد *bard* (illness) **a cold**
مُؤخّراً *muʔaxxáran* **recently, lately**
بدأ *bádaʔ* [1s1] (+ imperfect) **to begin to**
اِهْتمّ بِـ *ihtámm bi-* [8g] (+ imperfect) **to be interested in**
فِهِم *fíhim* [1s4] **to understand**
ليْه *lē* **why**
مِرِض *míriḍ* [1s4] **to get sick**

➲ **Health and illnesses:** See *Egyptian Colloquial Arabic Vocabulary (section 11)*

18 عملْت أيْه النّهارْده الصُّبْح؟

3amált^ə ʔēh innahárda -ṣṣubḥ?

What did you do this morning?

عمل *3ámal* [1s2] **to do; to make**
أيْه *ʔē(h)* **what**
النّهارْده *innahárda* **today**
الصُّبْح *iṣṣúbḥ* **in the morning**
عملْتي أيْه النّهارْده الصُّبْح؟ *3amálti ʔē innahárda -ṣṣubḥ?* **What did you** (f.) **do this morning?**

على *3ála* **on; to**
عَ *3a* **on; to**

شُغْل *šuɣl* **work, job**
يوْم *yōm* (pl. أيّام *ayyām*) **day**

عمل *3ámal* [1s2] **to do; to make**
جهِّز *gáhhiz* [2s1] **to prepare, make ready**
نِزِل *nízil* [1s5] **to go out** (of the house)
صِحي *ṣíḥi* [1d4] **to wake up, get up**
فِطِر *fíṭir* [1s4] **to have breakfast**
راح *rāḥ* [1h1] **to go (to)**

كُلّ يوْم *kull^ə yōm* **every day**

Yomna

عملْت المُعْتاد بِتاع كُلّ يوْم. جهِّزْت السّنْدِوتْشات لِلوِلاد و نزِّلوا المدْرسة و لْبِسْت و نْزِلْت شُغْلي.

3amált ilmu3tād bitā3 kull^ə yōm. gahhízt issandiwitšāt li-lwilād wi nízlu -lmadrása wi lbíst, wi nzilt^ə šúɣli.

I did what I normally do every day: I prepared sandwiches for kids. They went to school. I got dressed and went to work.

المُعْتاد *ilmu3tād* **the usual**
بِتاع __ *bitā3* __ **of** __ (f. بِتاعِةْ __ *bitā3it* __)
سنْدِوِتْش *sandiwítš* **sandwich**

وَلد *wálad* (pl. وِلاد *wilād*) **son; boy**
مدْرسة *madrása* (pl. مدارِس *madāris*) **school**
لِبِس *líbis* [1s5] **to get dressed; to wear**

Mohamed

ولا حاجة. صِحيت السّاعة تمانْيَة زيّ كُلّ يوْم، فِطِرْت و اِسْتحمّيْت و رُحْت عَ الشُّغْل.

wála ɧāga. ṣiɧīt issā3a tamánya záyyᵊ kúllᵊ yōm, fiṭírtᵊ w istaɧammēt wi rúɧtᵊ 3a -ššúɣl.

Nothing. I woke up at 8 a.m. as usual, showered, and went to work.

ولا حاجة *wála ɧāga* **nothing**
السّاعة __ *issā3a* __ **at __ o'clock**
تمانْيَة *tamánya* **eight**
زيّ *zayy* **like, as, such as**
اِسْتحمّى *istaɧámma* [10.2d] **to bathe**

Dalia

النّهارْده أوِّل ما صْحيت فِطِرْت و شْرِبْت القهْوَة بِتاعْتي و عملْت شْويّةْ رِياضة عشان أعْرف أكمِّل يوْمي.

innahárda áwwil ma ṣɧīt fiṭírt, wi šríbt ilʔáhwa bitá3ti wi 3amáltᵊ šwáyyit riyāḍa 3ašān á3raf akámmil yōmi.

Today, as soon as I woke up, I had breakfast, drank my coffee, and did a little exercise so that I could get on with my day.

أوِّل ما *áwwil ma* **as soon as**
شِرِب *šírib* [1s4] **to drink**
قهْوَة *ʔáhwa* **coffee**
__ بِتاعي __ *bitā3i* (def. noun +) **my __** (f. بِتاعْتي *bitá3ti*)
__شُوَيِّةْ *šuwáyyit*__ **a little __**
رِياضة *riyāḍa* **physical activity, exercise; sport(s)**
عِرِف *3írif* [1s4] **to know**
كمِّل *kámmil* [2s1] **to carry on with, continue**

Andrew

أوِّل ما صْحيت أخدْت الشّنْطة و نْزِلْت على الشُّغْل و كلِّمْت النّاس أتابِع معاها شُغْل إمْبارِح بِاللّيْل.

áwwil ma ṣɧīt axádt iššánṭa wi nziltᵊ 3ála -ššúɣl. wi kallímt innās atābi3 ma3āha šuɣl imbāriɧ bi-llēl.

As soon as I woke up, I grabbed my bag, went to work, and talked to people to continue last night's work.

أخد *áxad* [i3] (also: خد *xad*) **to take**
شنْطة *šánṭa* (pl. شُنط *shúnaṭ*) **bag**
كلِّم *kállim* [2s1] **to talk with**
ناس *nās* **people**
تابع *tābi3* [3s] **to continue**
معاها *ma3āha* **with them; with her; with it** (f.)
بِاللّيْل *bi-llēl* **at night**

النّهارْده الصُّبح صِحيت و فْطِرْت، و بعْديْن رُحْت الشُّغْل. ده العادي في أُسْبوع شُغْل.

Aya

innahárda -şşúbɧ şiɧīt wi fţírt, wi ba3dēn ruɧt iššúɣl. da -l3ādi fi usbū3 šuɣl.

This morning, I woke up early, had breakfast, then went to work. This is the norm during the workweek.

بعْديْن *ba3dēn* **then, after that**
العادي *il3ādi* **the usual, the norm**
أُسْبوع *usbū3* (pl. أسابيع *asabī3*) **week**

صلّيْت و فْطِرْت و فْضِلْت قاعِد على الفيْسْبوك يَعْني معملْتِش أيّ حاجة مُفيدة.

Mahmoud

şallēt wi fţirtᵊ wi fḑiltᵊ ʔā3id 3ála -lfēsbūk yá3ni ma-3amáltiš ayyᵊ ɧāga mufīda.

I prayed, had breakfast, and just played on Facebook, so I didn't do anything useful.

صلّى *şálla* [2d] **to pray**
فِضِل *fíḑil* [1s4] (+ act. part.) **to keep __ing**
قاعِد *ʔā3id* **remaining; sitting**
الفيْسْبوك *ilfēsbūk* **Facebook**
يَعْني *yá3ni* **that is; you know**
ايّ حاجة *ayyᵊ ɧāga* **anything**
مُفيد *mufīd* **useful**

كُنْت في الشُّغْل بسّ النّهارْده كان يوْم تِقيل أوي، يا ربّ بُكْره يْكون أحْسن.

Rabab

kuntᵊ fi -ššuɣlᵊ bass innahárda kān yōm tiʔīl áwi, ya rabbᵊ búkra ykūn áɧsan.

I was at work, but it was quite a trying day. I hope tomorrow is better.

تِقيل *tiʔīl* **difficult, trying; heavy**
يا ربّ... *ya rabb...* **I hope...** (lit. O Lord)
بُكْره *búkra* **tomorrow**
أحْسن *áɧsan* **better**

Tamer

صِحيت مِن النّوْم في ميعاد الشُّغْل و رُحْت الشُّغل و أخّروني هِناك شُوَيّة و تقْريباً اليوْم ضاع هِناك.

ṣiɧīt min innōm fi m3ād iššúɣl^{ə} *wi ruɧt iššúɣl, w axxarūni hināk šuwáyya, wi taʔrīban ilyōm ḍā3 hināk.*

I woke up for work, went to work, and they kept me there a bit late, so the [whole] day was wasted there, more or less.

نوْم *nōm* **sleep**
ميعاد *mi3ād* (pl. مَواعيد *mawa3īd*) **set time, the time for __; appointment**
أخّر *áxxar* [2s2] **to delay, make late**
هِناك *hināk* **there**
ضاع *ḍā3* [1h2] **to be wasted; to be lost**

Shorouk

بعْد ما صْحيت فتحْت البْلاي سْتيْشِن و قعدْت أدوّر على ألْعاب عشان أنزِّلْها و ألْعب.

bá3d^{ə} *ma ṣɧīt, fatáɧt il-*PlayStation *wi ʔa3ádt adáwwar 3ála al3āb 3ašān anazzílha w ál3ab.*

After I woke up, I turned on the PlayStation and was looking for games to download and play.

بعْد ما *ba3d*^{ə} *ma* **after**
فتح *fátaɧ* [1s1] **to turn on; to open**
قعد *ʔá3ad* [1s3] (+ imperfect) **to keep __ing, continue to**
دوّر على *dáwwar 3ála* [2s2] **to look for**
لِعْبة *lí3ba* (pl. ألْعاب *al3āb*) **game**
نزِّل *názzil* [2s1] **to download**
لِعِب *lí3ib* [1s4] **to play**

Fouad

صِحيت، غِسِلْت وِشّي، فِطِرْت بطاطِس معَ بعْض حبّات البُرْتُقان و نْزِلْت أتمْشّى شْوَيّة.

ṣiɧīt, ɣasált^{ə} *wíšši, fiṭírt*^{ə} *baṭāṭis má3a ba3ḍ*^{ə} *ɧabbāt ilburtuʔān wi nzílt atmášša šwáyya.*

I woke up, washed my face, had potatoes for breakfast with a few oranges, and I went out for a walk.

غسِل *ɣásal* [1s2] **to wash**
وِشّ *wišš* (pl. وُشوش *wušūš*) **face**
بطاطِس *baṭāṭis* (coll.) **potatoes**
بعْض *ba3ḍ* **some**
حبّة *ɧábba* **piece** (of fruit, etc.)
بُرْتُقان *burtuʔān* (coll.) **oranges**
اِتْمشّى *itmášša* [5d] **to go for a walk, take a stroll**

بِتْفضّل أنْهي فصْل مِن السّنة؟ أيْه الجوّ اللي بِتْفضّلْه؟

bitfáḍḍal ánhi faṣlᵊ min issána? ʔēh ilgáww ílli bitfaḍḍálu?

What is your favorite season or kind of weather?

فضّل *fáḍḍal* [2s2] **to prefer**
أنْهي *ánhi* **which**
فصْل *faṣl* (pl. فُصول *fuṣūl*) **season**
سنة *sána* (pl. سِنين *sinīn*) **year**
أيْه *ʔē(h)* **what**
جوّ *gaww* **weather**
اللي *ílli* **that, which**
بِتْفضّلي أنْهي فصْل مِن السّنة؟ أيْه الجوّ اللي بِتْفضّليه؟
bitfaḍḍáli ánhi faṣlᵊ min issána? ʔēh ilgáww ílli bitfaḍḍalī? **What is your** (f.) **favorite season or kind of weather?**

حبّ *ḥabb* [1g3] **to like; to love**
بقى *báʔa* [1d1] **to become; to be**

حرّ *ḥarr* **hot; heat**

أكْتر مِن *áktar min* **more than**

فيه *fī* **in it** (m.)**; there is, there are**

خريف *xarīf* **autumn, fall**
السّقْعة *issáʔ3a* **the cold, cold weather**
صيْف *ṣēf* **summer**
بحْر *baḥr* (pl. بِحار *biḥār*) **sea**
شِتا *shíta* **winter**
ربيع *rabī3* **spring**
مصْر *maṣr* (f.) **Egypt**
إسْكِنْدِرية *iskindiríyya* **Alexandria**

Yomna

الخريف هُوَّ أَفْضل فصْل لِإنّ الجوّ بِيْكون فيه مُعْتدِل و مُناسِب لِلخُروج، و كمان عشان اِتْوَلدْت فيه.

ilxarīf húwwa áfḍal fáṣl, li-inn ilgáwwᵊ biykūn fī mu3tádil wi munāsib li-lxurūg, wi kamān 3ašān itwaládtᵊ fī.

Autumn is the best season because the weather is moderate and suitable for going out, and also because I was born then.

مُعْتدِل *mu3tádil* **moderate**
مُناسِب لِـ *munāsib li-* **appropriate, suitable for**

خُروج *xurūg* **going out**
اِتْوَلد *itwálad* [7s1] **to be born**

Mohamed

أنا مبحِبِّش السّقْعة. عشان كِده الصّيْف هُوَّ وَقْتي المُفضّل، بحْر و شمْس.

ána ma-baħíbbiš issáʔ3a. 3ašān kída -ṣṣēf húwwa wáʔti -lmufáḍḍal, baħr^{ə} wi šams.

I don't like the cold. That's why summer is my favorite time—the sea and sun.

عشان كِده *3ašān kída* **so, therefore, that's why**
وَقْت *waʔt* (pl. أَوْقات *awʔāt*) **time**
مُفضّل *mufáḍḍal* **favorite, preferred**
شمْس *šams* **sun**

Dalia

أنا بحِبّ فصْل الصّيْف. رغْم إنُّه حرّ بسّ أنا بحِبّ فيه الطّاقة اللي بِتْكون عنْدي.

ána baħíbb^{ə} faṣl iṣṣēf. raɣm ínnu ħarr^{ə} bass ána baħíbb^{ə} fī iṭṭāʔa ílli bitkūn 3ándi.

I like summer. Although it's hot, I love the energy I have during it.

رغْم إنّ *raɣm ínn* **in spite of the fact that, although**
طاقة *ṭāʔa* **energy**
عنْدي *3ándi* **I have**

Andrew

طبْعاً الشِّتا لإِنّ الجوّ عنْدِنا بِيِبْقى جميل و أقْدر أعْمل أنْشِطة أكْتر مِن الصّيْف.

ṭáb3an iššíta li-inn ilgáww^{ə} 3andína biyíbʔa gamīl w áʔdar á3mal anšíṭa áktar min iṣṣēf.

Winter, of course, because the weather here is nice, and I can do activities more than in the summer.

طبْعاً *ṭáb3an* **of course, naturally**
عنْدِنا *3andína* **where I'm from, in my country** (lit. at us, at our place); **we have**
جميل *gamīl* **nice; beautiful**
قِدِر *ʔídir* [1s4] **to be able to**
عمل *3ámal* [1s2] **to do; to make**
نشاط *našāṭ* (pl. أنْشِطة *anšíṭa*) **activity**

Aya

بفضّل فصْل الخريف. بِيْكون الجوّ فيه في مصْر مُتَوازِن جِدّاً.

bafáḍḍal faṣl ilxarīf. biykūn ilgáww^ə fī fi maṣr^ə mutawāzin gíddan.

I prefer autumn. The weather becomes balanced in Egypt then.

مُتَوازِن *mutawāzin* balanced

Mahmoud

الصّيْف، عشان جوّ في الصّيْف في مصْر حِلْو جِدّاً خاصةً في الأماكِن السّاحْلية.

iṣṣēf, 3ašān gaww^ə fi -ṣṣēf fi maṣr^ə ɦílw^ə gíddan xāṣatan fi -lʔamākin issaɦlíyya.

Summer, because the weather in Egypt is really nice, especially in coastal areas.

حِلْو *ɦilw* **nice; beautiful**

خاصةً *xāṣatan* **especially**

مكان *makān* (pl. أماكِن *amākin*) **place**

ساحْلي *sáɦli* **coastal**

Rabab

بفضّل الشِّتا. الجوّ خُصوصاً في إسْكِنْدِرية بِيْكون أكْتر مِن رائع و البحْر خلّاب.

bafáḍḍal iššíta. ilgáww^ə xuṣūṣan f iskindiríyya biykūn áktar min rāʔi3 wi -lbaɦr^ə xallāb.

I prefer winter. The weather, especially in Alexandria, is wonderful, and the sea is captivating.

خُصوصاً *xuṣūṣan* **especially**

أكْتر مِن رائع *áktar min rāʔi3* (lit. more than great) **absolutely amazing**

خلّاب *xallāb* **captivating**

Tamer

عادةً الإجابة بِتِبْقى الرّبيع أَوْ الصّيْف بسّ أنا بفضّل الشّتا. بيِبْقى الجوّ أحْسن في إسْكِنْدِرية.

3ādatan il?igāba bitíb?a -rrabī3 aw -ṣṣēf, bass ána bafáḍḍal iššíta. biyíb?a -lgáww^{ə} áɦsan f iskindiríyya.

The usual answer would be the spring or summer, but I prefer winter—the weather becomes better in Alexandria.

عادةً *3ādatan* **usually**
إجابة *igāba* **answer, reply**
أحْسن *áɦsan* **better**

Shorouk

بحِبّ الشّتا أوي عشان بحِبّ السّقْعة و البرْد أكْتر مِن الصّيْف و الحرّ اللي فيه.

baɦíbb iššíta áwi 3ašān baɦíbb issá?3a wi -lbárd áktar min iṣṣēf wi -lɦárr ílli fī.

I really like winter because I like cold more than summer and the heat then.

برْد *bard* **coldness, coolness**

Fouad

فصْل الصّيْف. نادِراً ما بْتِعْيا، و لكِن بِيِصْعب عليّا أكْتر المُحجّبات في الصّيْف عشان لِبْسُهم بِيْحرّرْهُم أوي.

faṣl iṣṣēf. nādiran ma btí3ya, wi lākin biyíṣ3ab 3aláyya áktar ilmuɦaggabāt fi -ṣṣēf 3alašān libsúhum biyɦarrárhum áwi.

The summer. Because you rarely get sick, but I feel sorry for women who wear hijab because their clothes are really hot for them.

نادِراً ما *nādiran ma* **rarely, hardly ever**
عِيي *3íyi* [1d4] **to get sick**
صِعِب على *ṣí3ib 3ála* [1s4] **to make feel sorry for**
عليّا *3aláyya* **for me; to me; on me**
مُحجّبة *muɦaggába* **covered woman (wearing hijab)**
لِبْس *libs* **clothes**
ـهُم *-hum, -úhum* (pronoun suffix) **them;** (possessive) **their**
حرّر *ɦárrar* [2s2] **to make (feel) hot**

➲ **Weather:** See *Egyptian Colloquial Arabic Vocabulary (section 43)*

20

بِتْحِبّ تْغنّي أَوْ تُرْقُص؟

bitɦíbb^{ə} tiɣánni ʔaw túrʔuʂ?

Do you like to sing or dance?

حبّ *ɦabb* [1g3] (+ imperfect) **to like; to love**
غنّى *ɣánna* [2d] **to sing**
أَوْ *aw* **or**
رقص *ráʔaʂ* [1s3] **to dance**
بِتْحِبّي تِغنّي أَوْ تُرْقُصي؟ *bitɦíbbi tiɣánni aw turʔúʂi?* **Do you** (f.) **like to sing or dance?**

غُنا *ɣúna* **singing**
رقْص *raʔʂ* **dancing, dance**
مزّيكا *mazzīka* **music**
أُغنية *uɣníyya* (pl. أغاني *aɣāni*) **song**

سِمِع *sími3* [1s4] **to listen to; to hear**

آه *ā, āh* **yes**

لِوَحْدُه *li-wáɦdu* **by oneself, alone**

Yomna

مليش في الغُنا خالِص بسّ بحِبّ أسْمعُه و بحِبّ الرّقْص. بعْتِبِرُه رِياضة مُسلّية و بِيْحسِّن المزاج.

ma-līš fi -lɣúna xāliʂ bass^{ə} baɦíbb asmá3u wi baɦíbb irráʔʂ. ba3tibíru riyāɖa musallíyya wi biyɦássin ilmazāg.

I don't care for singing, but I love listening to it, and I love to dance. I consider it fun exercise that puts me in a good mood.

ليه في *lī fi* **to care for, be concerned with**
خالِص *xāliʂ* (negative +) **not at all**
اِعْتبر *i3tábar* [8s1] **to consider**
رِياضة *riyāɖa* **physical activity, exercise; sport(s)**
مُسلّي *musálli* **fun, enjoyable**
حسِّن *ɦássin* [2s1] **to improve, make better**
مزاج *mazāg* **mood**

Mohamed

أه، أنا مِن أكْتر الحاجات اللي بحِبّها الرّقْص و المزّيكا.

āh, ána min áktar ilɦagāt ílli baɦibbáha -rraʔṣ^{ə} wi -lmazzīka.

Yes, dancing and music are among the things I love most.

حاجة *ɦāga* **thing, something**

اللي *ílli* **that, which**

Dalia

بحِبّ أغنّي معَ إنّ صوْتي وِحِش بسّ ببْقى مبْسوطة لمّا بغنّي و بلاقي نفْسي برْقُص تِلْقائيّاً.

baɦíbb aɣánni má3a inn^{ə} ṣōti wíɦiš bass^{ə} báb?a mabsūṭa lámma baɣánni wi balāʔi náfsi bárʔuṣ tilqaʔíyyan.

I love singing despite the fact that my voice is bad, but I feel happy when I sing and find myself dancing spontaneously.

معَ إنّ *má3a ínn* **despite the fact that, even though**

صوْت *ṣōt* (pl. أصْوات *aswāt*) **voice**

وِحِش *wíɦiš* **bad, ugly**

بقى *báʔa* [1d1] **to become; to be**

مبْسوط *mabsūṭ* **happy**

لمّا *lámma* **when**

لاقى *lāʔa* [3d] **to find**

نفْسُه *náfsu* **onself**

تِلْقائياً *tilqaʔíyyan* **spontaneously, automatically**

Andrew

أنا بحِبّ الغُنا جِدّاً و بحِبّ الأغاني القديمة و الحديثة. و أكْتر مُغنّي بسْمعْله هُوَّ مُحمّد مُنير.

ána baɦíbb ilɣúna giddan wi baɦíbb ilʔaɣāni -lʔadīma wi -lɦadīsa. w áktar muɣánni basmá3lu húwwa muɦámmad munīr.

I love singing a lot, and I love old and modern songs. The singer I listen to most is Mohammed Munir.

قديم *ʔadīm* **old**

حديث *ɦadīs* **modern**

مُغنّي *muɣánni* **singer**

Aya

بحِبّ أغنّي و أرْقُص، لكِن و أنا لِوَحْدي عشان مبحِبِّش حدّ يِتْفرّج أَوْ يِسْمع.

baħíbb aɣánni w árʔuṣ, lākin w ána li-wáħdi 3ašān ma-baħíbbiš ħaddᵊ yitfárrag aw yísma3.

I love singing and dancing, but [just] when I'm by myself, because I don't want anyone watching or listening.

و أنا... *w ána...* **when I...**
حدّ *ħadd* **someone**
اِتْفرّج على *itfárrag 3ála* [5s2] **to watch; to look at**

Mahmoud

بحِبّ الرّقْص بسّ في المُناسْبات زيّ الأفْراح و أعْياد الميلاد.

baħíbb irráʔṣᵊ bassᵊ fi -lmunasbāt zayy ilʔafrāħ w a3yād ilmilād.

I like dancing on special occasions, such as weddings and birthdays.

مُناسْبة *munásba* **special occasion**
فرْح *farħ* (pl. أفْراح *afrāħ*) **wedding**
عيد ميلاد *3īd milād* (pl. أعْياد ميلاد *a3yād milād*) **birthday**

Rabab

بحِبّ أرْقُص جِدّاً بسّ لِسّه مخدْتِش الخطْوَة إنيّ أتْعلِّم بِجدّ.

baħíbb árʔuṣ gíddan bassᵊ líssa ma-xádtiš ilxáṭwa ínni at3állim bi-gádd.

I love dance, but I still haven't taken the [first] step to learn it seriously.

أخد *áxad* [i3] (also: خد *xad*) **to take**
خطْوَة *xáṭwa* **step**
اِتْعلِّم *it3állim* [5s1] **to learn**
بِجدّ *bi-gádd* **seriously**

Tamer

بحِبّ الرّقْص أوي و كمان بحِبّ المزّيكا بْكُلّ أشْكالْها حتّى المزّيكا الغرْيبة شْوَيّة عنّنا.

baɦíbb irráʔṣ^{ə} áwi wi kamān baɦíbb ilmazzīka b-kúll aškálha, ɦátta -lmazzīka -lɣarība šwáyya 3annína.

I really like dance, and I like music of all kinds, even exotic music.

بْكُلّ اشْكالْها *bi-kúll aškálha* **of all kinds** (lit. in all its shapes)
حتّى *ɦátta* **even**
غريب عن *ɣarīb 3an* **strange for, unfamiliar to**
عنّنا *3annína* **from us**

Shorouk

أه، بحِبّ أغنّي و أرْقُص جِدّاً بِالذّات أغاني الكرْتون بِتاعِةْ سْبيْسْتون زمان. بحِبّ أغنّيها أوي.

āh, baɦíbb aɣánni w árʔuṣ gíddan bi-zzāt aɣāni -kkartūn bitā3it Spacetoon *zamān. baɦíbb aɣannīha áwi.*

Yes, I love singing and dancing, especially the old cartoon songs on the Spacetoon channel. I really like their songs.

بِالذّات *bi-zzāt* **especially, particularly**
كرْتون *kartūn* **cartoon**
بِتاع __ *bitā3* __ **of** __ (f. بِتاعِةْ __ *bitā3it* __)
زمان *zamān* **(from) long ago, in the past**

Fouad

أه، بسّ لَوْ أنا لِوَحْدي أَوْ لَوْ معَ صديق عزيز عشان الرّقْص بِيْكون لِلاِسْتِمْتاع.

āh, báss^{ə} law ána li-waɦdi aw law má3a ṣadīq 3azīz 3ašān irráʔṣ^{ə} biykūn li-lʔistimtā3.

Yes, if I'm alone or with a good friend, because dancing is for having fun.

لَوْ *law* **if**
صديق *ṣadīq* (pl. أصْدِقاء *aṣdiqāʔ*) **friend**
عزيز *3azīz* **dear**
اِسْتِمْتاع *istimtā3* **fun, enjoyment**

21

لوْن شعْرك و عينْك أيْه؟

lōn šá3rak wi 3ēnak ʔē?

What color are your eyes and hair?

لوْن *lōn* (pl. ألْوان *alwān*) **color**
شعْر *šahr* **hair**
ـك *-ak* [m.] **your**
عينْ *3ēn* (pl. عِيون *3iyūn*, عينيْـ *3inē-*) **eye(s)**
أيْه *ʔē(h)* **what**
لوْن شعْرِك و عيْنك أيْه؟ *lōn šá3rik wi 3ēnik ʔē?* **What color are your** [f.] **eyes and hair?**

مصْر *maṣr* (f.) **Egypt**

بُنّي *búnni* **brown**
أخْضر *áxḍar* **green**
عسلي *3ásali* **hazel** (lit. honey-)
إسْوِد *íswid* **black** (f. سوْدا *sōda*)
أبْيَض *ábyaḍ* (hair) **gray** (lit. white)
أحْمر *áḫmar* **red**

غامِق *ɣāmiʔ* (pl. غَوامِق *ɣawāmiʔ*) **dark**
فاتح *fātiḫ* (color) **light**
صبغ *ṣábaɣ, sábaɣ* [1s3] **to dye**

Yomna

شعْري بُنّي و عينيّا فيها أخْضر و عسلي. و أنا صُغيّرة كان لوْن شعْري أفْتح.

šá3ri búnni wi 3ináyya fīha áxḍar wi 3ásali. wi ána ṣuɣayyára kān lōn šá3ri áftaḫ.

My hair is brown, and my eyes have green and hazel in them. When I was young, my hair was lighter.

و أنا... *w ána...* **when I was...**
صُغيّر *ṣuɣáyyar* **young; small, little**

أفْتح *áftaḫ* **lighter; the lightest**

Mohamed

لوْن شعْري إسْوِد. و لوْن عيْني بُنّي. بسّ أنا على طول بحْلق أقْرع.

lōn šá3ri íswid. wi lōn 3ēni búnni. bass ána 3ála ţūl báɦlaʔ áʔra3.

My hair color is black. And my eye color is brown, but I always shave [my head] bald.

على طول *3ála ţūl* **always**
حلق *ɦálaʔ* [1s1] **to shave**

أقْرع *áʔra3* **bald**

Dalia

لوْن شعْري إسْوِد و ساعات بصْبُغْه عشان يِبْقى بُنّي و لوْن عيْني بُنّي غامِق.

lōn šá3ri íswid wi sa3āt başbúɣu 3ašān yíbʔa búnni wi lōn 3ēni búnni ɣāmiʔ.

My hair is black, and sometimes I dye it brown. And my eyes are dark brown.

ساعات *sa3āt* **sometimes**
عشان *3ašān* (+ imperfect) **so that, in order to**

بقى *báʔa* [1d1] **to be; to become**

Andrew

لوْن شعْري إسْوِد و قُصيرّ و فيه شِويِّةْ شعْر أبْيَض و عينيّا لونْها إسْوِد و واسْعة.

lōn šá3ri íswid wi ʔuşáyyar wi fī šwáyyit ša3r ábyad̨ wi 3ináyya lúnha íswid wi wás3a.

My hair is black and short, and there is some gray. My eyes are dark and big.

قُصيرّ *ʔuşáyyar* **short**
فيه *fī* **there is, there are; in it** (m.)

شُوَيِّةْ__ *šuwáyyit*__ **a little __**
واسِع *wāsi3* **wide, big**

Aya

لوْن شعْري و لوْن عيْني بُنّي فاتِح زيّ ماما و بابا.

lōn šá3ri wi lōn 3ēni búnni fātiẖ, záyyᵊ māma wi bāba.

The color of my hair and eyes is light brown, like my mom's and dad's.

ماما *māma* **mom**

بابا *bāba* **dad**

Mahmoud

لوْن شعْري إسْوِد و عيْني بُنّي فاتِح. دي ألْوان مُعْظم العرب.

lōn šá3ri íswid wi 3ēni búnni fātiẖ. di alwān mú3ẓam il3árab.

My hair's black, and my eyes are light brown, which are the colors among most Arabs.

مُعْظم __ *mú3ẓam* __ **most __, the majority of __**

عربي *3árabi* (pl. عرب *3árab*) **Arab**

Rabab

لوْن شعْري إسْوِد و عيْني كمان سودا. أنا بحِبّ أوي لوْن شعْري.

lōn šá3ri íswid wi 3ēni kamān sōda. ána baẖíbb áwi lōn šá3ri.

My hair is black, and my eyes are very dark too. I love the color of my hair.

حبّ *ẖabb* [1g3] **to like, love**

شعْري لوْنُه إسْوِد و ناعِم، و عِيوني عسلية أَوْ بُنّي غامِق و دي تُعْتبر الصِّفات الرّئيسية في مصْر.

Tamer

šá3ri lōnu íswid wi nā3im, wi 3iyūni 3asalíyya aw búnni ɣāmiʔ wi di tu3tábar iṣṣifāt irraʔisíyya fi maṣr.

The color of my hair is black, and it's straight. My eyes are hazel or dark brown. These are considered the primary characteristics in Egypt.

ناعِم *nā3im* **straight**
اِعْتبر *i3tábar* [8s1] **to consider**
تُعْتبر *tu3tábar* (passive) **it** (f.) **is considered; they are considered**
صِفة *ṣífa* **characteristic, trait**
رئيسي *raʔīsi* **primary, main**

شعْري لوْنُه إسْوِد بسّ أنا صبغْتُه حالِيّاً أحْمر أمّا عيْني فا لونْها بُنّي غامِق.

Shorouk

šá3ri lōnu íswid bass ána ṣabáɣtu ɧalíyyan áɧmar ámma 3ēni fa lúnha búnni ɣāmiʔ.

My hair's black, but I've died it red now. As for my eyes, they're dark brown.

حالِيّاً *ɧalíyyan* **now, presently**
أمّا __ فا... *ámma __ fa...* **as for __, ...**

لوْن شعْري إسْوِد و لوْن عيْني بُنّي غامِق. بِيْكون نادِراً ما تْلاقي ألْوان تانْيَة في مصْر.

Fouad

lōn šá3ri íswid wi lōn 3ēni búnni ɣāmiʔ. biykūn nādiran ma tlāʔi alwān tánya f maṣr.

My hair is black, and my eyes are dark brown. You'll rarely find other colors in Egypt.

نادِراً ما *nādiran ma* **rarely, hardly ever**
لاقى *lāʔa* [3d] **to find**
تاني *tāni* **another, other** (f. تانْيَة *tánya*)

➲ **Colors:** See *Egyptian Colloquial Arabic Vocabulary (section 46)*

➲ **Eyes and hair:** See *Egyptian Colloquial Arabic Vocabulary (section 5)*

مِن بينْ الأجازات السّنَوية، أيْه أجازْتك المُفضّلة؟

min bēn ilʔagazāt issanawíyya, ʔē ʔagáztak ilmufaḍḍála?

What is your favorite holiday of the year?

مِن بينْ *min bēn* **from among**
أجازة *agāza* **holiday, vacation**
سنَوي *sánawi* **annual, yearly, of the year**
مُفضّل *mufáḍḍal* **favorite, preferred**
مِن بينْ الأجازات السّنَوية، أيْه أجازْتِك المُفضّلة؟ *min bēn ilʔagazāt issanawíyya, ʔē ʔagáztik ilmufaḍḍála?* **What is your** (f.) **favorite holiday of the year?**

سنة *sána* (pl. سِنين *sinīn*) **year**
عيد *3īd* (pl. أعْياد *a3yād*) **holiday, festival**
عيْله *3ēla* **family**
صيْف *ṣēf* **summer**
وَقْت *waʔt* (pl. أوْقات *awʔāt*) **time**
بحْر *baḫr* (pl. بِحار *biḫār*) **sea**

قضّى *ʔáḍḍa* [2d] **to spend** (time)
اِتْجمّع *itgámma3* [5s1] **to gather, get together**
أخد *áxad* [i3] (also: خد *xad*) **to take**

كِبير *kibīr* **big, large**

كِتير *kitīr* **a lot, much, many**
كُلّ *kull* **every, all**

لإِنّ *li-inn* **because**

فيها *fīha* **in it** (f.)**; during it**
عنْدي *3ándi* **I have**

Yomna

أجازْتي المُفضّلة هِيَّ أجازِةْ عيد الأضْحى. بِتْكون أجازة طَويلة بشوف فيها ناس كِتير واحْشينّي.

agázti -lmufaḍḍála híyya agāzit 3īd ilʔáḍḫa. bitkūn agāza ṭawīla bašūf fīha nās kitīr waḫšínni.

My favorite holiday is the Sacrifice Feast. It's a long holiday, during which I see a lot of people that I missed.

عيد الأضْحى *3īd ilʔáḍḫa* **the Sacrifice Feast, Eid Al-Adha**
طَويل *ṭawīl* **long**

شاف *šāf* [1h1] **to see**
ناس *nās* **people**
واحِش *wāḫiš* **being missed by**

Mohamed

أجازةْ راس السّنة، عشان الواحِد يِحْتِفِل بِالاجازات السّنة اللي فاتِت.

agāzit rās issána, 3ašān ilwāɦid yiɦtífil bi-lʔagazāt issána ílli fātit.

New Year's, because you celebrate all the holidays of the previous year.

راس السّنة *rās issána* **New Year's**
الواحِد *ilwāɦid* (impersonal) **one, you**
اِحْتفل بِـ *iɦtáfal bi-* [7s1] **to celebrate**
اللي فاتِت __ __ *ílli fātit* (f. noun +) **last __, the previous __**
فات *fāt* [1h1] **to pass**

Dalia

بيْكون عنْدي أجازات سنَوية كِتير بسّ أنا بحِبّ دايْماً أجازةْ العيد لإِنّي بقضّيها معَ عيْلْتي.

biykūn 3ándi agazāt sanawíyya kitīr bass ána baɦíbbᵊ dáyman agázt il3īd li-ínni baʔaḍḍīha má3a 3ílti.

I get a lot of annual holidays, but I always love the Eid Al-Fitr holiday because I spend it with my family.

سنَوي *sánawi* **annual, yearly**
دايْماً *dáyman* **always**

Andrew

أجازةْ الصّيْف طبْعاً لإِنّ فيها بْتِتْجمّع العيْلة كُلّها و كمان بِنْقضّي أغْلب أَوْقاتْنا على البحْر.

agāzit iṣṣēf ṭáb3an li-innᵊ fīha btitgámma3 il3ēla kulláha wi kamān binʔáḍḍi áɣlab awʔátna 3ála -lbáɦr.

The summer holiday, of course, because the whole family gets together then, and we spend most of our time by the sea.

طبْعاً *ṭáb3an* **of course, naturally**
أغْلب __ *áɣlab __* (+ noun) **most of __**

Aya

أجازْتي المُفضّلة في الصَيْف، لمّا ناخُد أجازة و نْسافِر سَوا نْروح البحْر.

agázti -lmufaḍḍála fi -lṣēf, lámma nāxud agāza wi nsāfir sáwa nrūħ ilbáħr.

My favorite holiday is in the summer, when we take a vacation and travel together to go to the coast.

لمّا *lámma* **when**
سافِر *sāfir* [3s] **to travel**
سَوا *sáwa* **together**
راح *rāħ* [1h1] **to go (to)**

Mahmoud

الأجازة الكِّبيرة. دي بِتْكون مُدِّتْها تلات شُهور بعْد كُلّ سنة دِراسية.

ilʔagāza -kkibīra. di bitkūn muddítha tálat šuhūr ba3d[ə] kull[ə] sána dirasíyya.

The big holiday, which lasts for three months after every school year.

مُدّة *múdda* **period (of time), duration**
تلات *tálat* (+ pl. noun) **three**
شهْر *šahr* (pl. شُهور *šuhūr*) **month**
بعْد *ba3d* **after**
دِراسي *dirāsi* **academic, school-**

Rabab

كانِت في هولنْدا. قضّيْت وَقْت مُمْتِع معَ جَوْزي و أصْحابْنا.

kānit fi hulánda. ʔaḍḍēt waʔt[ə] múmti3 má3a gōzi w aṣħábna.

It was in the Netherlands, I had a great time with my husband and our friends.

هولنْدا *hulánda* **Holland, the Netherlands**
مُمْتِع *múmti3* **great, wonderful**
جوْز *gōz* **husband**
صاحِب *ṣāħib* (pl. صُحاب *ṣuħāb*) **friend**

Tamer

أكْتر أجازة بحِبّها هِيَّ العيد الصُّغيرّ و العيد الكِبير عشان العيْلة كُلّها بِتِتْجمّع.

áktar agāza baɦibbáha híyya -l3īd iṣṣuɣáyyar wi -l3īd ilkibīr 3ašān il3ēla kulláha bititgámma3.

The holiday I like most is the Lesser Eid and the Greater Eid because the whole family gets together.

العيد الصُّغيرّ *il3īd iṣṣuɣáyyar* **the Lesser Eid, Eid Al-Fitr**

العيد الكِبير *il3īd ilkibīr* the Greater Eid**, Eid Al-Adha, the Sacrifice Feast**

Shorouk

آخِر حاجة طْلِعْناها كانِت معَ العيْلة و صاحْبِتي المُقرّبة و صيِّفْنا في إسْكِنْدِرية.

áxir ɦāga ṭli3nāha kānit má3a -l3ēla wi ṣaɦbíti -lmuqarrába wi ṣayyífna f iskindiríyya.

The last one we had was with family and my close friend, and went to the beach in Alexandria.

حاجة *ɦāga* **thing, something**

طِلِع *ṭíli3* [1s4] **to go (on a trip)**

صاحْبة *ṣáɦba* **(female) friend**

مُقرّب *muqárrab* **close, intimate**

صيِّف *ṣáyyif* [2s1] **to summer, spend the summer**

إسْكِنْدِرية *iskindiríyya* **Alexandria**

Fouad

أجازِةْ العيد عشان كِده كِده بِيْكونوا أجازة فا باخُد قبْلُهُم أجازة كمان فا يِبْقى عنْدي أجازة كْبيرة.

agāzit il3īd 3ašān kída kída biykūnu ayyām agāza fā bāxud ʔablúhum agāza kamān fa yíbʔa 3ándi agāza kbīra.

The Feast holiday [the Lesser Eid], as it's already a holiday, so I take a vacation prior to it so I have a long vacation.

كِده كِده *kída kída* **anyway, already, as it is**

فا *fa, fā* **(and) so, therefore**

قبْل *ʔabl* **before, prior to**

بقى *báʔa* [1d1] **to be; to become**

➲ **Holidays:** See *Egyptian Colloquial Arabic Vocabulary (section 50)*

23

بِتِعْرف تِسوق؟

bití3raf tisūʔ?

Can you drive?

عِرِف *3írif* [1s4] (+ imperfect) **to be able to, know how to**
ساق *sāʔ* [1h1] **to drive**
بِتِعْرفى تْسوقى؟ *biti3ráfi tsūʔi?* **Can you** (f.) **drive?**

عربية *3arabíyya* **car**
سِواقة *siwāʔa* **driving**
رُخْصة *rúxṣa* (pl. رُخص *rúxaṣ*) **license**
سنة *sána* (pl. سِنين *sinīn*) **year**
تمانْتاشر *tamantāšar* **eighteen**
زحْمة *záḫma* **traffic, congestion; crowdedness**
مصْر *maṣr* (f.) **Egypt**

اِشْترى *ištára* [8d] **to buy**
اِتْعلِّم *it3állim* [5s1] **to learn**
طلّع *ṭálla3* [2s2] **to get, obtain**
نِفْسي *nífsi* (+ imperfect) **I want**
شاف *šāf* [1h1] **to see**

لِلأسف *li-lʔásaf* **unfortunately**

آه *ā, āh* **yes**
أَيْوَه *áywa* **yes**
لا *láʔ, láʔa* **no**

فا *fa, fā* **(and) so, therefore**

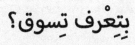

Yomna

بعْرف أسوق. سنةْ ألْفينْ و سبْعة اِشْتريْت عربية صْغيرّة و اِتْعلِّمْت عليْها السِّواقة معَ بابايا.

bá3raf asūʔ. sánit alfēn wi sáb3a ištarēt 3arabíyya ṣɣayyára w it3allímtᵊ 3alēha -ssiwāʔa má3a babāya.

Yes, I know how to drive. I bought a small car in 2007, and in it, I learned to drive with my father.

سنةْ __ *sánit* __ **in the year __**
ألْفينْ *alfēn* **two-thousand**
سبْعة *sáb3a* **seven**
صُغيرّ *ṣuɣáyyar* **small**
عليْها *3alēha* **in it** (f.)**; on it**
بابايا *babāya* **my dad**

أه، بعْرف أسوق. طلّعْت رُخْصة أوِّل ما كمِّلْت تمانْتاشر سنة بِالظّبْط.

āh, bá3raf asūʔ. ṭallá3tᵊ rúxṣa áwwil ma kammíltᵊ tamantāšar sána bi-ẓẓábṭ.

Mohamed

Yes, I can drive. I got my driver's license right after I turned 18.

أوِّل ما *áwwil ma* **as soon as**
كمِّل *kámmil* [2s1] **to turn __ (years old)**
بِالظّبْط *bi-ẓẓábṭ* **exactly, precisely**

مبعْرفْش أسوق لِلأسف و نِفْسي أتْعلِّم جِدّاً لإِنّ مِن أحْلامي إنّي أشْترِي عربية فا عايْزة أتْعلِّم.

ma-ba3ráfš asūʔ li-lʔásaf. wi nífsi at3állim gíddan li-ínnᵊ min aħlāmi ínni aštíri 3arabíyya fa 3áyza at3állim.

Dalia

I don't know how to drive, but I really want to learn because one of my dreams is to buy a car, so I want to learn.

مِن __ *min* __ (+ plural noun) **one of** __
حِلْم *ħilm* (pl. أحْلام *aħlām*) **dream**
عايِز *3āyiz* (+ imperfect) **want to** (f. عايْزة *3áyza*)

لِلأسف لا، بسّ ضروري هتْعلِّم السِّواقة لإِنّ أغْلبيةْ شُغْلي في الشّارِع.

li-lʔásaf laʔ, bássᵊ ḍarūri hat3állim issiwāʔa li-inn aɣlabíyyit šúɣli fi -ššāri3.

Andrew

Unfortunately not, but I'll definitely learn to drive because most of my work is outside [of the office].

ضروري *ḍarūri* **definitely**
أغْلبِيِّة __ *aɣlabíyyit* __ **most __, the majority of __**
شُغْل *šuɣl* **job, work**
في الشّارِع *fi -ššāri3* **outside, out and about** (lit. on the street)

Aya

أَيْوَه بعْرف أسوق. و معايا رُخْصة و عربية مِن أوِّل ما كُنْت تمانْتاشر سنة.

áywa, bá3raf asū?. wi ma3āya rúxṣa wi 3arabíyya min áwwil ma kúntᵊ tamantāšar sána.

Yes, I can drive. I've had a license and car ever since I was 18 years old.

معايا *ma3āya* **I have** (lit. with me)

مِن أوِّل ما *min áwwil ma* **ever since**

Mahmoud

أه، بحِبّ السِّواقة بسّ الزّحْمة اللي مَوْجودة على طول في الشّوارِع بِتْكرّهْني فيها.

āh, baħíbb issiwā?a bass izzáħma ílli mawgūda 3ála ṭūl fi -ššawāri3 bitkarráhni fīha.

Yes, I love driving, but the ever-present congestions on the roads make me hate it.

مَوْجود *mawgūd* **present, existing**

على طول *3ála ṭūl* **always**

شارِع *šāri3* (pl. شَوارِع *šawāri3*) **street**

كرّه __ في *kárrah __ fi* [2s2] **to make __ hate**

Rabab

لا، مِش بعْرف. بسّ ناوْيَة أتْعلِّم عشان السِّواقة لا غِنى عنْها في مصْر.

la?, miš bá3raf. bássᵊ náwya at3állim 3ašān issiwā?a la ɣína 3ánha fi maṣr.

No, I don't. But intend to learn because there's no avoiding driving in Egypt.

ناوي *nāwi* (+ imperfect) **to intend to** (f. ناوْيَة *náwya*)

لا غِنى عن *la ɣína 3an* **cannot do without**

Tamer

بعْرف أسوق كُوَيِّس بسّ بكْرهْ السِّواقة بِسبب الزّحْمة و كمان السّوّاقين مِش بيِلْتِزْموا بِأداب السِّواقة.

bá3raf asūʔ kuwáyyis bássᵊ bákrah issiwāʔa bi-sábab izzáɦma wi kamān issawwaʔīn miš biyiltízmu bi-adāb issiwāʔa.

I can drive well, but I hate driving because of traffic and drivers who don't abide by driving etiquette.

كِرِهْ *kírih* [1s4] **to hate**
بِسبب *bi-sábab* **because of**
سوّاق *sawwāʔ* **driver**
اِلْتزم بِـ *iltázam bi-* [8s1] **to abide by, follow, obey**
أداب *adāb* (pl.) **etiquette, manners**

Shorouk

لا، بسّ نِفْسي أتْعلِّم أوي. هُوَّ أنا شُفْت قريبي بِيْعلِّم أخويا فا أخدْت حبِّةْ معْلومات مِنُّه.

laʔ, bássᵊ nífsi at3állim áwi. húwwa ána šuftᵊ ʔarībi biy3állim axūya, fa axádtᵊ ɦábbit ma3lumāt mínnu.

No, but I really want to learn. I've watched a relative teach my brother to drive, so I've gotten some information from him.

هُوَّ *húwwa* (emphatic particle, untranslated)
قريب *ʔarīb* (pl. قرايِب *ʔarāyib*) **relative**
علِّم *3állim* [2s1] **to teach**
أخويا *axūya* **my brother**
أخد *áxad* [i3] (also: خد *xad*) **to take**
حبِّةْ __ *ɦábbit* __ **a little __, a bit of __**
معْلوم *ma3lūm* **information**
مِنُّه *mínnu* **from him**

Fouad

آه، بسّ لِسّه مطلّعْتِش رُخْصة. مُعْظم الشّباب في مصْر بيْتعلِّموا السِّواقة هِنا في سِنّ مُبكِّر.

āh, bassᵊ lissa ma-ṭallá3tiš rúxṣa. mú3ẓam iššabāb fi maṣrᵊ byit3allímu -ssiwāʔa hína f sinnᵊ mubákkir.

Yes, but I still haven't gotten a license. Most young people here in Egypt learn to drive at an early age.

لِسّه *líssa* **still**
مُعْظم __ *mú3ẓam* __ **most __, the majority of __**
شباب *šabāb* (pl.) **young people, youth**
هِنا *hína* **here**
سِنّ *sinn* **age**
مُبكِّر *mubákkir* **early, premature**

24

بِتْقابِل أصْحابك فينْ؟

bit?ābil aṣħābak fēn?

Where do you meet your friends?

قابِل *ʔābil* [3s] **to meet**
صاحِب *ṣāħib* (pl. صُحاب *ṣuħāb*) **friend**
ـك *-ak* (m.) **your**
فينْ *fēn* **where**
بِتْقابْلي أصْحابِك فينْ؟ *bitʔábli aṣħābik fēn?* **Where do you** (f.) **meet your friends?**

راح *rāħ* [1h1] **to go (to)**
اِتّفق *ittáfaʔ* [8s1] (+ imperfect) **to agree on/to**
خرج *xárag* [1s3] **to go out; to exit**
نِزِل *nízil* [1s5] **to go out** (of the house)
اِتْمشّى *itmášša* [5d] **to go for a walk**
أكل *ákal* [i3] (also: كل *kal*) **to eat**

بيْت *bēt* (pl. بِيوت *biyūt*) **house**
نادي *nādi* **club**
كافيْه *kafē* **café**
صاحِب *ṣāħib* (pl. صُحاب *ṣuħāb*) **friend**
مكان *makān* (pl. أماكِن *amākin*) **place**
موْل *mōl* **shopping mall**
شارِع *šāri3* (pl. شَوارِع *šawāri3*) **street**

عادةً *3ādatan* **usually**

أيّ *ayy* **any**

Yomna

عادةً بِنِتْقابِل في بيْت واحْدة فينا و ساعات بِنْروح في نادي أَوْ كافيْه.

3ādatan binitʔābil fi bēt wáħda fīna wi sa3āt binrūħ fi nādi aw kafē.

We usually meet at one of our houses, and sometimes we go to the club or a café.

واحْدة *wáħda* (f.) **one (woman)**
واحِد فينا *wāħid fīna* **one of us** (f. واحْدة فينا *wáħda fīna*)

ساعات *sa3āt* **sometimes**

في القهْوَة. أيّ شابّ مصْري بِيْقدِّس القهْوَة و عارِف أهمِّيِّتها.

Mohamed

fi -lʔáhwa. ayy^{ə} šabb^{ə} máṣri biyqáddis ilʔáhwa wi 3ārif ahammiyyítha.

In the coffee house. Any young Egyptian man dedicates time to the coffee house and knows its importance.

قهْوَة *ʔáhwa* **(traditional) coffee house**
عارِف *3ārif* **knowing**
أهمّية *ahammíyya* **importance**

دايْماً بحِبّ أقابِل صُحابي في كافيْه و بِنتِّفِق نِتْقابِل في مكان مُعيّن و نُخْرُج نِروح أيّ موْل.

Dalia

dáyman baħíbb aʔābil ṣuħābi fi kafē, wi binittífiʔ nitʔābil fi makān mu3áyyan wi núxrug nirūħ ayy^{ə} mōl.

I always like to meet my friends at a café. Or we agree to meet in a specific place and then go to the mall.

دايْماً *dáyman* **always**
حبّ *ħabb* [1g3] (+ imperfect) **to like**
مُعيّن *mu3áyyan* **specific, specified**

عادةً عنْدي في البيْت أَوْ بِنِنْزِل نِتْمشّى في الشّارِع أَوْ بِنْروح أيّ موْل.

Andrew

3ādatan 3ándi fi -lbēt aw binínzil nitmášša fi -ššāri3 aw binrūħ ayy^{ə} mōl.

Usually at my house. Or go out for a walk on the street or we go to whichever mall.

عنْدي *3ándi* **at my house; I have**

Aya

بقابِل أصْحابي في الموْل. بِيْكون مكان مُناسِب إنِّنا نِتْمشّى و ناكُل و نِتْفرّج على لِبْس.

baʔābil aṣḥābi fi -lmōl. biykūn makān munāsib innína nitmášša wi nākul wi nitfárrag 3ála libs.

I meet my friends at the mall. It's a good place for walking around, and we eat and look at clothes.

مُناسِب *munāsib* **proper, appropriate, suitable**
اِتْفرّج على *itfárrag 3ála* [5s2] **to look at; to watch**
لِبْس *libs* **clothes**

Mahmoud

في قهْوَة عنْدِنا في المدينة عشان مكان بِيْكون هادي و أسْعار الطّلبات رخيصة.

fi ʔáhwa 3andína fi -lmadīna 3ašān makān biykūn hādi w as3ār iṭṭalabāt raxīṣa.

At a local café in the city because it's a quiet location and the menu prices are low.

عنْدِنا *3andína* **where I'm from** (lit. at us, at our place); **we have**
مدينة *madīna* (pl. مُدُن *múdun*) **city**
هادي *hādi* **quiet, calm**
سِعْر *si3r* (pl. أسْعار *as3ār*) **price**
طلب *ṭálab* **order, item ordered**
رخيص *raxīṣ* **cheap**

Rabab

في البيْت أَوْ الكافيْه أَوْ النّادي بِنُقْعُد نِرْغي و نْجيب في سيرِةْ كُلّ النّاس.

fi -lbēt aw ilkafē aw innādi binúʔ3ud níryi wi ngīb fi sīrit kull innās.

At home, a café, or the club. We sit and chat and gossip about everyone.

قعد *ʔá3ad* [1s3] **to sit**
رغى *ráya* [1d2] **to chat**
جاب في سيرِةْ __ *gāb fi sīrit* __ [1h2] **to gossip about __**
كُلّ النّاس *kull innās* **everyone** (lit. all the people)

Tamer

مكان المُقابْلة المِعْتاد هُوَّ القهْوَة، مُعْظمْنا مِتْجوِّزين و بِيِبْقى صعْب نِبْعِد عن بِيوتْنا كِتير.

makān ilmuʔábla -lmi3tād húwwa -lʔáhwa, mu3ẓámna mitgawwizīn wi biyíbʔa ṣa3bᵊ níb3id 3an biyútna kitīr.

The usual meeting place is the coffee house. Most of us are married, and it's hard for us to go far from home very often.

مُقابْلة *muʔábla* **meeting, get-together, meet-up**
مِعْتاد *mi3tād* **usual, habitual**
مُعْظمْنا *mu3ẓámna* **most of us**
مِتْجوِّز *mitgáwwiz* **married**
بقى *báʔa* [1d1] **to be; to become**
صعْب *ṣa3b* **difficult, hard**
بِعِد عن *bí3id 3an* [1s5] **to be away from**
كِتير *kitīr* **often, a lot**

Shorouk

يا إمّا في الجامْعة و بعْد كِده نُخْرُج، أَوْ في بيْت حدّ مِنْهُم أَوْ عَ الشّارِعَ و نِتْمشّى.

ya-ímma fi -lgám3a wi ba3dᵊ kída núxrug, aw fi bēt ḥaddᵊ mínhum aw 3a -ššāri3 wi nitmášša.

Either at the university and then we leave, or at someone's house or on the street and then we go for a walk.

يا إمّا... أَوْ... *ya-ímma... aw...* **either... or...**
جامْعة *gám3a* **university, college**
بعْد كِده *ba3dᵊ kída* **then, after that**
حدّ مِنْهُم *ḥaddᵊ mínhum* **one of them**
عَ *3a* **on**

Fouad

بقابِلْهُم في مهْرجانات قِصص مِصوّرة في مصْر أَوْ مُمْكِن نِتِّفِق نُخْرُج نِشوف فيلْم سينِما و ناكُل.

baʔabílhum fi mahraganāt qíṣaṣ miṣawwára fi maṣr aw múmkin nittífiʔ núxrug nišūf fílmᵊ sínima wi nākul.

I meet them at comic book conventions in Egypt. Or we might make plans to go out to see a movie and eat.

مهْرجان *mahragān* **fair, festival**
قِصّة *qíṣṣa* (pl. قِصص *qíṣaṣ*) **story**
مِصوّر *miṣáwwar* **drawn, illustrated; photographed**
مصْر *maṣr* (f.) **Egypt**
مُمْكِن *múmkin* (+ imperfect) **may, might, could; possibly**
فيلْم سينِما *filmᵊ sínima* **movie**

➲ **Free time activities:** See *Egyptian Colloquial Arabic Vocabulary (section 21)*

25

أيْه الأكْل اللي مِش بِتْحِبّ تاكْله؟

ʔēh ilʔákl ílli miš bitħíbbə táklu?

Is there anything you don't like eating?

أيْه *ʔē(h)* **what**
أكْل *akl* **food**
اللي *ílli* **that, which**
مِش *miš* **not; don't**
حبّ *ħabb* [1g3] (+ imperfect) **to like**
أكل *ákal* [i3] (also: كل *kal*) **to eat**
أيْه الاكْل اللي مِش بِتْحِبّي تاكْليه؟ *ʔēh ilʔákl ílli miš bitħíbbi taklī?* **Is there anything you** (f.) **don't like eating?**

نوْع *nō3* (pl. أنْواع *anwā3*) **kind, type, sort**
بلد *bálad* (pl. بِلاد *bilād*) **country; land, place**
كوسة *kūsa* **zucchini**
طعْم *ṭa3m* **taste, flavor**
سبانخ *sabānix* **spinach**
فاصولْيا *faṣúlya* **beans**
حاجة *ħāga* **thing, something**
كَوارِع *kawāri3* (dish) **cows' feet**

جميل *gamīl* **nice; beautiful**

مفيش *ma-fīš* **there isn't, there aren't**

كُلّ *kull* **every, all**
أيّ *ayy* **any**

بِالرّغْم مِن *bi-rráɣm[ə] min* **despite, in spite of**

Yomna

مفيش أكْل مِش بحِبُّه. الأكْل كُلُّه جميل بِكُلّ أنْواعُه و مِن كُلّ البِلاد.

ma-fīš akl[ə] miš baħíbbu. ilʔákl[ə] kúllu gamīl bi-kúll anwā3u wi min kull ilbilād.

There's no food I do not like. All food is lovely in all its varieties and from all countries.

كُلُّه *kúllu* **all of it** (m.)

Mohamed

أنا قِشْطة بحِبّ آكُل مُعْظم الأكْل. الكوسة و القرْنبيط مِش بحِبُّهُم.

ána ʔíšṭa baɦíbb ākul múʒẓam ilʔákl. ilkūsa wi -lʔarnabīṭ miš baɦibbúhum.

I love most food, but I don't like zucchini or cauliflower.

قِشْطة *ʔíšṭa* (slang) **really; okay**
مُعْظم__ *múʒẓam__* **most of __**
قرْنبيط *ʔarnabīṭ* **cauliflower**

Dalia

مبحِبِّش آكُل الكوسة و مبحِبِّش كمان السّبانِخ لإِنّ طعْمها بِالنِّسْبة لي مِش حِلْو زيّ الأكْلات السّريعة.

ma-baɦíbbiš ākul ilkūsa wi ma-baɦíbbiš kamān issabānix li-ínnᵊ ṭaʒmáha bi-nnisbā-li miš ɦilwᵊ zayy ilʔaklāt issarīʒa.

I don't like zucchini or spinach because it doesn't taste good to me like fast food does.

بِالنِّسْبة لي *bi-nnisbā-li* **for me**
حِلْو *ɦilw* **nice; beautiful**
الأكْلات السّريعة *ilʔaklāt issarīʒa* **fast food**

Andrew

طبْعاً البِصارة و السّبانِخ و الكَوارِع و الرِّنْجة و الفِسيخ و بِالرّغْم مِن فَوايِدْهُم إلّا إنّ ريحِتْهُم بِتْخلّيني أبْعِد عنْهُم.

ṭábʒan ilbiṣāra wi -ssabānix wi -lkawāriʒ wi -rrínga wi -lfisīx wi bi-rráɣmᵊ min fawayídhum, ílla inn riɦíthum bitxallīni ábʒid ʒánhum.

Of course, I don't like bisara, spinach, cows' feet, smoked herring, or fesikh, despite their [health] benefits. However, their smell keeps me away from them.

بصارة *biṣāra* **bisara** (fava bean puree)
رِنْجة *rínga* **smoked herring**
فِسيخ *fisīx* **fesikh** (salted gray mullet fish)
فايْدة *fáyda* (pl. فَوايْد *fawāyid*) **benefit, advantage**
إلّا إنّ *ílla inn* **however, although**
ريحة *rīɦa* **smell**
خلّى *xálla* [2d] **to make, cause**
بِعِد عن *bíʒid ʒan* [1s5] **to stay away from, avoid**

Aya

مِش بحِبّ آكُل الفاصولْيا الخضْرا بِالصّلْصلة. كُلّ طعْمها بِيْضيع، لكِن بحِبّها سلطة.

miš baɧíbb ākul ilfaṣúlya -lxáḑra bi-ṣṣalṣála. kull^{ə} ṭa3máha biyḑī3, lākin baɧibbáha sálaṭa.

I do not like green beans with tomato sauce because they lose their flavor. But I love them as a salad.

أخْضر *áxḑar* **green** (f. خضرا *xáḑra*)
صلْصلة *ṣalṣála* **tomato sauce**
ضاع *ḑā3* [1h2] **to be lost; to be wasted**
سلطة *sálaṭa* **salad**

Mahmoud

مِش بحِبّ الفاصولْيا و السّبانِخ في الخُضار و اللّحْمة البارْدة.

miš baɧíbb ilfaṣúlya wi -ssabānix fi -lxuḑār wi -lláɧma -lbárda.

Among vegetables, I don't like beans and broccoli. And [I don't like] cold meat.

خُضار *xuḑār* (coll.) **vegetables**
لحْمة *láɧma* **meat**
بارِد *bārid* **cold**

Rabab

مفيش حاجة مبحِبِّش آكُلْها. الأكْل كُلُّه جميل و لازِم أجرّب كُلُّه.

ma-fīš ɧāga ma-baɧíbbiš akúlha. ilʔákl^{ə} kúllu gamīl wi lāzim agárrab kúllu.

There's no food I don't like. All food is beautiful, and I should try it all.

لازِم *lāzim* (+ imperfect) **should; to have to, must**
جرّب *gárrab* [2s2] **to try (out)**

مِش بحِبّ أيّ نوْع سمك. محدِّش بِيْصدّق لإنّي مِن إسْكِنْدِرية و هِيَّ بلد مشْهورة بِالسّمك.

Tamer

miš baħíbb ayy^{ə} nō3 sámak, ma-ħáddiš biyṣádda? li-ínni min iskindiríyya wi híyya bálad mašhūra bi-ssámak.

I don't like any kind of fish. No one believes it because I'm from Alexandria, which is renowned for its fish.

سمك *sámak* **fish**
محدِّش *ma-ħáddiš* **nobody**
صدّق *ṣádda?* [2s2] **to believe**
مشْهور بِـ *mašhūr bi-* **famous for**

الكَوارِع و الفِشّة و الكِرْشة و أيّ حاجة مِن مُشْتقات الحَيَوانات دي.

Shorouk

ilkawāri3 wi -lfíšša wi -lkírša w ayy^{ə} ħāga min muštaqāt ilħayawanāt di.

Cows' feet, lungs, tripe, and any organ meats [lit. derivatives of these animals].

فِشّة *físša* (food) **lungs, lights of animals**
كِرْشة *kírša* **tripe**
مُشْتق *múštaq* **derivative**
حَيَوان *ħayawān* **animal**

مِش بحِبّ آكل البِتِنْجان. و بِرغْم مِن كِده والْدِتي بِتْعِمْله بسّ باكْلُه عشان متِزْعلْش.

Fouad

miš baħíbb ākul ilbitingān. wi bi-ráɣm^{ə} min kída waldíti bit3ímlu bass^{ə} báklu 3ašān ma-tiz3álš.

I don't like eggplant. In spite of this, my mother makes it, but I eat it so she doesn't get upset.

بِتِنْجان *bitingān* **eggplant**
بِرغْم مِن كِده *bi-ráɣm^{ə} min kída* **in spite of this**
والْدة *wálda* **mother**
عمل *3ámal* [1s2] **to make; to do**
زِعِل *zí3il* [1s4] **to get upset, get angry**

➲ **Food:** See *Egyptian Colloquial Arabic Vocabulary (section 8)*

26

بِتْخاف مِن أيْه؟

bitxāf min ʔē?

What are you afraid of?

خاف مِن *xāf min* [1h4] **to be afraid of, fear**
أيْه *ʔē(h)* **what**
بِتْخافي مِن أيْه؟ *bitxāfi min ʔē?* **What are you** (f.) **afraid of?**

موْت *mōt* **death**
وَحْدة *wáħda* **isolation, lonliness, being alone**
حاجة *ħāga* **thing, something**
حشرة *ħášara* **insect**

قِدِر *ʔídir* [1s4] **to be able to**

لِوَحْدُه *li-wáħdu* **by oneself, alone**
خالِص *xāliṣ* (negative +) **not at all**

مِ الـ *mi -l-* (also: مِن الـ *min il-*) **from the**
اللي *ílli* **that which, those which; what**

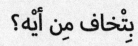

Yomna

بخاف مِن الإيذاء، إنّ أنا أَوْ حدّ مِن أُسْرِتي يِتْعرّض لإيذاء بدني أَوْ نفْسي.

baxāf min ilʔizāʔ, innᵊ ána aw ħaddᵊ min usríti yit3árraḍ li-izāʔ bádani aw náfsi.

I'm afraid of being hurt—that I or someone in my family might be exposed to physical or psychological harm.

إيذاء *izāʔ* **harm**
حدّ *ħadd* **someone**
أُسْرة *úsra* **family**
اِتْعرّض لِـ *it3árraḍ li-* [5s2] **to be faced with, be exposed to**

بدني *bádani* **physical, bodily**
نفْسي *náfsi* **psychological**

Mohamed

أنا بخاف مِ الموْت. فِكْرِةْ الموْت بِنِسْبة لي مُخيفة جِدّاً. مِش بقْدر أسْتحْمِلْها.

ána baxāf mi -lmōt. fíkrit ilmōt bi-nisbā-li muxīfa gíddan. miš báʔdar astaɧmílha.

I am afraid of death. The idea of death is very frightening for me. I cannot bear it.

فِكْرة *fíkra* **idea**
بِالنِّسْبة لي *bi-nnisbā-li* **for me**
مُخيف *muxīf* **scary, frightening**
اِسْتحْمِل *istáɧmil* [10s1] **to bear, tolerate, put up with**

Dalia

بخاف مِن الموْت و الفِراق و المرض. بخاف أفْشل في حَياتي و إنّي مقْدرْش أحقّق اللي نِفْسي فيه.

baxāf min ilmōt wi -lfirāʔ wi -lmáraḍ. baxāf áfšal fi ɧayāti w ínni ma-ʔdárš^ə aɧáʔʔaʔ ílli nífsi fī.

I'm afraid of death, separation, and illness. I am afraid of failure in my life and not being able to achieve what I want in it.

فِراق *firāʔ* **separation, parting, farewell**
مرض *máraḍ* **illness, disease**
فِشِل *fíšil* [1s4] **to fail**
حَياة *ɧáya* **life**
حقّق *ɧáʔʔaʔ* [2s2] **to get, obtain, win, achieve**
نِفْسـ *nifs-* (+ pronoun suffix) **to want**
فيه *fī* **in it** (m.)

Andrew

بخاف مِن القرارات السّريعة في لحْظات الغضب و بِتْكون فيها نوْع مِن أنْواع العِنْد.

baxāf min ilqararāt issarīʕa fi laɧẓāt ilɣáḍab wi bitkūn fīha nōʕ min anwāʕ ilʕínd.

I am afraid of quick decisions in moments of anger, and these contain a kind of stubbornness.

قرار *qarār* **decision**
سريع *sarīʕ* **quick, fast**
لحْظة *láɧẓa* **moment**
غضب *ɣádab* **anger**
فيها *fīha* **in them; in it** (f.)
نوْع مِن أنْواع __ *nōʕ min anwāʕ* __ **a kind of** __
عِنْد *ʕind* **stubbornness, obstinacy**

Aya

بخاف مِن الوَحْدة و الاِكْتِئاب. الإنْسان متْخلّقْش علشان يِعيش لِوَحْدُه ولا يِعيش طول عُمْرُه حزين.

baxāf min ilwáɦda wi -lʔiktiʔāb. ilʔinsān ma-txalláʔšᵊ 3alašān yi3īš li-wáɦdu wála yi3īš ţūl 3úmru ɦazīn.

Fear of loneliness and depression, because the human being wasn't created to live alone or live all his life sad.

اِكْتِئاب *iktiʔāb* **depression, gloom**
إنْسان *insān* **person, human being**
اِتْخلّق *itxállaʔ* [5s2] **to be created**
علشان *3ašān* (+ imperfect) **so that, in order to**
عاش [1h2] *3āš* **to live**
طول *ţūl* **throughout**
عُمْر *3umr* **lifetime; age**
حزين *ɦazīn* **sad**

Mahmoud

إنِّي أسْقط في مادّة أَوْ أشيل سنة في الكُلّية. دي أكْتر حاجة بخاف مِنْها.

ínni ásʔaţ fi mádda aw ašīl sána fi -lkullíyya. di áktar ɦāga baxāf mínha.

That I'll fail a subject or [have to] repeat a year at college. This is what I'm most afraid of.

سقط في *sáʔaţ fi* [1s1] **to fail**
مادّة *mádda* (pl. موَادّ *mawádd*) **subject**
شال *šāl* [1h2] **to fail, not pass; to carry, lift**
كُلّية *kullíyya* **college, university**

Rabab

بخاف أكون لِوَحْدي. مبحِبِّش الوَحْدة خالِص. بحِسّ بِكآبة و حُزْن و أنا قاعْدة لِوَحْدي.

baxāf akūn li-wáɦdi. ma-baɦíbbiš ilwáɦda xāliş. baɦíssᵊ b-kaʔāba wi ɦúzn, w ána ʔá3da l-wáɦdi.

I am afraid of being alone. I don't like being alone at all. I feel depressed and sad when I am alone.

حبّ *ɦabb* [1g3] (+ imperfect) **to like**
حسّ بِـ *ɦass bi-* [1g3] (+ noun) **to feel**
كآبة *kaʔāba* **depression, gloom**
حُزْن *ɦuzn* **sadness**
و أنا... *w ána...* **when I...**
قعد *ʔá3ad* [1s3] **to remain, stay; to sit**

Tamer

مِن صُغْري و أنا عنْدي فوبْيا مِن التّعابين و العقارِب و كُنْت بحْلم بِكَوابيس كِتير بيهُم.

min ṣúɣri w ána 3ándi fōbiya min itta3abīn wi -l3aʔārib wi kúntᵊ báɧlam bi-kawabīs kitīr bīhum.

Since my childhood, I've been afraid of snakes and scorpions, and I used to have many nightmares about them.

صُغْر *ṣuɣr* **childhood, youth; smallness**
عنْدي *3ándi* **I have**
فوْبِيا *fōbiya* **phobia**
تِعْبان *ti3bān* (pl. تعابين *ta3abīn*) **snake**
عقْرب *3áʔrab* (pl. عقارِب *3aʔārib*) **scorpion**
حِلِم بِـ *ɧílim bi-* [1s4] **to dream (about)**
كابوس *kabūs* (pl. كَوابيس *kawabīs*) **nightmare**

Shorouk

لا، مِش بخاف مِن حاجة خالِص، لا حَيَوانات مثلاً أَوْ حشرات أَوْ ضلْمة، وَلا حاجة.

laʔ, miš baxāf min ɧāga xāliṣ, la ɧayawanāt másalan aw ɧašarāt aw ḍálma, wála ɧāga.

No, I'm not afraid of anything at all—not animals, for example, or insects or the dark. Nothing at all.

لا... أوْ... *la... aw...* **neither... nor...**
حَيَوان *ɧayawān* **animal**
مثلاً *másalan* **for example, for instance**
ضلْمة *ḍálma* **darkness**
وَلا حاجة *wála ɧāga* **nothing (at all)**

Fouad

بخاف مِ الحشرات الكِبيرة، خُصوصاً اللي ليها أجْنحة و عنْدها اِسْتِعْداد تِطير.

baxāf mi -lɧašarāt ilkibīra, xuṣūṣan ílli līha agnáɧa wi 3andáha isti3dād tiṭīr.

I'm scared of big insects, especially those that have wings and are prone to fly.

كِبير *kibīr* **big, large**
خُصوصاً *xuṣūṣan* **especially**
ليها *līha* **they have; it** (f.) **has**
جناح *ginā ɧ* (pl. أجْنحة *agnáɧa*) **wing**
عنْدها *3andáha* **they have; it** (f.) **has**
اِسْتِعْداد *isti3dād* **disposition, inclination**
طار *ṭār* [1h2] **to fly**

27

إحْساسك أيْه النّهارْده؟

iɦsāsak ʔēh innahárda?

How do you feel today?

إحْساس *iɦsās* **feeling**
ـك *-ak* (m.) **your**
أيْه *ʔē(h)* **what**
النّهارْده *innahárda* **today**
إحْساسِك أيْه النّهارْده؟ *iɦsāsik ʔē innahárda?* **How do you (f.) feel today?**

شُغْل *šuɣl* **job, work**
حاجة *ɦāga* **thing**
يوْم *yōm* (pl. أيّام *ayyām*) **day**

خلّى *xálla* [2d] **to make, cause**
حقّق *ɦáʔʔaʔ* [2s2] **to achieve;** لِـ *li-* **to grant**

عايِز *3āyiz* (+ imperfect) **want to** (f. عايْزة *3áyza*)

مبْسوط *mabsūṭ* **happy**
حاسِس *ɦāsis* **feeling** (f. حاسّة *ɦássa*)
مُتفائِل *mutafāʔil* **optimistic**

Yomna

إحْساس بِالنّشاط. الصّحَيان بدْري و الرّوتين اليَوْمي بِيْخلّيني مِركِّزة في شُغْلي و مبْسوطة.

iɦsās bi-nnašāṭ. iṣṣaɦayān bádri wi -rrutīn ilyáwmi biyxallīni mirakkíza fi šúɣli wi mabsūṭa.

I feel energetic. Waking up early and my daily routine makes me happy and focused on my job.

نشاط *našāṭ* **activeness, energy; activity**
صحَيان *ṣaɦayān* **waking up**
بدْري *bádri* **early**
روتين *rutīn* **routine**
يَوْمي *yáwmi* **daily**
مِركِّز في *mirákkiz fi* **focused on**

Mohamed

أنا النّهارْده تعْبان. بطْني واجْعاني أوي مِن إمْبارِح. مِش عارِف ليْه.

ána -nnahárda ta3bān. báṭni wag3āni áwi min imbāriḫ. miš 3ārif lē.

I'm unwell today. My stomach's been hurting since yesterday. I don't know why.

تعْبان *ta3bān* **sick; tired**
بطْن *baṭn* **stomach**
واجِع *wāgi3* **hurting**
إمْبارِح *imbāriḫ* **yesterday**
عارِف *3ārif* **knowing**
ليْه *lē* **why**

Dalia

أنا حاسّة إنّ أنا مبْسوطة أوي النّهارْده لإنّي قِدِرْت أحقّق حاجات كِتير كان نفْسي فيها.

ána ḫássa innᵊ ána mabsūṭa áwi -nnahárda li-ínni ʔidírt aḫáʔʔaʔ ḫagāt kitīr kān nífsi fīha.

I feel very happy today because I was able to achieve many things I wanted.

قِدِر *ʔídir* [1s4] **to be able to**
كان نِفْسي *kān nífsi* **I wanted**

Andrew

مُتفائِل زيّ كُلّ يوْم الصُّبْح. و ده بِيْخلّيني أكمِّل بقِيِّةْ اليوْم نشيط في الشُّغْل.

mutafāʔil zayyᵊ kullᵊ yōm iṣṣúbḫ. wi da biyxallīni akámmil baʔíyyit ilyōm našīṭ fi -ššúɣl.

Optimistic, like every morning, which lets me get on with the rest of the day active at work.

كُلّ يوْم *kúllᵊ yōm* **every day**
الصُّبْح *iṣṣúbḫ* **in the morning**
كمِّل *kámmil* [2s1] **to carry on with, continue**
بقِيِّةْ *baʔíyyit* (+ def. noun) **the rest of**
نشيط *našīṭ* **active, energetic**

Aya

حاسّة النّهارْده بِالتّعْب علشان أخدْت دوْر برْد مِن تغْيير الجوّ.

ɦássa innahárda bi-ttá3b, 3alašān axádtᵊ dōr bardᵊ min taɣyīr ilgáww.

I feel tired today because I have a cold because of the change in the weather.

طعْب *ta3b* **tiredness**
أخد *áxad* [i3] (also: خد *xad*) **to take**
دوْر برْد *dōr bárd* **a cold**
تغْيير *taɣyīr* **change**
جوّ *gaww* **weather**

Mahmoud

إنيّ مبْسوط، الحمْدُ لله. ربِّنا بدأ يِحقّقْلي حاجات كُنْت مِسْتنّيها.

ínni mabsūṭ, ilɦámdu li-llāh. rabbína báda? yiɦa??á?li ɦagāt kuntᵊ mistannīha.

I am happy, thanks to God. The Lord has begun to grant me many things I'd been waiting for.

الحمْدُ لله *ilɦámdu li-llāh* **praise (be to) God**
ربّ *rabb* **lord**
بدأ *báda?* [1s1] (+ imperfect) **to begin to**
اِسْتنّى *istánna* [10.2i] **to wait for**

Rabab

عايْزة أنام. كان يوْم شُغْل مُرْهِق جِدّاً و أخيراً عدّى بْسلام.

3áyza -nām. kān yōm šuɣlᵊ múrhiq gíddan w axīran 3ádda b-salām.

I want to sleep. It's been a very stressful day at work, but it finally passed by peacefully.

نام *nām* [1h3] **to sleep**
مُرْهِق *múrhiq* **tiring, stressful**
أخيراً *axīran* **finally, in the end**
عدّى *3ádda* [2d] **to pass by**
سلام *salām* **peace**

Tamer

حاسِس النّهارْده بِملل شديد لِإنّ اليوْم كان طَويل جِدّاً مِن ناحْيِةْ الشُّغْل و الحَياة العملية.

ɧāsis innahárda bi-málal šadīd li-inn ilyōm kān ṭawīl gíddan min náɧyit iššúɣlᵊ wi -lɧáya -l3amalíyya.

I feel extremely bored today because the day was very long in terms of my job and working life.

ملل *málal* **boredom**
شديد *šadīd* **extreme, intense**
طَويل *ṭawīl* **long**
مِن ناحْيِةْ *min náɧyit* **in terms of**
حَياة *ɧáya* **life**
عملي *3ámali* **work-, working; practical**

Shorouk

عادي، يَعْني زيّ أيّ يوْم بسّ مْصدّعة شْوَيّة و ده مْخلّيني في موود مِش كُوَيِّس.

3ādi, yá3ni zayy ayyᵊ yōm bassᵊ mṣaddá3a šwáyya wi da mxallīni fi mūd miš kuwáyyis.

So-so, you know, like any other day, but I have a bit of a headache, which puts me in a bad mood.

عادي *3ādi* **normal, usual**
يَعْني *yá3ni* **that is; you know**
أيّ *ayy* **any**
مِصدّع *miṣáddi3* **having a headache**
شُوَيّة *šuwáyya* **somewhat, a little**
موود *mūd* **mood**
كُوَيِّس *kuwáyyis* **good**

Fouad

مِتْفائِل. صعْب الواحِد يِلاقي اللي عايْزُه بِالضّبْط بسّ ساعات بِيْلاقي أقْرب حاجة تِسْعِدُه.

mutafāʔil. ṣa3b ilwāɧid yilāʔi -lli 3áyzu bi-ḍḍábṭ, bassᵊ sa3āt biylāʔi áʔrab ɧāga tis3ídu.

Optimistic. It's difficult to find exactly what you want, but sometimes you find it's what's right in front of you that makes you happy.

صعْب *ṣa3b* **difficult, hard**
الواحِد *ilwāɧid* (impersonal) **one, you**
لاقى *lāʔa* [3d] **to find**
بِالضّبْط *bi-ḍḍábṭ* (also: بِالظّبْط *bi-ẓẓábṭ*) **exactly, precisely**
ساعات *sa3āt* **sometimes**
أقْرب *aʔrab* **the closest**
سعد *sá3ad* [1s2] **to make happy**

➲ **Feelings:** See *Egyptian Colloquial Arabic Vocabulary (section 32)*

28

ناوي تِعْمِل أيْه بُكْره؟

nāwi tí3mil ʔē búkra?

What are you going to do tomorrow?

ناوي *nāwi* (+ imperfect) **to intend to, plan to** (f. ناوْيَة *náwya*)
عمل *3ámal* [1s2] **to make; to do**
أيْه *ʔē(h)* **what**
بُكْره *búkra* **tomorrow**
ناوْيَة تِعْمِلي أيْه بُكْره؟ *náwya ti3míli ʔē búkra?* **What are you** (f.) **going to do tomorrow?**

أُسْبوع *usbū3* (pl. أسابيع *asabī3*) **week**
شُغْل *šuɣl* **job, work**
صاحِب *ṣāḥib* (pl. صُحاب *ṣuḥāb*) **friend**
حاجة *ḥāga* **thing, something**

راح *rāḥ* [1h1] **to go (to)**
رِجِع *rígi3* [1s4] **to return, go back (home)**
صِحي *ṣíḥi* [1d4] **to wake up, get up**
نِزِل *nízil* [1s5] **to go out** (of the house)
اِشْترى *ištára* [8d] **to buy**
خرج *xárag* [1s3] **to go out; to exit**

بدْري *bádri* **early**

عنْد *3and-* (+ pronoun suffix) **to have**

Yomna

روتيني خِلال الأُسْبوع ثابِت. بروح الشُّغْل الصُّبْح و أرْجع أجهِّز الغدا و أقْعد معَ أُسْرِتي لِحدّ النّوْم.

rutīni xilāl ilʔusbū3 sābit. barūḥ iššúɣl iṣṣúbḥᵊ w árga3 agáhhiz ilɣáda w áʔ3ad má3a usríti li-ḥadd innōm.

I have a fixed routine during the week. I go to work in the morning and go back home to fix lunch and sit around with my family until bedtime.

روتين *rutīn* **routine**
خِلال *xilāl* **during**
ثابِت *sābit* **fixed, determined; stable**
الصُّبْح *iṣṣúbḥ* **in the morning**
جهِّز *gáhhiz* [2s1] **to prepare, make ready**

غدا *ɣáda* **lunch**
قعد *ʔá3ad* [1s3] **to sit**
أُسْرة *úsra* **family**
لِحدّ *li-ḥadd* **until**
نوْم *nōm* **sleep**

Mohamed

بُكْره أنا مِسافر. رايِح إسْكِنْدِرِية أزور أهْلي و أشوف صُحابي.

búkra ána misāfar. rāyiḫ iskindiríyya azūr áhli w ašūf ṣuḫābi.

Tomorrow I'll be traveling. I'm going to Alexandria to visit my family and see my friends.

مِسافِر *misāfir* **traveling, on the road**
رايِح *rāyiḫ* **going**
إسْكِنْدِرِية *iskindiríyya* **Alexandria**
زار *zār* [1h1] **to visit**
أهْل *ahl* **family, parents**
شاف *šāf* [1h1] **to see**

Dalia

ناوْيَة أصْحى بدْري و أفْطر و أعْمِل رِياضة و أشْتغل و أنْزِل أشْترِي حاجات و أطْبُخ و أنضّف البيْت.

náwya áṣḫa bádri wi áfṭar w á3mil riyāḍa w aštáɣal w ánzil aštíri ḫagāt w áṭbux w anáḍḍaf ilbēt.

I intend to wake up early, have breakfast, exercise, work, go out to buy stuff, cook, and clean the house.

فِطِر *fíṭir* [1s4] **to have breakfast**
عمل *3ámal* [1s2] **to do; to make**
رِياضة *riyāḍa* **physical activity, exercise; sport(s)**
اِشْتغل *ištáɣal* [8s2] **to work**
طبخ *ṭábax* [1s3] **to cook**
نضّف *náḍḍaf* [2s2] **to clean**
بيْت *bēt* (pl. بِيوت *biyūt*) **house**

Andrew

أهمّ حاجة مُتابْعِةْ باقي الشُّغْل علشان كُلّ التّحرُّكات تِكون سليمة و عاوِز أروح الجّيم.

ahámmᵊ ḫāga mutáb3it bāʔi -ššúɣlᵊ 3alašān kull ittaḫarrukāt tikūn salīma wi 3āwiz arūḫ ižžīm.

The most important thing is following up on the rest of the work to make sure everything is going well. And I also want to go to the gym.

أهمّ *ahámm* **the most important; more important** (elative of مُهِمّ *muhímm*)
مُتابْعة *mutá3ba* **follow-up, resumption**
باقي *bāʔi* (+ def. noun) **the rest of**
تحرُّك *taḫarruk* **movement**
سليم *salīm* **in good condition, sound, correct**
عاوِز *3āwiz* (+ imperfect) **want to**
جيم *žīm* **gym**

Aya

ناوْيَة أخْرُج معَ صاحْبِتي و أُخْتي. نِروح السّينِما و ناكُل برّه.

náwya áxrug má3a ṣaḫbíti w úxti. nirūḫ issínima w nākul bárra.

I'm going out with my friend and my sister. We're going to the movies and eating out.

صاحْبِة *ṣáḫba* **(female) friend**
أُخْت *uxt* (pl. إخْوات بنات *ixwāt banāt*) **sister**
سينما *sínima* **cinema, movie theater**
أكل *ákal* [i3] (also: كل *kal*) **to eat**
برّه *bárra* **outside**

Mahmoud

ناوي أذاكِر عشان عنْدِنا اِمْتِحانات نُص التّيرْم هتِبْدأ كمان أُسْبوع.

nāwi azākir 3ašān 3andína imtiḫanāt nuṣṣ ittírm hatíbdaʔ kamān usbū3.

I plan to study because we have mid-terms that will start in a week.

ذاكِر *zākir* [3s] **to study**
اِمْتِحان *imtiḫān* **exam, test**
نُصّ *nuṣṣ* **half**
تيرْم *tirm* **term, semester**
بدأ *bádaʔ* [1s1] **to begin, start**
كمان *kamān* **in... more; also, too**

Rabab

ناوْيَة أروح الشُّغْل و يا ربّ يِكون يوْم كُوَيِّس مِش زيّ النّهارْده.

náwya arūḫ iššúɣl, wi ya rábbᵊ yikūn yōm kuwáyyis miš zayy innahárda.

I intend to go to work, and I hope that it will be a good day, unlike today.

يا ربّ *ya rabb* (+ imperfect) **will hopefully**
يوْم *yōm* (pl. أيّام *ayyām*) **day**
كُوَيِّس *kuwáyyis* **good**

Tamer

ناوي أصْحى أروح الشُّغْل و أحاوِل أرْجع بدْري عشان عايِز أغيرّ جوّ و أخْرُج في أيّ حِتّة.

nāwi ʔáṣḥa arūḥ iššúɣl, w aḥāwil árga3 bádri 3ašān 3āyiz aɣáyyar gáwwᵊ w áxrug fi ʔáyyᵊ ḥítta.

I intend to wake up to go to work, and I'll try to go back home early because I want to change my mood and then I'll go out somewhere.

حاوِل *ḥāwil* [3s] **to try**
عايِز *3āyiz* (+ imperfect) **want to**
غيرّ *ɣáyyar* [2s2] **to change**
جوّ *gaww* **mood; atmosphere; weather**
في أيّ حِتّة *fi ʔayyᵊ ḥítta* **anywhere**
حِتّة *ḥítta* **place**

Shorouk

كُنْت ناوْيَة أنْزِل وِسْط البلد معَ صاحْبِتي أشْترِي قُماش بسّ هِيَّ عنْدها شُغْل فا الخُطّة أتْغيرِّت.

kuntᵊ nawy- ánzil wisṭ ilbálad má3a ṣaḥbíti aštíri ʔumāš bassᵊ híyya 3andáha šuɣl, fa -lxúṭṭa -tɣayyárit.

I was going to go downtown with my friend to buy fabric, but she has work, so the plan has changed.

وِسْط البلد *wisṭ ilbálad* **downtown**
قُماش *ʔumāš* **fabric, cloth**
فا *fa, fā* **(and) so, therefore**
خُطّة *xúṭṭa* (pl. خُطط *xúṭaṭ*) **plan**
اِتْغيرّ *itɣáyyar* [5s2] **to be changed, change**

Fouad

أنا عُموماً بحِبّ أتْعلِّم حاجة جِديدة كُلّ يوْم. أكمِّل حاجة كُنْت بتْعلِّمْها. ناوي أكمِّل رسْمة.

ána 3umūman baḥíbb at3állim ḥāga gidīda kullᵊ yōm. akámmil ḥāga kúntᵊ bat3allímha. nāwi akámmil rásma.

In general, I like to learn something new every day. I'll work on something I've been learning. I intend to finish a drawing.

عُموماً *3umūman* **in general, generally**
حبّ *ḥabb* [1g3] (+ imperfect) **to like**
اِتْعلِّم *it3állim* [5s1] **to learn**
جديد *gidīd* **new**
كُلّ يوْم *kullᵊ yōm* **every day**
كمِّل *kámmil* [2s1] **to carry on with, continue; complete, finish**
رسْمة *rásma* **drawing, picture**

29 أيْه هِوايْتك المفُضّله؟

ēʔ hiwáytak ilmufaḍḍála?

What is your favorite hobby?

أيْه *ʔē(h)* **what**
هِوايَة *hiwāya* **hobby**
ـك *-ak* (m.) **your**
مُفضّل *mufáḍḍal* **favorite, preferred**
أيْه هِوايْتِك المفُضّلة؟ *ēʔ hiwáytik ilmufaḍḍála?* **What is your** (f.) **favorite hobby?**

شُغْل *šuɣl* (pl. أشْغال *ašɣāl*) **work, craft; job**
حاجة *ḥāga* **thing, something**
قِرايَة *ʔirāya* **reading**
رَسْم *rasm* **drawing**
وَقْت *waʔt* (pl. أوْقات *awʔāt*) **time**
ناس *nās* **people**

حبّ *ḥabb* [1g3] **to like;** (+ imperfect) **to like to**
اِتْعلِّم *it3állim* [5s1] **to learn**
عمل *3ámal* [1s2] **to make; to do**
قِدِر *ʔídir* [1s4] **to be able to**

يَدَوي *yádawi* **manual, hand-**

اللي *ílli* **that, who; which**

Yomna

بحِبّ الأشْغال الفنّية اليَدَوية. بنْدِمِج فيها جِدّاً و بتْعلِّمْها بِشغف. آخِر حاجة كُنْت بعْمِلْها الإسْكوبيدو.

baḥíbb ilʔašɣāl ilfanníyya -lyadawíyya. bandímig fīha gíddan wi bat3allímha bi-šáɣaf. āxir ḥāga kúntᵊ ba3mílha, ilʔiskubīdu.

I love doing art handicrafts. I get engrossed in it and learn it out of real love. The last thing I was making was a scoubidou.

فنّي *fánni* **artistic**
اِنْدمج في *indámag fi* [7s2] **to get engrossed in, lose oneself in**
شغف *šáɣaf* **passion, zeal**

آخِر __ *āxir* __ (+ noun) **the last __**
الإسْكوبيدو *ilʔiskubīdu* **scoubidou** (knotting plastic thread)

Mohamed

أنا بحِبّ الجّيتار. عشان كِده هِوايْتي المُفضّلة هِيَّ العزْف عَ الجّيتار.

ána baɦíbb iggitār. 3ašān kída hiwáyti -lmufaɖɖála híyya -l3azf^{ə} 3a -ggitār.

I love guitar. That's why my favorite hobby is playing the guitar.

جيتار *gitār* **guitar**
عشان كِده *3ašān kída* **so, therefore, that's why**
عزْف على *3azf 3ála* **playing** (an instrument)

Dalia

أنا بحِبّ جِدّاً الطّبْخ و إنّي أتْعلِّم أكلات جِديدة. و مِن هِواياتي القِرايَة. بحِبّ أقْرا كْتير.

ána baɦíbb^{ə} gíddan iʈʈábx^{ə} w ínni at3állim akalāt gidīda. wi min hiwayāti, ilʔirāya. baɦíbb áʔra ktīr.

I love cooking and learning [to make] new dishes. One of my favorite hobbies is reading. I love reading.

طبْخ *ʈabx* **cooking**
أكْلة *ákla* **dish, food**
جِديد *gidīd* **new**
مِن *min* **one of**
قرا *ʔára* [1d1] **to read**

Andrew

أنا بحِبّ الرّسْم جِدّاً و السِّباحة، بسّ مِش بقْدر أنمّيهُم علشان الشُّغْل واخِد أغْلبية الوَقْت.

ána baɦíbb irrásm^{ə} giddan wi -ssibāɦa, bass^{ə} miš báʔdar anammīhum 3alašān iššúɣl^{ə} wāxid aɣlabíyyit ilwáʔt.

I love drawing and also swimming, but I can't develop them because my job takes up most of my time.

برْضُه *bárɖu, bárdu* **also, too, as well**
سِباحة *sibāɦa* **swimming**
نمّى *námma* [2d] **to develop**
واخِد *wāxid* **taking**
أغْلبيِّة __ *aɣlabíyyit* __ (+ noun) **most of __**

Aya

هِوايْتي المُفضّلة هِيَّ إني أخْرُج معَ أصْحابي و النّاس اللي بحِبّها. بِيْكون وَقْت مُمْتِع جِدّاً.

hiwáyti -lmufaḍḍála híyya ínni áxrug má3a aṣḫābi wi -nnās ílli baḫibbáha. biykūn waʔt[ə] múmti3 gíddan.

My favorite hobby is going out with my friends and loved ones. We have a great time.

خرج *xárag* [1s3] **to go out; to exit**
صاحِب *ṣāḫib* (pl. صُحاب *ṣuḫāb*) **friend**
مُمْتع *múmti3* **fun, enjoyable, interesting**

Mahmoud

ألْعب رِياضة. دي الحاجة اللي بسْتمْتِع و بحِسّ إنيّ فرْحان و أنا بعْمِلْها.

ál3ab riyāḍa. di -lḫāga ílli bastámti3 wi baḫíss[ə] ínni farḫān w ána ba3mílha.

I play sports. It's what I enjoy, and I feel happy when I'm doing it.

لِعِب *lí3ib* [1s4] **to play**
رِياضة *riyāḍa* **sport(s); physical activity, exercise**
اِسْتمْتع بِ *istámta3 bi-* [10s1] **to enjoy**
حسّ *ḫass* [1g3] **to feel**
فرْحان *farḫān* **happy**
و أنا... *w ána...* **when I...**

Rabab

معنْديش هِوايات. كُلّ وَقْتي لِلبيْت و الشُّغْل فا معنْديش وَقْت ألاقي هِوايْتي.

ma-3andīš hiwayāt. kull[ə] wáʔti li-lbēt wi -ššuɣl, fa ma-3andīš waʔt alʔáʔi hiwáyti.

I don't have any hobbies. All my time is for the house and my work, so I don't have time to find a hobby.

معنْديش *ma-3andīš* **I don't have**
لِ *li-* **for**
بيْت *bēt* (pl. بِيوت *biyūt*) **house**
فا *fa, fā* **(and) so, therefore**
لاقى *lāʔa* [3d] **to find**

Tamer

هِوايْتي المُفضّلة القِرايَة و الكُمْبيوتر. دوْل الحاجْتيْن اللي مقْدرْش أسْتغْنى عنْهُم.

hiwáyti -lmufaḍḍála ilʔirāya wi -lkumbyūtar. dōl ilḫagtēn ílli ma-ʔdárš astáɣna 3ánhum.

My hobbies are reading and computers. Those are the two things I can't live without.

كُمْبيوتر *kumbyūtar* **computer**
دوْل *dōl* **these, those, they**
حاجْتيْن *ḫagtēn* **two things**
اِسْتغْنى عن *istáɣna 3an* [10d1] **to get along without, live without**

Shorouk

الرّسْم و صْناعِةْ حاجات يَدَوية مِن أيّ حاجة بقى صلْصال أَوْ قُماش أَوْ وَرق.

irrásmᵊ wi ṣnā3it ḫagāt yadawíyya min ayyᵊ ḫāga báʔa ṣalṣāl aw ʔumāš aw wáraʔ.

Drawing and making things by hand out of any material, whether clay, fabric, or paper.

صِناعة *ṣinā3a* **production, making**
أيّ حاجة *ayyᵊ ḫāga* **anything**
بقى *báʔa* **then**
صلْصال *ṣalṣāl* **clay**
قُماش *ʔumāš* **fabric, cloth**
وَرق *wáraʔ* **paper**

Fouad

الرّسْم و خُصوصاً رسْم القِصص المِصوّرة. بحِبّ أرْسِم تعْبيرات الوِشّ و أَوْصِل فِكْرة بِالرّسْم.

irrásm, wi xuṣūṣan rasm ilqíṣaṣ ilmiṣawwára. baḫíbb ársim ta3birāt ilwíššᵊ wi áwṣil fíkra bi-rrásm.

Drawing, in particular drawing comic books. I love drawing facial expressions and conveying an idea through drawing.

خُصوصاً *xuṣūṣan* **especially**
قِصّة *qíṣṣa* (pl. قِصص *qíṣaṣ*) **story**
مِصوّر *miṣáwwar* **drawn, illustrated; photographed**
رسم *rásam* [1s2] **to draw**
تعْبير *ta3bīr* **expression**
وِشّ *wišš* (pl. وْشوش *wušūš*) **face**
وصّل *wáṣṣal* [2s2] **to convey, deliver**
فِكْرة *fíkra* **idea**

➲ **Likes and dislikes:** See *Egyptian Colloquial Arabic Vocabulary (section 34)*
➲ **Activities:** See *Egyptian Colloquial Arabic Vocabulary (sections 21-23)*

30

تِقْدر تِوْصِف شخْصِيِّتك بِأَيْه؟

tíʔdar tíwṣif šaxṣiyyítak bi-ʔē?

How would you describe your personality?

قِدِر *ʔídir* [1s4] **to be able to**
وَصف __ بِـ *wáṣaf __ bi-* [1s2] **to describe __ as**
شخْصية *šaxṣíyya* **personality**
ـك *-ak* (m.) **your**
بِـ *bi-* **with, by; in, at**
أَيْه *ʔē(h)* **what**
تِقْدري تِوْصِفي شخْصِيِّتِك بِأَيْه؟ *tiʔdári tiwṣífi šaxṣiyyítik bi-ʔē?* **How would you** (f.) **describe your personality?**

ناس *nās* **people**
شُغْل *šuɣl* **work, job**
حاجة *ḫāga* **thing, something**

حبّ *ḫabb* [1g3] **to like;** (+ imperfect) **to like to**

اِجْتِماعي *igtimā3i* **sociable; social**

Yomna

أنا شخْصية هادْيَة، مُحِبّة لِلنِّظام و الهُدوء و شِديدة المُلاحْظة لِلتّفاصيل. حسّاسة جِدّاً و حالِمة.

ána šaxṣíyya hádya, muḫíbba li-nniẓām wi -lhudūʔ wi šadīda -lmuláḫẓa li-ttafaṣīl, ḫassāsa gíddan wi ḫālíma.

I am a quiet. I'm fond of order and tranquility. And [I'm] meticulous, very sensitive, and a dreamer.

هادي *hādi* **quiet, calm** (f. هادْيَة *hádya*)
مُحِبّ لِـ *muḫíbb li-* **fond of**
نِظام *niẓām* **order, orderliness; organization**
هُدوء *hudūʔ* **tranquility, calm**
شِديد *šidīd* **intense, strong**
مُلاحْظة *muláḫẓa* **observation, noticing**
تفْصيل *tafṣīl* (pl. تفاصيل *tafaṣīl*) **detail**
حسّاس *ḫassās* **sensitive**
حالِم *ḫālim* **dreamy, romantic** (f. حالِمة *ḫālíma*)

أنا شخْص مُنظّم جِدّاً. يَعْني أنا شخْص بْتاع أرْقام و مُعادْلات.

Mohamed

ána šaxṣᵊ munáẓẓam gíddan. yá3ni ána šaxṣᵊ btā3 arqām wi mu3adlāt.

I am a very organized person, you know, a numbers and calculations person.

شخْص *šaxṣ* (pl. أشْخاص *ašxāṣ*) **person**
مُنظّم *munáẓẓam* **organized**
يَعْني *yá3ni* **that is; you know**
بِتاع *bitā3* **tending toward; belonging to**
رقم *ráqam* (pl. أرْقام *arqām*) **number**
مُعادْلة *mu3ádla* **calculation**

أقْدر أوْصِف شخْصِيِّتي بِإنّها شخْصية مرِحة و اِجْتِماعية و لكِن في نفْس الوَقْت جدّية وَقْت الشُّغْل.

Dalia

áʔdar áwṣif šaxṣiyyíti bi-innáha šaxṣíyya maríḫa w igtima3íyya wi lākin fi nafs ilwáʔt, gaddíyya waʔt iššúɣl.

I can describe my personality as cheerful and sociable, but at the same time serious while working.

مرِح *máriḫ* **cheerful**
في نفْس الوَقْت *fi nafs ilwáʔt* **at the same time**
جدّي *gáddi* **serious**
وَقْت *waʔt* (pl. أوْقات *awʔāt*) **time**

بقْدونِس. لإنّ البقْدونِس بِتْلاقية في أكْلات كِتير و أنا كمان بحِبّ أكون مِشارِك في أيّ حاجة.

Andrew

baʔdūnis, li-inn ilbaʔdūnis bitlaʔī f aklāt kitīr w ána kamān baḫíbbᵊ akūn mišārik fi ʔayyᵊ ḫāga.

Parsley, because you can find it in many dishes, and I too love to participate in everything.

بقْدونس *baʔdūnis* **parsley**
لاقى *lāʔa* [3d] **to find**
أكْلة *ákla* **dish, food**
مِشارِك في *mišārik fi* **participating in**
أيّ حاجة *ayyᵊ ḫāga* **anything**

Aya

أقْدر أَوْصِف شخْصِيِّتي بِإِنّها مِتْوَتّرة بسّ مُتحمِّلة لِلمسْؤولية جِدّاً. و ده رأْي ناس كِتير فِيّا.

áʔdar áwṣif šaxṣiyyíti bi-innáha mitwattára bassᵊ mutaɧammíla li-lmasʔulíyya gíddan. wi da raʔyᵊ nās kitīr fíyya.

I can describe my personality as anxious but responsible. And this is the opinion many people have of me.

مِتْوَتّر *mitwáttar* **nervous, tense, anxious**
مُتحمِّل لِـ *mutaɧámmil li-* **taking upon onself**
مسْؤولية *masʔulíyya* **responsibility**
رأْي *raʔy* **opinión, view**
فِيّا *fíyya* **about me; in me, at me**

Mahmoud

مِتْكلِّم. لمّا بقْعُد في أيّ مكان معَ ناس معْرفْهاش بعْرف أفْتح معاهُم مَواضيع.

mutakállim. lámma báʔ3ud fi ayyᵊ makān má3a nās ma-3rafhāš, bá3raf áftaɧ ma3āhum mawaḍī3.

A talker. When I remain in any place with people I don't know, I can talk with them about [various] topics.

مُتكلِّم *mutakállim* **speaker, talker**
لمّا *lámma* **when**
قعد *ʔá3ad* [1s3] **to sit**
في أيّ مكان *fi ʔayyᵊ makān* **anywhere**
عِرِف *3írif* [1s4] **to know;** (+ imperfect) **to be able to**
فتح *fátaɧ* [1s1] **to open**
مَوْضوع *mawḍū3* (pl. مَواضيع *mawaḍī3*) **subject, topic**

Rabab

أنا شخْصية طيِّبة و محْبوبة و اِجْتِماعية و غاوْيَة شُغْل.

ána šaxṣíyya ṭayyíba wi maɧbūba w igtima3íyya wi ɣáwya šuɣl.

I am good person, likeable and sociable, and hard-working.

طيِّب *ṭáyyib* **good, kind**
محْبوب *maɧbūb* **beloved, popular, well-liked**
غاوي *ɣāwi* **enthusiast, fan (of)**

Tamer

أنا عصبي جِدّاً لِلأسف، شخصِيِّتي مُنْطَوية شْوَيّة و مِش مِن السّهْل أثِق في حدّ.

ána 3áṣabi giddan li-lʔásaf. šaxaṣiyyíti munṭawíyya šwáyya wi miš min issáhl ásiq fi ħadd.

I'm quite nervous, unfortunately, a bit introverted, and it's not easy for me to trust anyone.

عصبي *3áṣabi* **nervous, timid**
لِلأسف *li-lʔásaf* **unfortunately**
مُنْطَوي *munṭáwi* **introverted**
سهْل *sahl* **easy**
وَثق *wásaq* [(1s2)] **to trust**
حدّ *ħadd* **someone**

Shorouk

أنا شخْصية بسيطة، مِش بحِبّ أنافِق و بحِبّ المرح و الضِّحْك.

ána šaxṣíyya basīṭa, miš baħíbb anāfiʔ wi baħíbb ilmáraħ wi -ḍḍíħk.

I am uncomplicated. I dislike being hypocritical, and I love fun and laughter.

بسيط *basīṭ* **simple, uncomplicated**
نافِق *nāfiʔ* [3s] **to be hypocritical**
مرح *máraħ* **fun, enjoyment**
ضِحْك *ḍiħk* **laughter**

Fouad

عادِل. العدْل بِالنِّسْبة لي حاجة مُهِمّة لإِنّ مِن غيْرُه النّاس هتِظْلِم بعْض و تِكْرَهْ بعْض.

3ādil. il3ádlᵊ bi-nnisbā-li ħāga muhímma li-ínnᵊ min ɣēru -nnās hatíẓlim ba3ḍᵊ wi tíkrah ba3ḍ.

Fair. To me, being fair is important because without it people will behave unjustly toward each other and hate each other.

عادِل *3ādil* **just, fair**
عدْل *3adl* **justice, fairness**
بِالنِّسْبة لي *bi-nnisbā-li* **for me**
مُهِمّ *muhímm* **important**
مِن غيْر *min ɣēr* **without**
ظلم *ẓálam* [1s2] **to wrong, oppress**
بعْض *ba3ḍ* **each other**
كِرِه *kírih* [1s4] **to hate**

➲ **Personality:** See *Egyptian Colloquial Arabic Vocabulary (section 33)*

Appendix A: Numbers

١	واحِد *wāḫid* (f. واحْدة *wáḫda*) **one**	٦	ستّة *sítta* (ستّ *sitt*) **six**
٢	اِتْنين *itnēn* **two**	٧	سبْعة *sáb3a* (سبع *sába3*) **seven**
٣	تلاتة *talāta* (تلات *tálat*) **three**	٨	تمانْية *tamánya* (تمان *táman*) **eight**
٤	أرْبعة *arbá3a* (أرْبع *árba3*) **four**	٩	تِسْعة *tís3a* (تِسع *tísa3*) **nine**
٥	خمْسة *xámsa* (خمس *xámas*) **five**	١٠	عشرة *3ášara* (عشر *3ášar*) **ten**

When modifying a noun:

- the number 1 follows the noun and agrees in gender.
- the number 2 can be followed a plural noun, but more commonly the dual suffix ـين *-ēn* is used instead of the number.
- the numbers 3-10 have shortened forms (shown in parentheses above) and are followed by plural nouns.

١١	حِداشر *ḫidāšar* **eleven**	١٦	سِتّاشر *sittāšar* **sixteen**
١٢	اِتْناشر *itnāšar* **twelve**	١٧	سبعْتاشر *saba3tāšar* **seventeen**
١٣	تلتّاشر *talattāšar* **thirteen**	١٨	تمانْتاشر *tamantāšar* **eighteen**
١٤	أرْبعْتاشر *arba3tāšar* **fourteen**	١٩	تِسعْتاشر *tisa3tāšar* **nineteen**
١٥	خمسْتاشر *xamastāšar* **fifteen**		

٢٠	عِشْرين *3išrīn* **twenty**	٦٠	سِتّين *sittīn* **sixty**
٣٠	تلاتين *talatīn* **thirty**	٧٠	سبْعين *sab3īn* **seventy**
٤٠	ارْبِعين *arbi3īn* **forty**	٨٠	تمانين *tamanīn* **eighty**
٥٠	خمْسين *xamsīn* **fifty**	٩٠	تِسْعين *tis3īn* **ninety**

Compund numbers (21, 75, etc.) are formed literally as "one and twenty", "five and seventy", etc. The number 1-9 in its full form (that is, not the shortened form) precedes و *wi:* واحِد و عِشْرين *wāḫid wi 3išrīn* **twenty-one**; خمْسة و سبْعين *xámsa w sab3īn* **seventy-five**.

Appendix B: Dates

Days of the Week

الحدّ *ilḫádd* **Sunday**
الاِتْنين *ilʔitnēn* **Monday**
التّلات *ittalāt* **Tuesday**
الأرْبع *ilʔárba3* **Wednesday**
الخميس *ilxamīs* **Thursday**
الجُمْعة *ilgúm3a* **Friday**
السّبْت *issábt* **Saturday**

Months of the Year

يَنايِر *yanāyir* **January**
فِبْرايِر *fibrāyir* **February**
مارِس *māris* **March**
إبْريل *ibrīl* **April**
مايو *māyu* **May**
يونْيو *yúnyu* (also: يونْيَة *yúnya*) **June**
يوليو *yúlyu* (also: يولْيَة *yúlya*) **July**
أغُسْطُس *aɣústus* **August**
سِبْتِمْبِر *sibtímbir* **September**
أُكْتوْبِر *uktōbir* **October**
نوفِمْبِر *nuvímbir* **November**
ديسِمْبِر *disímbir* **December**

Egyptians also commonly refer to months by number.

Years

ألْف تُسْعُمية (و)... *alfᵉ tus3umíyya (wi)...* **19_ _**
ألْفيْن (و)... *alfēn (wi)...* **20_ _**

The و *wi* (shown above in parentheses) is present unless the following number is compound (21-29, 31-39, etc.), in other words a number which already contains و *wi.*

Appendix C: The Egyptian Arabic Texts

1

إسمك أيه؟

إسمك أيه؟

يمنى: إسمي يمنى. بحب إسمي لإنه مش منتشر و كمان معناه حلو.

محمد: أنا إسمي محمد. أكيد إنتو عارفين إن ده أشهر إسم في العالم.

داليا: أنا إسمي داليا. و بحب إسمي جدا لإن داليا هي إسم زهرة شكلها و لونها حلو.

أندرو: أنا إسمي أندرو و الإسم ده نادر في مصر و من صغري بيقولولي دورا علشان رجلي صغيرة.

آيه: أنا إسمي آية. و معناه معجزة أو دليل زي الآيات في القرآن.

محمود: محمود أسامة، و معنى إسم محمود هو الشخص اللي بيمدح في الناس كتير.

رباب: إسمي رباب محمود. رباب يعني السحاب الأبيض و ممكن كمان يكون معناه ربابة (آلة موسيقية).

تامر: إسمي تامر. الإسم تركي الأصل و غالبا معظم الناس على النت بيفتكروني تركي.

شروق: إسمي شروق و معنى إسمي جاي من شروق الشمس و صحابي بينادوني شيرو.

فؤاد: إسمي فؤاد و ده إسم قديم شوية و معناه القلب. و اتسميت بيه تيمنا بجدي الله يرحمه.

2 إنت منين؟ إنتي منين؟

يمنى: أنا من مصر، و تحديدا من القاهرة العاصمة. و عشت أغلب حياتي في محافظة الجيزة الملاصقة للقاهرة.

محمد: أنا أصلا من إسكندرية، بلد البحر المتوسط الرايق و البنات.

داليا: أنا من مصر و تحديدا القاهرة العاصمة و كمان أنا طول عمري عايشة في الجيزة و هي جمبها.

أندرو: أنا من شبرا و هو حي شعبي موجود من أكتر من ميتين سنة في القاهرة.

آيه: أنا من مصر الجديدة في القاهرة، حي راقي جدا و هادي.

محمود: من مصر. دي أحسن بلد في العالم و فيها تلتين أثار العالم.

رباب: أنا من مصر، تحديدا من محافظة الإسكندرية، أجمل محافظات مصر.

تامر: أنا من إسكندرية من حي العجمي، منطقة في غرب إسكندرية كانت زمان من أفضل المصايف.

شروق: أنا من القاهرة في مصر بس كنت عايشة فترة طفولتي في الإمارات.

فؤاد: من القاهرة، مدينة نصر في الأساس، و لكن أصل العيلة نفسه غير معروف بالنسبة لي.

3

سنك كام؟

سنك كام؟

يمنى: أنا سني خمسة و تلاتين سنة. و في شهر نوفمبر الجاي هتم ستة و تلاتين. إنما بالتقويم الهجري هكون تميت ستة و تلاتين خلاص.

محمد: أنا مكمل سبعة و عشرين سنة، كمان أسبوع بالظبط، يوم اتنين إبريل هو عيد ميلادي.

داليا: أنا عندي اتنين و عشرين سنة. اتولدت يوم واحد أكتوبر ألف تسعمية تلاتة و تسعين و كمان اتولدت في القاهرة.

أندرو: أنا عندي تسعة و عشرين سنة لإني اتولدت في أكتوبر سنة ألف تسعمية ستة و تمانين و بالأخص في اليوم تلتمية في السنة.

آيه: أنا عندي تلاتة و عشرين سنة. بس العمر مجرد رقم. الشباب في الروح.

محمود: واحد و عشرين سنة، عشان أنا مولود سنة ألف تسعمية أربعة و تسعين، يعني كمان شهرين هكمل اتنين و عشرين سنة.

رباب: أنا عندي سبعة و عشرين سنة و عيد ميلادي هيكون في شهر مايو.

تامر: عندي أربعة و تلاتين سنة و ست شهور و حداشر يوم تقريبا.

شروق: دلوقتي اتنين و عشرين سنة و هتم التلاتة و عشرين شهر عشرة الجاي ده إن شاء الله.

فؤاد: ستة و عشرين سنة. و لكن ناس كتير بيقولولي إنت شكلك صغير أوي. ده بسبب شكل وشي طفولي أوي.

4

تاريخ ميلادك إمتى؟

تاريخ ميلادك إمتى؟

يمنى: أنا من مواليد ١٤ نوفمبر ١٩٨٠. و بالتقويم الهجري ٧ محرم ١٤٠١. مش بحتفل عادة بيوم ميلادي بس بحب الهدايا.

محمد: تاريخ ميلادي يوم ٢ إبريل. اتولدت يوم حد في رمضان.

داليا: أنا تاريخ ميلادي ١ أكتوبر ١٩٩٣ و اتولدت يوم جمعة و بحب تاريخ ميلادي لإنه مميز و أول الشهر.

أندرو: يوم ٢٧ من شهر أكتوبر سنة ١٩٨٦.

آيه: تاريخ ميلادي واحد واحد ١٩٩٣. كان دايما عيد ميلادي بيكون في وقت الامتحانات.

محمود: سبعة خمسة ١٩٩٤، يوم سبعة و شهر خمسة و اتولدت في السعودية مدينة الرياض.

رباب: اتولدت يوم ٢٥ مايو سنة ١٩٨٨.

تامر: أنا من مواليد شهر سبتمبر سنة ٨٢ و برجي هو العذراء.

شروق: أنا اتولدت يوم ٣ من شهر أكتوبر اللي هو عشرة من سنة ١٩٩٣.

فؤاد: اتناشر اتناشر ١٩٨٩، و لكن دي حاجة خلتني أخش الدراسة بدري أوي و كنت ببقى مع ناس أكبر مني.

5

بتشتغل أيه؟

بتشتغلي أيه؟

يمنى: أنا مهندسة معمارية. بشتغل في مشروع إنشاء المتحف المصري الكبير.

محمد: أنا بشتغل مهندس اتصالات. أنا شغال في شركة اتصالات مصر.

داليا: أنا بشتغل مترجمة في شركة ترجمة في المهندسين و بشتغل فيها بقالي ست شهور و باخد خبرة كويسة.

أندرو: أنا بشتغل في شركة مشروبات غازية في قسم التسويق التجاري.

آيه: بشتغل محللة في مجال أبحاث السوق. بنحلل بيانات عن طبيعة استهلاك المنتجات مثلا.

محمود: بشتغل جرافيك ديزاينر مستقل متخصص في عمل اللوجوهات للشركات الجديدة.

رباب: بشتغل مهندسة شبكات في شركة أورنج، من أقوى و أنجح الشركات العالمية.

تامر: أنا بشتغل مدير شبكات و نظم في شركة ملاحة بقالي تلات سنين.

شروق: كنت بشتغل في عيادة و سبتها عشان تعبت فترة و حاليا بشتغل فري لانسر.

فؤاد: بشتغل حاليا في العمل الحر و خصوصا رسم الكوميكس الياباني و ألعاب الأندرويد.

6

عايش فين؟

عايشة فين؟

يمنى: عايشة في مصر، تحديدا في محافظة الجيزة قريب أوي من الأهرامات.

محمد: أنا أصلا من إسكندرية بس أنا عايش في القاهرة عشان شغلي.

داليا: أنا عايشة في الجيزة في منطقة إسمها المهندسين و دي منطقة تعتبر راقية عن مناطق تانية.

أندرو: أنا عايش في القاهرة و هي عاصمة مصر و القاهرة من المدن اللي مش بتنام.

آيه: عايشة في مدينة نصر في القاهرة. ده حي كبير و قريب من كل حاجة.

محمود: في الجيزة، و معنى كلمة الجيزة في اللغة العربية هي الوادي.

رباب: عايشة في القاهرة في المعادي، أهدى مكان في القاهرة. أنا محظوظة إني ساكنة في المعادي.

تامر: أنا عايش في بيت عيلة في إسكندرية، أبويا و أمي في الدور الأول و أنا في التاني.

شروق: دلوقتي أنا عايشة في القاهرة في مصر بس و أنا صغيرة كنت عايشة في الإمارات.

فؤاد: عايش في الرحاب. الحدائق هنا كتير و بتساعد أوي في راحة البال لما بتمشي فيها الصبح.

7

إنت متجوز؟
إنتي متجوزة؟

يمنى: أنا متجوزة من حوالي ست سنين و عندي طفلين. الطريق لأسرة سعيدة هو إظهار الحب، التفاهم و الاحترام.

محمد: أه، متجوز. اتجوزت و أنا سني صغير و أنا عندي أربعة و عشرين سنة.

داليا: لا، مش متجوزة ولا كمان مخطوبة و كنت هتخطب بس الظروف و النصيب منعوا الخطوبة.

أندرو: لا و كل الناس مستنية اليوم ده لإن سني بقى كبير شوية.

آيه: لا، أنا مش متجوزة لكن مرتبطة و ممكن أتجوز خلال سنتين.

محمود: لا، معظم الناس في مصر بيتجوز عند سن خمسة و عشرين عقبال ما يتخرج و يقدر يكون نفسه.

رباب: أيوه. أنا متجوزة بقالي سنتين و مبسوطة جدا معاه. هو إنسان أكتر من رائع.

تامر: أنا الحمد لله متجوز و عندي ولدين، آسر و عدي، و عمرهم أربع سنين و سنتين.

شروق: لا، أنا لسه سينجل و اتخطبت مرة بس فركشت الخطوبة عشان مكانش مناسب ليا.

فؤاد: لا، لسه بدري عليا في موضوع الزواج علشان دي مسؤولية كبيرة و بتحتاج ماديات و اتزان نفسي.

8

عندك إخوات؟

عندك إخوات؟

يمنى: عندي أخت و أخ أصغر مني. مش بشوفهم كتير نتيجة انشغالنا بس بنحاول نلاقي طرق للقاء.

محمد: أنا عندي أخ واحد أصغر مني بأربع سنين، لسه في الكلية.

داليا: عندي أخ واحد بس و معنديش إخوات بنات و كان نفسي يكون عندي إخوات كتير ألعب معاهم.

أندرو: عندي أخ و أخت و هما الاتنين أكبر مني و متجوزين و كل واحد فيهم عنده بنت.

آيه: أيوه عندي خمس إخوات كلهم بنات. دايما بنتخانق مع بعض بس منقدرش نستغنى عن بعض.

محمود: أه، عندي أخين، واحد أكبر مني و مخلص كلية و تاني أصغر مني بسنتين.

رباب: عندي أخ أصغر مني بسبع سنين يعني عنده واحد و عشرين سنة.

تامر: عندي أخ و أختين. أنا أكبرهم و بعدي أخت و بعدها أخ و أصغرنا أخت.

شروق: أه، عندي. هما بنتين و ولد. الفرق بين كل واحد فينا سنتين و أنا أكبرهم.

فؤاد: عندي اتنين و أنا الوسطاني. صعب تلاقي حد ملوش أخ أو أخت في مصر.

9

بتتكلم لغات؟

بتتكلمي لغات؟

يمنى: اللغة العربية هي لغتي الأم و بعرف أتكلم إنجليزي. الفرنساوي أعرفه شوية و نفسي أتعلمه كويس.

محمد: بتكلم عربي و إنجليزي بطلاقة و شوية فرنساوي مكسر على قدي.

داليا: بتكلم لغات زي الإنجليش و العربي و الفرنساوي و بتعلم لغات زي الأسباني و الإيطالي و الألماني.

أندرو: طبعا العربي و هي اللغة الأم و بتكلم إنجليزي و أعرف شوية فرنساوي بحكم الدراسة لمدة سبع سنين.

آيه: أيوه، بتكلم عربي و إنجليزي. اتعلمت الإنجليزي كويس من الأفلام و المسلسلات.

محمود: أه، بتكلم لغتين: اللغة الأولى عربي و اللغة التانية إنجليزي.

رباب: بتكلم إنجليزي كويس جدا. بستخدمه طول الوقت في الشغل عشان بتعامل مع مستخدمين بره مصر.

تامر: بتكلم إنجليزي كويس، يمكن أكتر من العربي و الفرنساوي يعني شوية.

شروق: هو مش لغات أوي يعني بتكلم إنجليزي و شوية كلمات ياباني و لسه بتعلم.

فؤاد: بتكلم اللغة الإنجليزية بطلاقة و دي حاجة مهمة جدا لأي مصري نظرا لإننا بلد سياحي.

10

أيه هو أكتر لون بتفضله؟

أيه هو أكتر لون بتفضليه؟

يمنى: بفضل تلات ألوان: الأخضر و البنفسجي و البمبي. لكن اختياري للالوان مرتبط عادة بحالتي المزاجية.

محمد: أكتر لون بحبه هو الأحمر. و كمان بحب الأخضر، لون الزرع.

داليا: أنا بحب اللون الإسود لإني بحس إنه ملك الألوان و بحب كمان البنفسجي و الأحمر و الكحلي و الأبيض.

أندرو: أكتر لون بفضله هو الأحمر علشان بيحسسني بالفرحة و حتى النادي اللي بشجعه بيلبس أحمر.

آيه: أكتر لون بحبه هو الأزرق الغامق، لون البحر، و بحسه لون نقي جدا.

محمود: الأزرق، ده أكتر لون بيوحي بالفخامة و العظمة و الهدو و سكون الليل.

رباب: الإسود. أنا أعشق الإسود لإنه بيمثل الأناقة و الشياكة بالنسبة لي.

تامر: الإسود هو أكتر لون بحبه بالرغم من إن ناس كتير بتقول إنه كئيب.

شروق: بحب الإسود و الجراي و البنفسجي جدا بدرجاته كلها و البينك بس الغوامق أكتر.

فؤاد: لوني المفضل هو الإسود. اللون الإسود هو لون بيدل على الغموض.

11

بتلعب رياضة؟

بتلعبي رياضة؟

يمنى: حاليا لا. لكن كنت بمارس المشي و السباحة و بحاول أمارسهم كل ما تتاحلي الفرصة.

محمد: بلعب سباحة في النادي، و بروح الجيم تلات أو أربع أيام.

داليا: بلعب رياضة بس مش دايما يعني ممكن الصبح ألعب رياضة شوية أو ممكن أنزل و أمشي.

أندرو: لا، بس زمان كنت بلعب بينج بونج و اشتركت مرة في مسابقة الجامعة بس محققتش جوايز.

آيه: أه، بلعب إسكواش. رياضة جميلة جدا محتاجة تركيز و رد فعل سريع.

محمود: أه، بلعب سباحة و في فريق النادي بقالي اتناشر سنة و دخلت بطولات كتير.

رباب: أيوه. بلعب سلاح و دي لعبة تحتاج سرعة و دقة عشان تغلب خصمك.

تامر: كنت بلعب كورة قدم و كونغ فو و أنا صغير بس جالي إصابة في ركبتي من الكورة.

شروق: أه، حاليا بلعب زومبا و زمان أيام المدرسة كنت مشتركة في فريق كرة سلة.

فؤاد: بلعب رفع أثقال و دي غالبا أكتر رياضة مفضلة عند المصريين و ليها شعبية كبيرة أوي في مصر.

12

أكلت أيه ع الغدا إمبارح؟

أكلتي أيه ع الغدا إمبارح؟

يمنى: أكلت إمبارح فراخ بانيه و مكرونة بالصلصة و البصل و طبق سلطة ضخم.

محمد: أكلت مكرونة بشاميل و فراخ مشوية و شوية خضار سوتيه.

داليا: إمبارح على الغدا كلت محشي و ملوخية و شوربة و فراخ مشوية و بطاطس و سلطة و عيش و مخلل و بتنجان.

أندرو: إمبارح علشان كنت في الشغل أكلت على الغدا كشري و دي أكلة شعبية مصرية.

آيه: أكلت إمبارح على الغدا رز و فراخ و كوسة. أختي هي اللي عملت الأكل لإنها مش بتشتغل.

محمود: كلت مكرونة و رز و لحمة في الصلصة و بانيه و ديك رومي.

رباب: أكلنا أنا و جوزي لحمة مشوية و سبانخ و رز و سلطة.

تامر: إمبارح أكلت محشي و هو الأكلة المفضلة للشعب المصري و كان معاه فراخ محمرة.

شروق: إمبارح كنت في مهرجان، فا أكلت بره مع صحابي رز و كفتة داوود باشا.

فؤاد: أكلت كنتاكي و زودت ليه رز مامتي كانت عاملاه علشان أنا بحب الرز الأبيض أوي.

13

متعود تصحى الساعة كام؟

متعودة تصحي الساعة كام؟

يمنى: عادة بصحى ستة الصبح. آخر الأسبوع بنحاول نصحى متأخر لكن كل البيت بيكون متعود يصحى بدري.

محمد: أنا بصحى على تمانية الصبح. أفطر و أستحمى و أروح الشغل.

داليا: أنا متعودة أصحى كل يوم الساعة تسعة الصبح و اتعودت أصحى كده لإن بيكون عندي شغل.

أندرو: عادة بصحى الساعة تمانية الصبح علشان الشغل و في الأجازات ممكن أصحى على عشرة.

آيه: متعودة أصحى الساعة سبعة الصبح، معاد مناسب إني أجهز و أروح الشغل.

محمود: متعود أصحى الساعة سبعة الصبح عشان ألحق أركب المواصلات و أروح الكلية.

رباب: الساعة سبعة عشان أتوبيس الشغل بيجيلي الساعة تمانية و بكون في الشغل الساعة تسعة.

تامر: المفروض أصحى للشغل الساعة سبعة الصبح بس ساعات ولادي بيصحوني قبل كده كمان.

شروق: غالبا بصحى بعد الضهر عشان بسهر كتير بس الأيام دي بصحى بدري بسبب الجامعة.

فؤاد: متعود أصحى الساعة تسعة الصبح. لازم ألحق أتمشى في الشمس عشان دي حاجة الجسم محتاجها.

14

أيه هي أكلتك المفضلة؟

أيه هي أكلتك المفضلة؟

يمنى: الأكل كله بالنسبة لي مفضل. أنا باعتبر الأكل من أجمل نعم ربنا علينا.

محمد: أنا بحب السمك. أكتر أكلة بحبها شوية سمك على سبيط على جمبري.

داليا: أكلتي المفضلة هي البيتزا الأيطالي رغم إن فيه أكل مصري برضه يجنن زي الكشري و الفلافل.

أندرو: بحب أوي الفول و الجبنة بالسلطة و دول أكتر اتنين ممكن أكل منهم من غير ما أشبع.

آيه: أكلتي المفضلة هي ورق عنب معاه لحمة مشوية. الأكلة دي بتتعمل كتير في العزومات.

محمود: البسلة. هي نوع من النباتات تبع الفصيلة البقولية من رتبة الفوليات.

رباب: السبيط. أنا بموت فيه بجد، ممكن أقعد آكل منه إلى ما لا نهاية.

تامر: أكلتي المفضلة المحشي و الديك الرومي، خصوصا لو مطبوخ كويس بيبقى حلو أوي.

شروق: أنا بعشق حاجة إسمها مسقعة بالذات اللي بتكون بالبشاميل و بحب المكرونة جدا كمان.

فؤاد: بحب آكل المحاشي و خصوصا الكرونب. الكرونب من أرخص الأكلات المصرية و لكن صعبة التحضير.

15

مين الممثل أو الممثلة المفضلة ليك؟

مين الممثل أو الممثلة المفضلة ليكي؟

يمنى: بحب الممثلين الكبار زي فاتن حمامة و عمر الشريف و روبرت دينيرو و أل باتشينو.

محمد: ممثلي المفضل هو أل باتشينو. أنا بعشق أفلام المافيا بتاعته زي الأب الروحي.

داليا: من الممثلين المفضلين عندي، بحب أحمد السقا. بحب أفلامه الأكشن و بحب منى ذكي تمثل معاه.

أندرو: أنا مش متابع التمثيل بس بحب أتفرج على أفلام أحمد حلمي لإنه بيقدم أفلام هادفة.

آيه: الممثل المفضل ليا هو آسر ياسين. بحبه علشان بيتقمص الدور كويس أوي و نظراته معبرة و وسيم.

محمود: أحمد حلمي، ده أكتر ممثل كوميدي في مصر و الشرق الأوسط.

رباب: بحب عمر الشريف الله يرحمه. كان ممثل أكتر من رائع و فنان فعلا موهوب.

تامر: الممثلة المفضلة ليا هي ياسمين عبد العزيز، تقريبا كل جيلي بيحب الممثلة دي.

شروق: مفيش حد معين بصراحة بس بحب سكارلت جوهانسن بتاعة فيلم لوسي جدا.

فؤاد: ويل سميث. بتعجبني أفلامه أد أيه. بتكون هادفة و إنه بيحاول يبني حاجة مع عيلته.

16

لابس أيه النهارده؟

لابسة أيه النهارده؟

يمنى: لابسة جيبة بني فاتح و قميص كحلي سادة و طرحة بمبي. بحب أدخل كذا لون في لبسي.

محمد: النهارده عشان رحت الشغل فا أنا لازم ألبس سيمي كاجوال. يعني قميص و بنطلون.

داليا: النهارده كنت لابسة بنطلون جينز و عليه بلوزة لونها كحلي منقطة بأبيض و الحقيقة برتاح فيها و بحبها.

أندرو: النهارده الجو حلو. لابس بلوفر رمادي خفيف و بنطلون جينز و كوتشي.

آيه: لابسة بنطلون إسود و بلوزة رمادي فاتح و جزمة رمادي. اخترت اللبس ده علشان مريح.

محمود: لابس تي شرت و جاكيت عشان الجو متقلب شوية حر و شوية برد.

رباب: لابسة بنطلون إسود و بلوفر إسود و طرحة بيضا و جاكيت إسود.

تامر: و أنا خارج بفضل اللبس الكاجوال أكتر من الرسمي و في البيت بلبس ترنج أو بيجامة.

شروق: لابسة لبس بيت عبارة عن بنطلون ليجن إسود و سويت شيرت واسع مقلم ألوان كتير.

فؤاد: لابس لبس مريح في الحركة. مش بحب يكون لبسي ضيق أو واسع أو فيه رسومات.

17

بتعيا كام مرة في السنة؟

بتعيي كام مرة في السنة؟

يمنى: حوالي تلاتأربع مرات في السنة. عادة حد من الولاد بيعيا و بعدين باقي البيت بيتعدي منه.

محمد: مش عارف. عمري ما حسبتها الصراحة. ربنا ميجيبش عيا لحد.

داليا: الحمد لله أنا صحتي كويسة و بحافظ على أكلي و الرياضة فا مش بعيا أكتر من مرتين في السنة.

أندرو: حوالي أربع مرات و عادة بيكون مع تغيير الفصول و عادة بيكون جيوب أنفية.

آيه: بعيا مثلا خمس مرات في السنة. أغلبهم مع تغيير الجو عشان عندي حساسية.

محمود: مرة واحدة تقريبا عشان عامل عملية اللوز و مناعتي كويسة.

رباب: قليل يعني تقريبا تلات مرات بالسنة بس لما بعيا العيا بيكون جامد أوي.

تامر: مجربتش أعد الصراحة قبل كده بس أنا عموما صحتي كويسة، يعني مش بعيا بسهولة.

شروق: لا، كام مرة دي متعدش. أنا بعيا أكتر من أي حاجة تانية في حياتي.

فؤاد: ممكن تمان أو تسع مرات و بيكونوا برد. و لكن مؤخرا بدأت أهتم بصحتي أكتر و أفهم أكتر ليه بنمرض.

18

عملت أيه النهارده الصبح؟

عملتي أيه النهارده الصبح؟

يمنى: عملت المعتاد بتاع كل يوم. جهزت السندوتشات للولاد و نزلوا المدرسة و لبست و نزلت شغلي.

محمد: ولا حاجة. صحيت الساعة تمانية زي كل يوم، فطرت و استحميت و رحت ع الشغل.

داليا: النهارده أول ما صحيت فطرت و شربت القهوة بتاعتي و عملت شوية رياضة عشان أعرف أكمل يومي.

أندرو: أول ما صحيت أخدت الشنطة و نزلت على الشغل و كلمت الناس أتابع معاها شغل إمبارح بالليل.

آيه: النهارده الصبح صحيت و فطرت، و بعدين رحت الشغل. ده العادي في أسبوع شغل.

محمود: صليت و فطرت و فضلت قاعد على الفيسبوك يعني معملتش أي حاجة مفيدة.

رباب: كنت في الشغل بس النهارده كان يوم تقيل أوي، يا رب بكره يكون أحسن.

تامر: صحيت من النوم في ميعاد الشغل و رحت الشغل و أخروني هناك شوية و تقريبا اليوم ضاع هناك.

شروق: بعد ما صحيت فتحت البلاي ستيشن و قعدت أدور على ألعاب عشان أنزلها و ألعب.

فؤاد: صحيت، غسلت وشي، فطرت بطاطس مع بعض حبات البرتقان و نزلت أتمشى شوية.

19

بتفضل أنهي فصل من السنة؟ أيه الجو اللي بتفضله؟

بتفضلي أنهي فصل من السنة؟ أيه الجو اللي بتفضليه؟

يمنى: الخريف هو أفضل فصل لإن الجو بيكون فيه معتدل و مناسب للخروج، و كمان عشان اتولدت فيه.

محمد: أنا مبحبش السقعة. عشان كده الصيف هو وقتي المفضل، بحر و شمس.

داليا: أنا بحب فصل الصيف. رغم إنه حر بس أنا بحب فيه الطاقة اللي بتكون عندي.

أندرو: طبعا الشتا لإن الجو عندنا بيبقى جميل و أقدر أعمل أنشطة أكتر من الصيف.

آيه: بفضل فصل الخريف. بيكون الجو فيه في مصر متوازن جدا.

محمود: الصيف، عشان جو في الصيف في مصر حلو جدا خاصة في الأماكن الساحلية.

رباب: بفضل الشتا. الجو خصوصا في إسكندرية بيكون أكتر من رائع و البحر خلاب.

تامر: عادة الإجابة بتبقى الربيع أو الصيف بس أنا بفضل الشتا. بيبقى الجو أحسن في إسكندرية.

شروق: بحب الشتا أوي عشان بحب السقعة و البرد أكتر من الصيف و الحر اللي فيه.

فؤاد: فصل الصيف. نادرا ما بتعيا، و لكن بيصعب عليا أكتر المحجبات في الصيف عشان لبسهم بيحررهم أوي.

20

بتحب تغني أو ترقص؟

بتحبي تغني أو ترقصي؟

يمنى: مليش في الغنا خالص بس بحب أسمعه و بحب الرقص. بعتبره رياضة مسلية و بيحسن المزاج.

محمد: أه، أنا من أكتر الحاجات اللي بحبها الرقص و المزيكا.

داليا: بحب أغني مع إن صوتي وحش بس ببقى مبسوطة لما بغني و بلاقي نفسي برقص تلقائيا.

أندرو: أنا بحب الغنا جدا و بحب الأغاني القديمة و الحديثة. و أكتر مغني بسمعله هو محمد منير.

آيه: بحب أغني و أرقص، لكن و أنا لوحدي عشان مبحبش حد يتفرج أو يسمع.

محمود: بحب الرقص بس في المناسبات زي الأفراح و أعياد الميلاد.

رباب: بحب أرقص جدا بس لسه مخدتش الخطوة إني أتعلم بجد.

تامر: بحب الرقص أوي و كمان بحب المزيكا بكل أشكالها حتى المزيكا الغريبة شوية عننا.

شروق: أه، بحب أغني و أرقص جدا بالذات أغاني الكرتون بتاعة سبيستون زمان. بحب أغنيها أوي.

فؤاد: أه، بس لو أنا لوحدي أو لو مع صديق عزيز عشان الرقص بيكون للاستمتاع.

21

لون شعرك و عينك أيه؟

لون شعرك و عينك أيه؟

يمنى: شعري بني و عينيا فيها أخضر و عسلي. و أنا صغيرة كان لون شعري أفتح.

محمد: لون شعري إسود. و لون عيني بني. بس أنا على طول بحلق أقرع.

داليا: لون شعري إسود و ساعات بصبغه عشان يبقى بني و لون عيني بني غامق.

أندرو: لون شعري إسود و قصير و فيه شوية شعر أبيض و عينيا لونها إسود و واسعة.

آيه: لون شعري و لون عيني بني فاتح زي ماما و بابا.

محمود: لون شعري إسود و عيني بني فاتح. دي ألوان معظم العرب.

رباب: لون شعري إسود و عيني كمان سودا. أنا بحب أوي لون شعري.

تامر: شعري لونه إسود و ناعم، و عيوني عسلية أو بني غامق و دي تعتبر الصفات الرئيسية في مصر.

شروق: شعري لونه إسود بس أنا صبغته حاليا أحمر أما عيني فا لونها بني غامق.

فؤاد: لون شعري إسود و لون عيني بني غامق. بيكون نادرا ما تلاقي ألوان تانية في مصر.

22

من بين الأجازات السنوية، أيه أجازتك المفضلة؟

من بين الأجازات السنوية، أيه أجازتك المفضلة؟

يمنى: أجازتي المفضلة هي أجازة عيد الأضحى. بتكون أجازة طويلة بشوف فيها ناس كتير واحشيني.

محمد: أجازة راس السنة، عشان الواحد يحتفل بالاجازات السنة اللي فاتت.

داليا: بيكون عندي أجازات سنوية كتير بس أنا بحب دايما أجازة العيد لإني بقضيها مع عيلتي.

أندرو: أجازة الصيف طبعا لإن فيها بتتجمع العيلة كلها و كمان بنقضي أغلب أوقاتنا على البحر.

آيه: أجازتي المفضلة في الصيف، لما ناخد أجازة و نسافر سوا نروح البحر.

محمود: الأجازة الكبيرة. دي بتكون مدتها تلات شهور بعد كل سنة دراسية.

رباب: كانت في هولندا. قضيت وقت ممتع مع جوزي و أصحابنا.

تامر: أكتر أجازة بحبها هي العيد الصغير و العيد الكبير عشان العيلة كلها بتتجمع.

شروق: آخر حاجة طلعناها كانت مع العيلة و صاحبتي المقربة و صيفنا في إسكندرية.

فؤاد: أجازة العيد عشان كده كده بيكونوا أجازة فا باخد قبلهم أجازة كمان فا يبقى عندي أجازة كبيرة.

23 بتعرف تسوق؟
بتعرفي تسوقي؟

يمنى: بعرف أسوق. سنة ألفين و سبعة اشتريت عربية صغيرة و اتعلمت عليها السواقة مع بابايا.

محمد: أه، بعرف أسوق. طلعت رخصة أول ما كملت تمانتاشر سنة بالظبط.

داليا: مبعرفش أسوق للأسف و نفسي أتعلم جدا لإن من أحلامي إني أشتري عربية فا عايزة أتعلم.

أندرو: للأسف لا، بس ضروري هتعلم السواقة لإن أغلبية شغلي في الشارع.

آيه: أيوه بعرف أسوق. و معايا رخصة و عربية من أول ما كنت تمانتاشر سنة.

محمود: أه، بحب السواقة بس الزحمة اللي موجودة على طول في الشوارع بتكرهني فيها.

رباب: لا، مش بعرف. بس ناوية أتعلم عشان السواقة لا غنى عنها في مصر.

تامر: بعرف أسوق كويس بس بكره السواقة بسبب الزحمة و كمان السواقين مش بيلتزموا بأداب السواقة.

شروق: لا، بس نفسي أتعلم أوي. هو أنا شفت قريبي بيعلم أخويا فا أخدت حبة معلومات منه.

فؤاد: آه، بس لسه مطلعتش رخصة. معظم الشباب في مصر بيتعلموا السواقة هنا في سن مبكر.

24

بتقابل أصحابك فين؟

بتقابلي أصحابك فين؟

يمنى: عادة بنتقابل في بيت واحدة فينا و ساعات بنروح في نادي أو كافيه.

محمد: في القهوة. أي شاب مصري بيقدس القهوة و عارف أهميتها.

داليا: دايما بحب أقابل صحابي في كافيه و بنتفق نتقابل في مكان معين و نخرج نروح أي مول.

أندرو: عادة عندي في البيت أو بننزل نتمشى في الشارع أو بنروح أي مول.

آيه: بقابل أصحابي في المول. بيكون مكان مناسب إننا نتمشى و ناكل و نتفرج على لبس.

محمود: في قهوة عندنا في المدينة عشان مكان بيكون هادي و أسعار الطلبات رخيصة.

رباب: في البيت أو الكافيه أو النادي بنقعد نرغي و نجيب في سيرة كل الناس.

تامر: مكان المقابلة المعتاد هو القهوة، معظمنا متجوزين و بيبقى صعب نبعد عن بيوتنا كتير.

شروق: يا إما في الجامعة و بعد كده نخرج، أو في بيت حد منهم أو ع الشارع و نتمشى.

فؤاد: بقابلهم في مهرجانات قصص مصورة في مصر أو ممكن نتفق نخرج نشوف فيلم سينما و ناكل.

25

أيه الأكل اللي مش بتحب تاكله؟

أيه الأكل اللي مش بتحبي تاكليه؟

يمنى: مفيش أكل مش بحبه. الأكل كله جميل بكل أنواعه و من كل البلاد.

محمد: أنا قشطة بحب آكل معظم الأكل. الكوسة و القرنبيط مش بحبهم.

داليا: مبحبش آكل الكوسة و مبحبش كمان السبانخ لإن طعمها بالنسبة لي مش حلو زي الأكلات السريعة.

أندرو: طبعا البصارة و السبانخ و الكوارع و الرنجة و الفسيخ و بالرغم من فوايدهم إلا إن ريحتهم بتخليني أبعد عنهم.

آيه: مش بحب آكل الفاصوليا الخضرا بالصلصلة. كل طعمها بيضيع، لكن بحبها سلطة.

محمود: مش بحب الفاصوليا و السبانخ في الخضار و اللحمة الباردة.

رباب: مفيش حاجة مبحبش آكلها. الأكل كله جميل و لازم أجرب كله.

تامر: مش بحب أي نوع سمك. محدش بيصدق لإني من إسكندرية و هي بلد مشهورة بالسمك.

شروق: الكوارع و الفشة و الكرشة و أي حاجة من مشتقات الحيوانات دي.

فؤاد: مش بحب آكل البتنجان. و برغم من كده والدتي بتعمله بس باكله عشان متزعلش.

26

بتخاف من أيه؟

بتخافي من أيه؟

يمنى: بخاف من الإيذاء، إن أنا أو حد من أسرتي يتعرض لإيذاء بدني أو نفسي.

محمد: أنا بخاف م الموت. فكرة الموت بنسبة لي مخيفة جدا. مش بقدر أستحملها.

داليا: بخاف من الموت و الفراق و المرض. بخاف أفشل في حياتي و إني مقدرش أحقق اللي نفسي فيه.

أندرو: بخاف من القرارات السريعة في لحظات الغضب و بتكون فيها نوع من أنواع العند.

آيه: بخاف من الوحدة و الاكتئاب. الإنسان متخلقش علشان يعيش لوحده ولا يعيش طول عمره حزين.

محمود: إني أسقط في مادة أو أشيل سنة في الكلية. دي أكتر حاجة بخاف منها.

رباب: بخاف أكون لوحدي. مبحبش الوحدة خالص. بحس بكآبة و حزن و أنا قاعدة لوحدي.

تامر: من صغري و أنا عندي فوبيا من التعابين و العقارب و كنت بحلم بكوابيس كتير بيهم.

شروق: لا، مش بخاف من حاجة خالص، لا حيوانات مثلا أو حشرات أو ضلمة، ولا حاجة.

فؤاد: بخاف م الحشرات الكبيرة، خصوصا اللي ليها أجنحة و عندها استعداد تطير.

27 إحساسك أيه النهارده؟

إحساسك أيه النهارده؟

يمنى: إحساس بالنشاط. الصحيان بدري و الروتين اليومي بيخليني مركزة في شغلي و مبسوطة.

محمد: أنا النهارده تعبان. بطني واجعاني أوي من إمبارح. مش عارف ليه.

داليا: أنا حاسة إن أنا مبسوطة أوي النهارده لإني قدرت أحقق حاجات كتير كان نفسي فيها.

أندرو: متفائل زي كل يوم الصبح. و ده بيخليني أكمل بقية اليوم نشيط في الشغل.

آيه: حاسة النهارده بالتعب علشان أخدت دور برد من تغيير الجو.

محمود: إني مبسوط، الحمد لله. ربنا بدأ يحققلي حاجات كنت مستنيها.

رباب: عايزة أنام. كان يوم شغل مرهق جدا و أخيرا عدى بسلام.

تامر: حاسس النهارده بملل شديد لإن اليوم كان طويل جدا من ناحية الشغل و الحياة العملية.

شروق: عادي، يعني زي أي يوم بس مصدعة شوية و ده مخليني في موود مش كويس.

فؤاد: متفائل. صعب الواحد يلاقي اللي عايزه بالضبط بس ساعات بيلاقي أقرب حاجة تسعده.

28

ناوي تعمل أيه بكره؟

ناوية تعملي أيه بكره؟

يمنى: روتيني خلال الأسبوع ثابت. بروح الشغل الصبح و أرجع أجهز الغدا و أقعد مع أسرتي لحد النوم.

محمد: بكره أنا مسافر. رايح إسكندرية أزور أهلي و أشوف صحابي.

داليا: ناوية أصحى بدري و أفطر و أعمل رياضة و أشتغل و أنزل أشتري حاجات و أطبخ و أنضف البيت.

أندرو: أهم حاجة متابعة باقي الشغل علشان كل التحركات تكون سليمة و عاوز أروح الجيم.

آيه: ناوية أخرج مع صاحبتي و أختي. نروح السينما و ناكل بره.

محمود: ناوي أذاكر عشان عندنا امتحانات نص التيرم هتبدأ كمان أسبوع.

رباب: ناوية أروح الشغل و يا رب يكون يوم كويس مش زي النهارده.

تامر: ناوي أصحى أروح الشغل و أحاول أرجع بدري عشان عايز أغير جو و أخرج في أي حتة.

شروق: كنت ناوية أنزل وسط البلد مع صاحبتي أشتري قماش بس هي عندها شغل فا الخطة أتغيرت.

فؤاد: أنا عموما بحب أتعلم حاجة جديدة كل يوم. أكمل حاجة كنت بتعلمها. ناوي أكمل رسمة.

29

أيه هوايتك المفضلة؟

أيه هوايتك المفضلة؟

يمنى: بحب الأشغال الفنية اليدوية. بندمج فيها جدا و بتعلمها بشغف. آخر حاجة كنت بعملها الإسكوبيدو.

محمد: أنا بحب الجيتار. عشان كده هوايتي المفضلة هي العزف ع الجيتار.

داليا: أنا بحب جدا الطبخ و إني أتعلم أكلات جديدة. و من هواياتي القراية. بحب أقرا كتير.

أندرو: أنا بحب الرسم جدا و السباحة، بس مش بقدر أنميهم علشان الشغل واخد أغلبية الوقت.

آيه: هوايتي المفضلة هي إني أخرج مع أصحابي و الناس اللي بحبها. بيكون وقت ممتع جدا.

محمود: ألعب رياضة. دي الحاجة اللي بستمتع و بحس إني فرحان و أنا بعملها.

رباب: معنديش هوايات. كل وقتي للبيت و الشغل فا معنديش وقت ألاقي هوايتي.

تامر: هوايتي المفضلة القراية و الكمبيوتر. دول الحاجتين اللي مقدرش أستغنى عنهم.

شروق: الرسم و صناعة حاجات يدوية من أي حاجة بقى صلصال أو قماش أو ورق.

فؤاد: الرسم و خصوصا رسم القصص المصورة. بحب أرسم تعبيرات الوش و أوصل فكرة بالرسم.

30

تقدر توصف شخصيتك بأيه؟

تقدري توصفي شخصيتك بأيه؟

يمنى: أنا شخصية هادية، محبة للنظام و الهدوء و شديدة الملاحظة للتفاصيل. حساسة جدا و حالمة.

محمد: أنا شخص منظم جدا. يعني أنا شخص بتاع أرقام و معادلات.

داليا: أقدر أوصف شخصيتي بإنها شخصية مرحة و اجتماعية و لكن في نفس الوقت جدية وقت الشغل.

أندرو: بقدونس. لإن البقدونس بتلاقية في أكلات كتير و أنا كمان بحب أكون مشارك في أي حاجة.

آيه: أقدر أوصف شخصيتي بإنها متوترة بس متحملة للمسؤولية جدا. و ده رأي ناس كتير فيا.

محمود: متكلم. لما بقعد في أي مكان مع ناس معرفهاش بعرف أفتح معاهم مواضيع.

رباب: أنا شخصية طيبة و محبوبة و اجتماعية و غاوية شغل.

تامر: أنا عصبي جدا للأسف، شخصيتي منطوية شوية و مش من السهل أثق في حد.

شروق: أنا شخصية بسيطة، مش بحب أنافق و بحب المرح و الضحك.

فؤاد: عادل. العدل بالنسبة لي حاجة مهمة لإن من غيره الناس هتظلم بعض و تكره بعض.

Appendix D: Modern Standard Arabic Translations

1 MSA

ما اسمك؟

ما اسمكِ؟

يمنى: اسمي يمنى. أحب اسمي لأنه ليس منتشرًا ومعناه جميل أيضًا.

محمد: أنا اسمي محمد، وأنتم تعرفون أنه أشهر اسم في العالم.

داليا: أنا اسمي داليا، وأحب اسمي لأن داليا هو اسم زهرة لها شكل ولون جميل.

أندرو: أنا اسمي أندرو وهذا الاسم نادر للغاية في مصر ومنذ أن كنت صغيرًا كانوا يطلقون عليّ دورا لأن قدميّ صغيرتان.

آيه: أنا اسمي آية، ومعنى اسمي المعجزة اَوْ دليل مثل آيات القرأن الكريم.

محمود: محمود أسامة، ومعنى محمود هو الشخص الذي يمدح الأشخاص كثيرًا.

رباب: اسمى رباب محمود ورباب هو السحاب الابيض ويمكن أيضًا أن يكون معنى رباب آلة الربابة وهي آلة موسيقية.

تامر: اسمى تامر. اسمي تركي الأصل، ويعتقد أغلب الأشخاص على شبكة الإنترنت أني تركي.

شروق: اسمى شروق ويأتى معنى اسمى من شروق الشمس ويدعوني أصدقائي باسم شيرو.

فؤاد: اسمي فؤاد، وهو من الأسماء القديمة نسبيًا ومعناه القلب، وقد سميت به تيمنًا بجدي رحمه الله.

2 MSA

من أين أنت؟

من أين أنتِ؟

يمنى: أنا من مصر، وتحديدًا من القاهرة العاصمة. وأقمت معظم حياتي بمحافظة الجيزة المجاورة للقاهرة.

محمد: أنا من الإسكندرية في الأصل، بلد البحر المتوسط الهادئ والفتيات.

داليا: أنا من مصر، وتحديدًا من القاهرة العاصمة وأيضًا أقيم بالجيزة منذ الصغر وتقع بجوار القاهرة.

أندرو: أنا من شبرا، وهي حي شعبي يوجد بالقاهرة منذ أكثر من مئتي عام.

آيه: أنا من مصر الجديدة، وهو حي راقي وهادئ للغاية.

محمود: من مصر، وهي أفضل دولة في العالم ويوجد بها ثلثي آثار العالم.

رباب: أنا من مصر، وتحديدًا من محافظة الاسكندرية وهي اروع محافظات مصر.

تامر: أنا من الإسكندرية من حي العجمى، وهي منطقة توجد بغرب الإسكندرية وكانت تعد من أفضل المصايف في السابق.

شروق: أنا من القاهرة في مصر ولكني قضيت فترة طفولتي بالإمارات العربية المتحدة.

فؤاد: من القاهرة، مدينة نصر في الأساس، ولكن منشأ العائلة نفسه مجهول بالنسبة لي.

3 كم عمركَ؟
MSA
كم عمركِ؟

يمنى: أبلغ من العمر خمسة وثلاثين عامًا. وسأصبح ستة وثلاثين في شهر نوفمبر القادم. ولكني أصبحت ستة وثلاثين بألفعل بناءً على التقويم الهجري.

محمد:

سأصبح سبعة وعشرين عامًا،

خلال أسبوع بالتحديد، وعيد مولدي في الثاني من إبريل.

داليا: أبلغ من العمر اثنين وعشرين عامًا. ولدت يوم واحد من أكتوبر عام ألف وتسعمائة وثلاثة وتسعين وولدت أيضًا في القاهرة.

أندرو: أبلغ من العمر تسعه وعشرين عامًا لأني ولدت في أكتوبر عام ألف وتسعمائة وستة ثمانين، وبالتحديد في اليوم المائتين من السنة.

آيه: أبلغ من العمر ثلاثة وعشرين عامًا. ولكن السن ليس إلا مجرد رقمًا، فالشباب يكمن في الروح.

محمود: أبلغ من العمر واحد وعشرين عامًا، فأنا ولدت عام ألف وتسعمائة أربعه وتسعين، ويعني هذا أني سأصبح اثنين وعشرين عامًا بعد شهرين من الآن.

رباب: أبلغ من العمر ثمانية وعشرين عامًا وسيكون عيد مولدي في شهر مايو.

تامر: أبلغ من العمر أربعه وثلاثين عامًا وستة أشهر وإحدى عشرة يومًا تقريبًا.

شروق: أبلغ من العمر اثنين وعشرين عامًا وسأصبح ثلاثة وعشرين في شهر أكتوبر القادم إن شاء الله.

فؤاد: أبلغ من العمر ستة وعشرين عامًا. ولكن يقول لي عدة أشخاص أني أبدو صغيرًا للغاية. وهذا بسبب شكل وجهي الطفولي للغاية.

4 MSA

ما هو تاريخ ميلادكَ؟

ما هو تاريخ ميلادكِ؟

يمنى: أنا من مواليد الرابع عشر من نوفمبر ألف وتسعمائة وثمانين. وبالتقويم الهجرى في السابع من محرم عام ألف وربعمائة وواحد. لا أحتفل عادةً بيوم مولدي ولكني أحب الهدايا.

محمد: تاريخ مولدي في الثاني من إبريل. وولدت يوم الأحد في رمضان.

داليا: تاريخ مولدي هو الأول من أكتوبر ألف وتسعمائة وثلاثة وتسعين وولدت يوم الجمعة وأحب تاريخ مولدي لأنه مميز وأول الشهر.

أندرو: في السابع والعشرين من شهر أكتوبر عام ألف وتسعمائة وستة وثمانين.

آيه: تاريخ مولدي هو الأول من يناير عام ألف وتسعمائة ثلاثة وتسعين. ودائمًا ما يأتي عيد مولدي في وقت الاختبارات.

محمود: في السابع من مايو ألف وتسعمائة وأربعة وتسعين، اليوم السابع من شهر مايو وولدت بالسعودية بمدينة الرياض.

رباب: ولدت في الخامس والعشرين من مايو عام ألف وتسعمائة وثمانين.

تامر: أنا من مواليد شهر سبتمبر عام اثنين وثمانين ومن مواليد برج العذراء.

شروق: أنا ولدت في الثالث من شهر أكتوبر وهو الشهر العاشر عام ألف وتسعمائة وثلاثة وتسعين.

فؤاد: في الثاني عشر من ديسمبر عام ألف وتسعمائة وتسعة وثمانين، ولكن كان هذا سببًا في بدئي للدراسة مبكرًا وكنت مع أشخاص أكبر مني سنًا.

5 MSA

ماذا تعمل؟

ماذا تعملين؟

يمنى: أنا أعمل كمهندسة معمارية. أنا أعمل على مشروع إنشاء المتحف المصري الكبير.

محمد: أنا أعمل كمهندس اتصالات. أنا أعمل في شركة اتصالات مصر.

داليا: أنا أعمل كمترجمة في شركة ترجمه بالمهندسين وأنا أعمل بها منذ ستة أشهر وأحصل على خبرة جيدة.

أندرو: أنا أعمل في شركة مشروبات غازية بقسم التسويق التجاري.

آيه: أنا أعمل كمحللة في مجال أبحاث السوق. نحلل بيأنات عن طبيعة استهلاك المنتجات كمثال.

محمود: أعمل كمصمم جرافيكس مستقل متخصص في عمل الشعارات للشركات الجديدة.

رباب: أعمل كمهندسة شبكات في شركة أورانج. وهي من أقوى وأكثر الشركات العالمية نجاحًا.

تامر: أنا أعمل كمدير شبكات ونظم في شركة ملاحة منذ ثلاث سنوات.

شروق: كنت أعمل في عيادة وتركتها بسبب مرضي وحاليًا أعمل في العمل الحر.

فؤاد: أعمل حاليًا في العمل الحر وخصوصًا رسم الكوميكس الياباني وألعاب الأندرويد.

6 أين تقيم؟

MSA

أين تقيمين؟

يمنى: أقيم في مصر. تحديدًا في محافظة الجيزة بالقرب من الأهرامات.

محمد: أنا في الأصل من الاسكندرية. ولكني أقيم في القاهرة من أجل عملي.

داليا: أقيم في الجيزة في منطقة تسمى المهندسين وهي منطقة تعد راقية عن مناطق أخرى.

أندرو: أقيم في القاهرة وهي عاصمة مصر وتعد القاهرة من المدن التي لا تنام.

آيه: أقيم في مدينة نصر في القاهرة. وهو حي كبير وقريب من كل شيء.

محمود: في الجيزة، ومعنى كلمة الجيزة في اللغة العربية هي الوادي.

رباب: أقيم في القاهرة في المعادي. وهي أهدى مكان في القاهرة. أنا محظوظة لأني أقيم في المعادى.

تامر: أقيم في منزل عائلي في الاسكندرية، ويسكن والداي في الدور الأول وأنا أسكن في الدور الثاني.

شروق: أقيم حاليًا في القاهرة في مصر ولكني كنت أقيم في الإمارات وأنا صغيرة.

فؤاد: أقيم في الرحاب. يوجد هنا العديد من الحدائق وتساعد كثيرًا على الاسترخاء عندما تسير بها في الصباح.

7 هل أنت متزوج؟

MSA

هل أنتِ متزوجة؟

يمنى: أنا متزوجة منذ ست سنوات ولدي طفلين. وإن إظهر الحب والتفاهم والاحترام هو الطريق لأسرة سعيدة.

محمد: نعم، متزوج، تزوجت في سن صغيرة وأنا أبلغ أربعة وعشرين عامًا.

داليا: لا، لست متزوجة ولست مخطوبة، وكنت على وشك الخطبة ولكن الظروف والنصيب منعوا ذلك.

أندرو: لا، وينتظر الجميع هذا اليوم لأن سني كبير بعض الشيء.

آيه: لا، لست متزوجة. ولكني مرتبطة ومن الممكن أن اتزوج خلال عامين.

محمود: لا، يتزوج معظم الأشخاص في مصر عند سن الخامسة والعشرين حتى يتخرج ويستطيع أن يكوّن نفسه.

رباب: نعم، أنا متزوجة منذ عامين وسعيدة جدًا معه فهو إنسان أكثر من رائع.

تامر: أنا متزوج الحمدلله ولدي ولدين، آسر وعدي، ويبلغون من العمر أربع سنوات وسنتين.

شروق: لا، ما زلت عذباء ولكني اتخطبت مرة فقط ولم أكمل لأنه لم يكن مناسبًا لي.

فؤاد: لا، ما زال من المبكر أن اتزوج لأنها مسئولية كبيرة وتحتاج إلى ماديات واتزان نفسي.

8 MSA

هل لديك أخوة؟

هل لديكِ أخوة؟

يمنى: لدي أخت وأخ أصغر مني. لا أراهم كثيرًا بسبب انشغالنا ولكننا نحاول إيجاد طريقة للقاء.

محمد: لدي أخ واحد، أصغر مني بأربع سنوات، وما زال يدرس في الكلية.

داليا: لدي أخ واحد فقط وليس لدي أخوات فتيات وكنت اتمنى لو يكون لي العديد من الأخوة لألعب معهم.

أندرو: لدي أخ وأخت، وهما أكبر مني ومتزوجين وكلٍّ منهما لديه فتاة.

آيه: نعم، لدي خمس أخوات فتيات، نتشاجر سويًا دائمًا ولكن لا نستطيع أن نعيش بدون إحدانا.

محمود: نعم، ولدَي أخين، واحد منهما أكبر مني وانتهى من دراسته والآخر أصغر مني بعامين.

رباب: لدي أخ أصغر مني بسبع سنوات وهذا يعني أنه يبلغ من العمر واحد وعشرين عامًا.

تامر: لدي أخ وأختين. أنا أكبرهم ويليني أخت ويليها أخ وأصغرنا أخت.

شروق: نعم، لدي أختين وأخ، ويوجد فرق بالعمر سنتين بين كلٍّ منا وأنا أكبرهم.

فؤاد: لدي أخين وأنا بالوسط. ومن الصعب أن تجد شخصًا ليس له أخ اَوْ أخت في مصر.

9
MSA

هل تتحدث لغات؟

هل تتحدثين لغات؟

يمنى: اللغة العربية هي لغتي الأم و أتحدث الإنجليزية. أعرف القليل من الفرنسية وأتمنى أن أتقنها.

محمد: أتحدث اللغة العربية والإنجليزية والقليل من الفرنسية.

داليا: أتحدث لغات مثل الإنجليزية والعربية والفرنسية وأيضًا أحاول أن أتقن الإسبانية والألمانية والإيطالية.

أندرو: اللغة العربية بالطبع وهي اللغة الأم وأتحدث الإنجليزية وأعرف القليل من الفرنسية بحكم الدراسة لمدة سبع سنوات.

آيه: نعم، أتحدث العربية والإنجليزية. تعلمت الإنجليزية من خلال الأفلام والدراما.

محمود: نعم، أتحدث لغتان وهي العربية الأولى والإنجليزية الثانية.

رباب: أتحدث الإنجليزية بشكل جيد. فأنا أتحدث الإنجليزية طوال الوقت بالعمل لأني أتعامل مع مستخدمين من خارج مصر.

تامر: أتحدث الإنجليزية جيدًا، وربما أكثر من العربية والقليل من الفرنسية.

شروق: ليست لغات بالمعنى المعروف ولكن القليل من الإنجليزية وبعض الكلمات اليابانية ومازلت أتعلم.

فؤاد: أتحدث الإنجليزية بطلاقة وهي شيئ هام لأي مصري لأننا بلد سياحي.

10
MSA

ما هو اللون المفضل بالنسبة إليكَ؟

ما هو اللون المفضل بالنسبة إليكِ؟

يمنى: أنا أفضل ثلاثة ألوان، الأخضر والبنفسجي والوردي. ولكن عادةً ما يكون اختياري للألوان مرتبطًا بحالتي المزاجية.

محمد: من أكثر الألوان التي أفضلها هو اللون الأحمر، كما أنني أحب اللون الأخضر فهو لون الزرع الرائع.

داليا: أنا أحب اللون الأسود، لأنني أشعر أنه ملك الألوان، كما أننى كذلك أحب اللون البنفسجي والأحمر والأزرق والأبيض.

أندرو: لوني المفضل هو الأحمر لأنه يشعرني بالبهجة، كما أنه اللون الذي يرتديه فريقي المفضل.

آيه: من أكثر الألوان التي أفضلها هو اللون الأزرق الغامق، فهو لون البحر الذي يشعرني بأنه لون شديد النقاء.

محمود: الأزرق، من أكثر الألوان التي تعبر عن الفخامة والعظمة كما يعبر عن الهدوء وسكون الليل.

رباب: أنا اعشق اللون الأسود لأنه عنوان الأناقة والجمال بالنسبة لي.

تامر: من أكثر الألوان التي أفضلها هو اللون الأسود، على الرغم من أن هناك الكثير من الأشخاص ممن يصفونه بالكئيب.

شروق: أحب اللون الأسود والرمادي والوردي والبنفسجي بجميع درجاته، ولكنني أفضل الألوان القاتمة أكثر من غيرها.

فؤاد: الأسود هو لوني المفضل، وهو اللون الذي يعبر عن الغموض.

11
MSA

هل تمارس الرياضة؟

هل تمارسين الرياضة؟

يمنى: حاليًا لا أمارس الرياضة، ولكنني كنت أمارس رياضة المشي والسباحة، وأقوم بممارستهم كلما أتيحت لي ألفرصة.

محمد: أمارس السباحة في النادي، وأقوم بالذهاب إلي صالة الرياضة ثلاثة اَوْ أربعة أيام.

داليا: أمارس الرياضة ولكنني لا أمارسها بأستمرار، فمن الممكن أن أقوم بممارسة الرياضة في الصباح الباكر، اَوْ أقوم بممارسة رياضة المشي.

أندرو: لا، ولكنني كنت ألعب كرة الطاولة منذ فترة طويلة، وقد قمت بالأشتراك ذات مرة في مسابقة الجامعة لكرة الطاوله، ولكنني لم أحقق فيها اي جوائز.

آيه: نعم، أمارس الأسكواش، فهو من الرياضات الجميلة التي تتطلب تركيزًا وردة فعل سريعة.

محمود: نعم، أمارس السباحة مع فريق النادي منذ اثنا عشر عامًا، وقد قمت بالأشتراك في الكثير من البطولات.

رباب: نعم، أمارس رياضة السلاح، وهي لعبة تحتاج إلي السرعة والدقة لكي تستطيع أن تتفوق علي خصمك.

تامر: كنت أمارس كرة القدم والملاكمة في طفولتي ولكنني تعرضت لإصابة في مفصلي أثناء لعب كرة القدم.

شروق: نعم، أمارس رياضة الزومبا، وقد كنت من المشتركين في فريق كرة السلة حينما كنت في المدرسة.

فؤاد: أمارس رياضة رفع الأثقال، وهي تعتبر من أكثر الرياضات التي يفضلها المصريين وهي تتمتع بشهرة كبيرة جدا في مصر.

12 MSA

ما الذي تناولته على الغداء بالأمس؟

ما الذي تناولتِه على الغداء بالأمس؟

يمنى: تناولت بالأمس دجاجًا مقليًا ومعكرونة بالصلصة والبصل، مع صحنًا كبيرًا من السلطة.

محمد: تناولت مكرونة بخلطة البشاميل مع الدجاج المشوي والقليل من الخضراوات المسلوقة.

داليا: تناولت أمس على الغداء المحشى والملوخية الخضراء وحساء من الشوربة ودجاجًا مشويًا مع البطاطس والسلطة والخبز والمخللات والباذنجان.

أندرو: في الأمس تناولت الكشري على الغداء لأنني كنت في العمل، وهو من الأكلات الشعبية المصرية الشهيرة.

آيه: في الأمس تناولت على الغداء الأرز والدجاج والكوسه، وقد قامت أختى بإعداد الطعام لأنها لا تعمل.

محمود: تناولت المعكرونة والأرز واللحم الممزوج بالصلصة مع الدجاج المقلي والديك الرومي.

رباب: تناولت أنا وزوجي اللحم المشوي والسبانخ مع الأرز والسلطة.

تامر: في الأمس تناولت المحشي، وهو من الأكلات المفضلة لدي الشعب المصري كله، كما تناولت معه دجاجًا مقليًا.

شروق: في الأمس كنت في أحتفال، فتناولت الطعام في الخارج مع أصدقائي، تناولنا الأرز وكفته داوود باشا الشهيرة.

فؤاد: تناولت الدجاج المقلي وقد قمت بإضافة الأرز إليه، لقد قامت والدتي بإعداده لأننى أحب الأرز الأبيض جدًا.

13
MSA

متى تستيقظ عادةً؟

متى تستيقظين عادةً؟

يمنى: عادةً أستيقظ في الساعة السادسة صباحًا، وفي نهاية الأسبوع أحاول أن أستيقظ متأخرًا، ولكن جميع من في المنزل يكونون قد أعتادوا علي الأستيقاظ مبكرًا.

محمد: أنا أستيقظ في الساعة الثامنة صباحًا، أتناول طعام الإفطار وأغتسل ثم أذهب إلي العمل.

داليا: أعتدت على أن أستيقظ كل يوم في الساعة التاسعة صباحًا، وقد أعتدت على ذلك للذهاب إلي العمل.

أندرو: عادة، أستيقظ في الساعة الثامنة صباحًا للذهاب إلي العمل، أما في أيام الأجازات فمن المحتمل أن أستيقظ في الساعة العاشرة صباحًا.

آيه: أعتدت على الأستيقاظ في الساعة السابعة صباحًا، حتى أستطيع الأستعداد ثم الذهاب إلي العمل.

محمود: أعتدت على الأستيقاظ في الساعة السابعة صباحًا، حتى أتمكن من ركوب المواصلات العامه والذهاب إلي الجامعة.

رباب: في الساعة السابعة صباحًا، لأن سيارة العمل تأتي في الساعة الثامنة صباحًا حتى أكون في العمل في تمام الساعة التاسعة.

تامر: من المفترض أن أستيقظ في الساعة السابعة صباحًا للذهاب إلي العمل، ولكن أحيانًا ما يقوم أولادي بإيقاظي قبل ذلك.

شروق: غالبًا ما أستيقظ بعد الظهر، لأنني أسهر كثيرًا، ولكن في هذه الأيام أستيقظ مبكرًا للذهاب إلي الجامعة.

فؤاد: أعتدت على الأستيقاظ في الساعة التاسعة صباحًا، حتى أتمكن من المشي تحت آشعة الشمس، لأن ذلك يعتبر من الأشياء التي يحتاجها الجسم.

14 MSA

ما هو طعامك المفضل؟
ما هو طعامكِ المفضل؟

يمنى: الطعام كله مفضل بالنسبة إلي، وأنا أعتبر الطعام من أجمل نعم الله التي أنعم بها علينا.

محمد: أنا أحب تناول السمك، ومن أكثر الأكلات التى أفضلها هي السمك المخلوط بالسبيط والجمبرى.

داليا: طعامي المفضل هو البيتزا الإيطالية، وذلك على الرغم من أن هناك العديد من الأكلات المصرية الرائعة مثل الكشرى والفلافل.

أندرو: أحب تناول الفول والجبن الممزوج بسلطة الخضروات، وهما من أكثر الأكلات التي من الممكن أن أتناولها دون شبع.

آيه: طعامي المفضل هو ورق العنب مع اللحم المشوي، وهي من الأكلات التى يتم تحضيرها كثيرًا في العزائم.

محمود: البازلاء هي نوع من النباتات التى تنتمي إلي فصيلة البقوليات، من رتبة الفوليات.

رباب: أنا أحب السبيط جدًا، ومن الممكن أن أقوم بتناوله دون شبع.

تامر: طعامي المفضل هو المحشى والديك الرومي، وبخاصة إذا كان مطهيًا بشكل جيد يكون رائع جدًا.

شروق: أنا أعشق تناول الباذنجان بالطماطم بشدة، وبخاصة عندما يضاف إليه البشاميل، وايضًا أحب تناول المعكرونة.

فؤاد: أحب تناول المحشي وبخاصة الكرنب، وهو من أرخص أنواع الأكلات المصرية التى من الصعب تحضيرها.

15 MSA

من هو الفنان اَوْ الفنانة المفضلة إليك؟

من هو الفنان اَوْ الفنانة المفضلة إليكِ؟

يمنى: أحب الفنانين الكبار مثل الفنانة فاتن حمامه والفنان عمر الشريف وروبرت دينيرو وال باتشينو.

محمد: الفنان المفضل بالنسبة لي هو ال باتشينو، فأنا أعشق أفلام المافيا الخاصة به فهو يشبه الأب الروحى لهذه الأفلام.

داليا: من الفنانين المفضلين لدي هو الفنان أحمد السقا، أحب أفلام الحركة الخاصه به، كما أحب أن تقوم الفنانة منى ذكي بالتمثيل معه.

أندرو: أنا لا أتابع التمثيل، ولكنني أحب أن أشاهد أفلام الفنان أحمد حلمى لأنه يقوم بتقديم أفلام هادفة.

آيه: الفنان المفضل بالنسبة لي هو الفنان آسر ياسين، أحبه لأنه يقوم بتقمص دوره بشكل ممتاز، كما أن نظراته معبرة ويتميز بوسامته.

محمود: أحمد حلمي هو من أفضل فنانين الكوميديا في مصر والشرق الأوسط.

رباب: أحب الفنان عمر الشريف رحمة الله عليه، فقد كان فنانًا رائعًا وموهوبًا جدًا.

تامر: الفنانة المفضلة بالنسبة لي هي الفنانة ياسمين عبد العزيز، فتقريبًا كان الجيل الذي أنتمي إليه يحب هذه الفنانة.

شروق: صراحة، لا يوجد فنان محدد، ولكنني أحب سكارلت جوهانسن جدًا التي قامت بفيلم لوسي.

فؤاد: أحب أفلام ويل سميث فهي من الأفلام الهادفة، حيث يحاول فيها أن يبني شيئًا ما مع عائلته.

16
MSA

ما الذي ترتديه اليوم؟

ما الذي ترتدينه اليوم؟

يمنى: أرتدي تنورة بنية اللون وقميصًا أزرق مع حجاب وردي اللون، كما أنني أحب أن أرتدي أكثر من لون.

محمد: اليوم أرتدي رداءً بسيطًا لأنني ذاهب إلي العمل، فأرتدي قميصًا وبنطال.

داليا: اليوم كنت أرتدي بنطال جينز، مع قميصًا أزرق بنقاط بيضاء، وفي الحقيقة أنا أحبه وأجد الراحة في أرتدائه.

أندرو: اليوم الطقس معتدل، أرتدي رداءً رماديًا من الصوف، وبنطال جينز مع حذاء رياضي.

آيه: أرتدي بنطال أسود اللون وقميصًا رماديًا من النوع الفاتح، مع حذاء رمادي، وقد قمت بأختيار هذه الملابس لأنها مريحة.

محمود: أرتدي قميصًا قطنيًا قصير الأكمام، مع سترة ثقيلة لأن الطقس غير مستقر فتارة يصبح حارًا وتارة أخري نجده باردًا.

رباب: أرتدي بنطال أسود ورداءً أسود من الصوف مع حجاب أبيض وسترة سوداء.

تامر: عند الخروج أفضل أرتداء الملابس الغير رسمية أكثر من الرسمية، أما في المنزل فأنا أرتدي ثوبًا للنوم.

شروق: أرتدي ملابس المنزل وهي عباره عن بنطال أسود وقميصًا قطنيًا واسعًا بألوان كثيرة.

فؤاد: أرتدي ملابس مريحة في الحركة، لأ أحب أن أرتدي ملابس ضيقة اَوْ واسعة اَوْ تحتوي على رسومات.

17 MSA

كم عدد المرات التى تصاب فيها بالمرض خلال العام؟

كم عدد المرات التى تصابين فيها بالمرض خلال العام؟

يمنى: حوالي ثلاثة أَوْ أربعة مرات في العام، وعادةً ما يصاب أحد الأبناء بالمرض ومن ثم يقوم بنقل العدوى لجميع من في المنزل.

محمد: لا أعلم، لم يكن الأمر في الحسبان بالنسبة لي، أتمني أن يبعد الله المرض عن الجميع.

داليا: الحمد لله، أنا أتمتع بصحة جيدة وأحافظ على تناول الطعام الصحى وممارسة الرياضة، لذلك فأنا لا أمرض أكثر من مرتين في العام.

أندرو: حوالي أربع مرات وعادةً ما يكون ذلك ناتجًا عن تغير الفصول، وعادةً ما أمرض بالجيوب الأنفية.

آيه: أمرض خمسة مرات في العام، ويكون ذلك ناتجًا عن تغير الطقس لأنني لدي حساسية من الأجواء المتغيرة.

محمود: مرة واحدة تقريبًا، لأنني قمت من قبل بإجراء عملية في اللوزتين وأتمتع بمناعة قوية.

رباب: أمرض قليلاً، ثلاثة مرات في العام تقريبًا، ولكنني حين أمرض يكون المرض شديدًا جدًا.

تامر: لم أقم بحساب ذلك من قبل، ولكنني أتمتع بصحة جيدة، لا أمرض بسهولة.

شروق: لم أحسب ذلك، ولكنني أمرض كثيرًا في حياتي.

فؤاد: ثماني أَوْ تسع مرات ويكون غالبًا بسبب البرد، ولكنني بدأت مؤخرًا بالأهتمام بصحتي بشكل كبير، وبدأت أفهم لماذا نمرض.

18 MSA

ماذا فعلت في صباح اليوم؟

ماذا فعلتِ في صباح اليوم؟

يمنى: قمت بعمل ما أعتدت علي فعله كل يوم، وقد قمت بتجهيز الطعام للأولاد وذهبوا إلي المدرسة، ثم ذهبت أنا إلي عملى.

محمد: لم أفعل شيء، أستيقظت في الساعة الثامنة كعادتي، تناولت الإفطار وأغتسلت ثم ذهبت إلى العمل.

داليا: اليوم أستيقظت من نومي ثم تناولت طعام الإفطار وشربت قهوتي الصباحية، ثم قمت بممارسة الرياضة حتى أستطيع أن أكمل باقي اليوم.

أندرو: عندما أستيقظت من النوم قمت بأخذ حقيبتي وذهبت إلى العمل مباشرة، وقد قمت بعمل مكالمات لبعض الناس لمتابعة الأعمال التى قاموا بها في مساء أمس.

آيه: اليوم أستيقظت في الصباح وتناولت وجبة الإفطار، ثم ذهبت إلى العمل، وهذا هو ما أعتدت على فعله في أسبوع العمل.

محمود: قمت بآداء الصلاة وتناولت وجبة الإفطار، ومن ثم جلست أتابع موقع التواصل الإجتماعي فيس بوك، لذلك فأنا لم أقم بأي شيء مفيد.

رباب: كنت في العمل، ولكن اليوم كان مرهقًا للغايه، أتمني أن يكون الغد أفضل.

تامر: أستيقظت من النوم في موعد العمل، ثم ذهبت إلي العمل الذي تأخرت فيه كثيرًا فأضاع يومي بأكمله.

شروق: بعد أن أستيقظت قمت بالبحث عن عدة العاب على جهاز الكمبيوتر لأقوم بتحميلها واللعب بها.

فؤاد: أستيقظت وقمت بغسل وجهي وتناولت الإفطار وهو عباره عن بطاطس مع بعض ثمرات البرتقال، ثم خرجت لأمارس رياضة المشي بعض الوقت.

19 MSA

ما هو الفصل المفضل في العام بالنسبة إليك؟ وما هو الطقس الذي تفضله؟

ما هو الفصل المفضل في العام بالنسبة إليكِ؟ وما هو الطقس الذي تفضلينه؟

يمنى: يعتبر الخريف هو أفضل الفصول، وذلك لأن الطقس فيه يكون معتدل ومناسب للخروج، وأيضًا لأنه هو الفصل الذي شهد الجميع فيه موعد ولادتى.

محمد: أنا لا أحب الطقس البارد، لذلك فالصيف هو فصلي المفضل، فهو فصل البحر والشمس.

داليا: أنا أفضل فصل الصيف وذلك على الرغم من أنه شديد الحرارة، ولكنني أحب الطاقة الكبيرة التى تكون لدي خلاله.

أندرو: فصل الشتاء بالطبع، لأن الطقس فيه يكون جميلاً، وتكون لدي القدرة على عمل العديد من الأنشطة خلاله أكثر من فصل الصيف.

آيه: أنا أفضل فصل الخريف، لأن الطقس فيه يكون معتدل جدًا في مصر.

محمود: فصل الصيف، وذلك لأن طقس الصيف في مصر رائع جدًا وبخاصة في المناطق الساحلية.

رباب: أفضل فصل الشتاء، الطقس في محافظة الأسكندرية يكون أكثر من رائع ويكون البحر خلاب وجميل.

تامر: عادةً ما تكون الإجابة على هذا السؤال هي فصل الربيع اَوْ فصل الصيف، ولكنني أفضل فصل الشتاء لأن الطقس يكون جميًلا في محافظة الأسكندرية.

شروق: أحب فصل الشتاء جدًا أكثر من فصل الصيف، لأنني أحب الطقس البارد ولا أحب الطقس الحار.

فؤاد: فصل الصيف، لأنه نادرًا ما نصاب بالأمراض، ولكن المحجبات هم أكثر من يعانون في فصل الصيف بسبب ما يرتدونه من ملابس تسبب لهم الحرارة الشديدة.

20 MSA

هل تحب الغناء أم الرقص؟

هل تحبين الغناء أم الرقص؟

يمنى: لا أمارس الغناء ولكنني أحب الأستماع له، وأحب الرقص وأعتبره رياضة مسلية حيث يساهم في تحسين الحالة المزاجية.

محمد: نعم، من أكثر الأشياء التى أفضلها هي الرقص والموسيقى.

داليا: أحب الغناء على الرغم من أن صوتى قبيح، ولكننى أكون سعيدة حين أغني، فأجد نفسي أرقص بشكل تلقائي.

أندرو: أنا أحب الغناء بشدة وأحب الأغاني القديمة والحديثة أيضًا، ويعتبر محمد منير من أكثر المغنيين الذين أقوم بسماعهم.

آيه: أحب الغناء والرقص ولكن عندما أكون وحيدًا، لأنني لا أحب أن يشاهدني اَوْ يسمعني أحد.

محمود: أحب الرقص ولكن في المناسبات؛ مثل الأفراح وأعياد الميلاد.

رباب: أحب الرقص جدًا، ولكنني لم أتخذ الخطوة الأولي لأتعلمه بشكل جدي.

تامر: أحب الرقص جدًا، وأيضًا أحب سماع الموسيقى بجميع أنواعها التى تشمل الموسيقى الغربية الغير تقليدية.

شروق: نعم أحب الغناء والرقص جدًا، وبخاصة أغاني الكارتون التي تخص كارتون سبيستون الشهير، كنت أحب أن أغنيها جدًا.

فؤاد: نعم، ولكن عندما أكون وحيدًا اَوْ مع صديق عزيز، وذلك لأن الرقص يكون بغرض الأستمتاع.

21 ما هو لون شعرك وعينيك؟

MSA

ما هو لون شعرِك وعينيكِ؟

يمنى: شعري بني اللون وعيناي بها اللون الأخضر والعسلي، وعندما كنت صغيرة كان شعرى يتميز باللون الفاتح.

محمد: لون شعري أسود، أما عيني فهي بنية اللون، ولكنني دائمًا ما أقوم بحلاقة شعري لأصبح أصلع.

داليا: شعري أسود اللون، وأحيانًا أقوم بوضع صبغة عليه ليصبح بني اللون، أما عيناى فلونهما بني داكن.

أندرو: لون شعري أسود وقصير، وهناك بعض الشعيرات البيضاء، أما عيناي فهما واسعتان باللون الأسود.

آيه: لون شعرى وعينيّ هو البني الفاتح، أشبه أبي وأمي في ذلك.

محمود: لون شعري هو الأسود، ولون عينيّ هو البني الفاتح، وعادةً ما تكون هذه الألوان هي التى يتميز بها العرب.

رباب: شعري أسود اللون وعيناي أيضًا، وأنا أحب لون شعري كثيرًا.

تامر: لون شعري هو الأسود ويتميز بنعومته، أما عيناي فهما عسليتان اَوْ بنيتان داكنتان، وتعتبر هذه الصفات من الصفات الأساسية في جمهورية مصر العربية.

شروق: لون شعري هو الأسود ولكنني قمت بوضع صبغة عليه ليصبح أحمر اللون، أما عيناي فلونهما هو البني الداكن.

فؤاد: لون شعري أسود أما عيناي فلونهما بني داكن، ونادرًا ما نجد ألوان أخرى في جمهورية مصر العربية.

22 MSA

من بين الإجازات السنوية، ما هي إجازتك المفضلة؟

من بين الإجازات السنوية، ما هي إجازتكِ المفضلة؟

يمنى: إجازتي المفضلة هي إجازة عيد الأضحي، وهي تكون إجازة طويلة أقوم فيها برؤية الكثير من الأشخاص الذين أشتقت لرؤيتهم.

محمد: إجازة رأس السنه، لأنني أقوم فيها بالأحتفال بجميع إجازات العام الماضي.

داليا: لدي العديد من الإجازات السنوية، ولكنني أفضل اجازة العيد أننا أقضيها مع عائلتي.

أندرو: إجازة الصيف بالتأكيد، لأن فيها تتجمع العائلة ونقوم بقضاء أغلب الوقت على البحر.

آيه: إجازتي المفضلة هي إجازة الصيف، عندما نقوم بأخذ الإجازة والسفرإلي البحر.

محمود: الإجازة الكبيرة، بعد كل عام دراسي، وتكون مدتها ثلاثة أشهر.

رباب: كانت الإجازة في هولندا، وقد قمت بقضاء وقت ممتع مع زوجي وأصدقائنا.

تامر: من أكثر الإجازات التى أفضلها هي إجازة العيد الصغير والعيد الكبير لأن العائلة تجتمع بهما.

شروق: آخر الإجازات التي قضيناها كانت مع العائلة وصديقتي المقربة وذهبنا إلي مصيف الأسكندرية.

فؤاد: إجازة العيد، لأنها بالفعل تكون إجازة، وأقوم أنا بأخذ إجازة أخري قبلها لتكون فترة الإجازة طويلة.

23 MSA

هل تعلمت قيادة السيارات؟

هل تعلمتِ قيادة السيارات؟

يمنى: نعم، أعرف القيادة، وقد قمت بشراء سيارة صغيرة في عام 2007 وتعلمت القيادة عليها مع أبي.

محمد: نعم، أعرف القيادة، وقد قمت بأستخراج رخصة قيادة بعد بلوغي ثمانية عشر عامًا بالظبط.

داليا: لا، أعرف القيادة، وأتمني أن أتعلمها كثيرًا لأنني أحلم بشراء سيارة.

أندرو: للأسف لا، ولكنني حتمًا سأتعلم القيادة لأن الغالبية العظمي من العمل الخاص بي يكون في الشارع.

آيه: نعم، أعرف القيادة، وأمتلك رخصة وسيارة منذ أن كنت في الثامنة عشر من عمري.

محمود: نعم، أحب القيادة، ولكن الأزدحام الشديد الموجود في الشوارع بأستمرار يجعلني أكرهها.

رباب: لا، ولكنني أنوي تعلمها وذلك لأن القيادة لا غنى عنها في جمهورية مصر العربية.

تامر: أعرف القيادة جيدًا، ولكنني أكره القيادة بسبب الأزدحام، كما أن قائدي السيارات لا يلتزمون بآداب المرور.

شروق: لا، ولكنني أرغب في تعلمها، وقد رأيت قريب لي يقوم بتعليم أخي القيادة فتعلمت بعض المعلومات منه.

فؤاد: نعم، ولكنني لم أقم بأستخراج رخصة قيادة، معظم شباب مصر يقومون بتعلم القيادة في سن مبكر.

24 MSA

أين تقابل أصدقاءك؟

أين تقابلين أصدقاءكِ؟

يمنى: عادةً نلتقي في منزل واحدة منا، واحيانًا نذهب إلي النادي اَوْ المقهي.

محمد: في المقهى، أي شاب مصري يقدس المقهي ويعلم أهميته.

داليا: دائمًا أحب أن أقابل أصدقائي في مقهي، كما نقوم بالأتفاق على مكان محدد ثم نذهب إلي مركز التسوق.

أندرو: عادةً ألتقي بهم في منزلي، اَوْ نذهب لممارسة رياضة المشي اَوْ إلي اي مركز للتسوق.

آيه: ألتقي بأصدقائي في مركز للتسوق، ويكون المكان مناسب للمشي وتناول الطعام ومشاهدة الملابس.

محمود: في مقهى لدينا في المدينة، لأنه مكان هاديء وأسعاره ليست مرتفعة.

رباب: في المنزل اَوْ المقهي اَوْ النادي، نجلس لنتحدث سويًا لنذكر جميع الناس أثناء حديثنا.

تامر: فى المقهي وهو المكان المعتاد للمقابلات، فمعظمنا متزوجين ومن الصعب أن نبتعد عن منازلنا لفترة طويلة.

شروق: في الجامعة ثم نقوم بالخروج، اَوْ في منزل أحد أصدقائي ثم نذهب للتمشية.

فؤاد: أقابلهم في أحتفالات قصص مصورة في جمهورية مصر العربية، ومن الممكن أيضًا أن نقوم بالأتفاق على الخروج لمشاهدة فيلم سينما وتناول الطعام.

25
MSA

ما هو الطعام الذي لا تحب تناوله؟

ما هو الطعام الذي لا تحبين تناوله؟

يمنى: لا يوجد طعام لا أحبه، فالطعام جميل بجميع أنواعه ومن جميع البلدان.

محمد: أنا احب تناول معظم الأطعمة، ولكنني لا احب تناول الكوسه والقرنبيط.

داليا: لا أحب تناول الكوسه والسبانخ لأن طعمها بالنسبة لي غير جميل بالمقارنة مع الآكلات السريعة.

أندرو: لا أحب البصارة والسبانخ والكوارع والسمك المملح وعلى الرغم من فوائد هذه الأطعمة إلا أن رائحتها هي السبب في جعلى أبتعد عن تناولها.

آيه: لا أحب تناول الفاصوليا الخضراء بصلصة الطماطم، لأن ذلك يضيع مذاقها، ولكنني أحب تناولها مثل السلطة.

محمود: لا أحب الفاصوليا والسبانخ في الخضروات واللحم البارد.

رباب: لا يوجد أطعمة لا أحب تناولها، جميع الأطعمة جميلة ولابد أن أقوم بتجريب جميع أنواعها.

تامر: لا أحب تناول اي نوع من أنواع السمك، وهذا ما لا يصدقه أحد لأنني من محافظة الأسكندرية التى تشتهر بالأسماك.

شروق: لا أحب الكوارع وأي شيء من مشتقات الحيوانات المختلفة.

فؤاد: لا أحب تناول الباذنجان، وعلى الرغم من ذلك حين تقوم والدتي بتحضيرة أقوم بتناوله حتي لا أجعلها تغضب منى.

26
MSA

ما هو الشيء الذي تخاف منه؟

ما هو الشيء الذي تخافين منه؟

يمنى: أخاف من الأذى، عندما أتعرض أنا اَوْ أحد من أسرتي للإيذاء البدني اَوْ النفسي.

محمد: أنا أخاف من الموت، ففكرة الموت تعتبر مخيفة جدًا بالنسبة لي، لا أستطيع تحملها.

داليا: أخاف من الموت والفراق والمرض، وأخاف من الفشل في حياتي وعدم قدرتي على تحقيق ما أرغب فيه.

أندرو: أخاف من القرارات السريعة في لحظات الغضب، وتكون هذه القرارات تحتوي على نوع من أنواع العند.

آيه: أخاف من الوحدة والأكتئاب، لأن الإنسان لم يخلق لكى يعيش وحيدًا حزينًا.

محمود: أخاف أن أفشل في أجتياز أختبار ما اَوْ أقوم بأعادةً عام في الجامعة، وهذه هي أكثر الأشياء التى أخاف منها.

رباب: أخاف أن أكون وحيدة، فلا أحب الوحدة لأنني أشعر خلالها بالحزن والكآبة.

تامر: منذ طفولتي وأنا أخاف من الثعابين والعقارب، وكنت أحلم بالعديد من الكوابيس بسببهم.

شروق: أنا لا أخاف من شيء، لا من حيوانات ولا من حشرات اَوْ ظلام اَوْ أى شيء على الإطلاق.

فؤاد: أخاف من الحشرات الكبيرة، وبخاصة الحشرات التى تمتلك أجنحة ولديها أستعداد للطيران.

27
MSA

ما هو شعورك اليوم؟

ما هو شعورِكِ اليوم؟

يمنى: أشعر بالنشاط، الأستيقاظ مبكرًا والروتين اليومي يجعلونني أكثر سعادةً وتركيزًا في العمل.

محمد: اليوم أشعر بالتعب، معدتي تؤلمني جدًا منذ الأمس، لا أعلم لماذا.

داليا: أشعر أنني سعيدة جدًا اليوم، لأنني أستطعت تحقيق أشياء كثيرة كنت أرغب بها.

أندرو: متفائل كعادتي كل يوم في الصباح الباكر، وذلك يجعلني أستكمل يومي بنشاط.

آيه: أشعر بالتعب اليوم لأنني أصبت بالبرد بسبب تغير الطقس.

محمود: أنا سعيد الحمد لله، لقد حقق الله لي أشياء كنت أنتظرها.

رباب: أريد النوم، لقد كان يومًا مرهقًا جدًا من العمل، وأخيرًا قد مر بسلام.

تامر: أشعر بملل شديد اليوم، لأن اليوم كان طويلاً جدًا من ناحية العمل والحياة العملية.

شروق: يومًا عاديًا، مثله كأي يوم آخر ولكنني أشعر بالصداع مما يجعلني في حالة مزاجية سيئة.

فؤاد: متفائل، من الصعب أن يجد أحد ما يريده بالضبط ولكنه من الممكن أن يجد أكثر الأشياء التي تجعله سعيدًا.

28 MSA

ما الذي تنوي القيام به في الغد؟
ما الذي تنوين القيام به في الغد؟

يمنى: لدي أعمال ثابتة أقوم بها خلال الأسبوع، أذهب إلى العمل صباحًا وأعود لتحضير الغداء ثم أجلس مع أسرتي حتى موعد النوم.

محمد: غدًا سأسافر، سأذهب إلي الأسكندرية لزيارة عائلتي ورؤية أصدقائي.

داليا: أنوي أن أستيقظ مبكرًا لتناول الإفطار وممارسة الرياضة والعمل والخروج لشراء مستلزماتي، ثم أقوم بطهي الطعام وتنظيف المنزل.

أندرو: أهم شيء هو متابعة العمل لتكون جميع التحركات سليمة، كما أنني أنوي الذهاب إلي صالة الرياضة.

آيه: أنوي الخروج مع صديقتي وأختي، نذهب إلى السينما ونتناول الطعام في الخارج.

محمود: أنوي أستذكار دروسي أستعدادًا لأمتحانات نصف الفصل الدراسي لأنها ستبدأ بعد أسبوع.

رباب: أنوي الذهاب إلى العمل، وأتمنى من الله أن يكون يومًا جيدًا لا يشبه اليوم.

تامر: أنوي الأستيقاظ للذهاب إلي العمل، وأحاول أن أعود مبكرًا حتى أستطيع تغيير الجو والخروج إلي أى مكان.

شروق: كنت أنوي الخروج في منطقة وسط البلد مع صديقتي لشراء الأقمشة، ولكنها لديها عمل ستقوم به لذلك فقد تغيرت خطتنا.

فؤاد: أنا أحب أن أتعلم الأشياء الجديدة كل يوم بشكل عام، أنوي تكملة شيء كنت أقوم بتعلمه وأقوم بأكمال رسم.

29 MSA
ما هي هوايتك المفضلة؟
ما هي هوايتكِ المفضلة؟

يمنى: أحب عمل الأشغال الفنية اليدوية، وأقوم بالأندماج فيها وتعلمها بشغف شديد، ومن الأشياء التي قمت بها مؤخرًا هو الأسكوبيدو.

محمد: أنا أحب الجيتار، لذلك فهوايتي المفضلة هي العزف على الجيتار.

داليا: أحب الطبخ جدًا وأقوم بتعلم أكلات جديدة، كما أن القراءة من هواياتي أيضًا.

أندرو: أحب الرسم كثيرًا والسباحة أيضاً، ولكنني للأسف لا أستطيع تنمية هذه الهوايات لأن العمل يأخذ الأغلبية العظمى من الوقت.

آيه: هوايتي المفضلة هي الخروج مع أصدقائي وجميع أحبابي، فيكون وقتًا ممتعًا جدًا.

محمود: أقوم بممارسة الرياضة، فهي الشيء الذي أستمتع به وأشعر بالسعادةً حين أمارسه.

رباب: لا أملك هوايات، كل أوقاتي للمنزل والعمل، فليس لدي وقت لأبحث عن هواياتي.

تامر: هواياتي المفضلة هما القراءة والحاسب الآلي، وهما الشيئين اللذان لا يمكنني الأستغناء عنهما.

شروق: الرسم وصناعة الأشياء اليدوية من أى مادة سواء الصلصال اَوْ الأقمشة اَوْ الأوراق.

فؤاد: الرسم، وبخاصة رسم القصص المصورة. أحب رسم تعبيرات الوجه لأوصل فكرة من خلال الرسم.

30 بماذا تستطيع أن تصف شخصيتك؟

MSA

بماذا تستطيعين أن تصفي شخصيتكِ؟

يمنى: أنا شخصية هادئة، أحب النظام والهدوء وأتميز بشدة الملاحظة للتفاصيل، حساسة جدًا وحالمة.

محمد: أنا شخص منظم جدًا، ويعني ذلك أنني شخص يهتم بالأرقام والمعادلات الحسابية.

داليا: أستطيع أن أصف شخصيتي بأنها شخصية مرحة وأجتماعية، ولكنها في نفس الوقت جادة في أوقات العمل.

أندرو: أصف نفسي بالبقدونس، لأنه يتواجد في العديد من الأكلات وأنا كذلك أحب أن أكون مشاركًا في جميع الأشياء.

آيه: أستطيع أن أصف شخصيتي بأنها متوترة ولكنها تتحمل المسئولية بشدة، وهذا هو رأي الكثير من الأشخاص.

محمود: متحدث، عندما أجلس في أى مكان مع أشخاص غير معروفين بالنسبة لي، أجدني أستطيع أن أتحدث معهم وأناقشهم في مواضيع مختلفة.

رباب: أنا شخصية طيبة وأجتماعية ومحبوبة من الجميع وأحب العمل بشدة.

تامر: للأسف أنا عصبي جدًا، ولدي شخصية انطوائية قليلاً، ويصعب عليها الثقة في أى شخص.

شروق: أنا شخصية بسيطة، لا أحب النفاق وأحب المرح والضحك.

فؤاد: أنا عادل، العدل بالنسبة لي من أهم الأشياء، لأن الغيرة بين الناس قد تجعلهم يظلمون ويكرهون بعضهم البعض.

lingualism

Visit our website for information on current and upcoming titles,

free excerpts, and language learning resources.

www.lingualism.com

Printed in Great Britain
by Amazon

47717240R00123